PENGUIN

THE POEMS OF MA

MARIANNE MOORE was born in Kirwood, Missouri, on November 15, 1887, and spent much of her youth in Carlisle, Pennsylvania. During her college years, her early poems appeared in Bryn Mawr publications, and, after her graduation, her poems began appearing in 1915 in *The Egoist* and in *Poetry*. In 1918 she moved to New York City, where she served as acting editor of *The Dial*, the preeminent American literary periodical. Marianne Moore's books of poetry include *Poems, Observations, Selected Poems, What Are Years, Nevertheless*, and *Collected Poems*, the last of which received all three of the major American poetry prizes: the Bollingen Award, the National Book Award, and the Pulitzer Prize. She went on to publish a verse translation of the complete *Fables of La Fontaine*, a collection of critical essays, and three more volumes of poems. Among the many awards Marianne Moore received are the National Institute of Arts and Letters Gold Medal for Poetry, the Poetry Society of America's Gold Medal for Distinguished Achievement, and the National Medal for Literature, America's highest literary honor. She died in New York City, in her eighty-fifth year, on February 5, 1972.

GRACE SCHULMAN, recipient of a Guggenheim Fellowship for Poetry, the Aiken Taylor Award for Modern Poetry, and the Delmore Schwartz Award for Poetry, is author, most recently, of *Days of Wonder: New and Selected Poems*. She is Distinguished Professor of English at Baruch College, City University of New York, poetry editor of *The Nation*, and former director of the 92nd Street Y Poetry Center.

Praise for *The Poems of Marianne Moore*

"The distinguished poet Grace Schulman has given poets and readers of poetry a very substantial gift: she has edited a definitive and inclusive volume of more than one hundred previously uncollected and unpublished poems of the extraordinary but elusive poet Marianne Moore. . . . Schulman, who knew Moore from an early age, provides a lively and often hilarious account of the poet's personality and a fascinating view of her politics. . . . Schulman's chronological recasting of these extraordinary poems in this collection amply and dramatically demonstrates her own passion for exactitude and her deep and lasting regard for an unforgettable and indisputably major American poet." —Carol Muske-Dukes, *Los Angeles Times*

"With her scrupulous vision and absolutely assured voice, Moore is one of the most appealing modernist poets; this new edition should bring her a new generation of admirers." —Adam Kirsch, *New York Sun*

"A splendid, much-needed edition . . . by one of the most witty, alert, scapular and truthful American modernists."
—Edward Hirsch, "Highly Recommended Poetry Books of 2003," *The Washington Post*

"[A] heroic accomplishment . . . What a task it must have been to get this refracting crystal palace of work assembled without benefit of instructions, and how beautifully and unpedantically Grace Schulman has accomplished it. Her introduction is short, insightful, and warmly personal, profiting from her friendship with Marianne Moore beginning when Schulman was fourteen and continuing until Moore's death in 1972."

—Kay Ryan, *Yale Review*

"How extraordinary was this woman whose poems could love the world so eagerly, embracingly, intoxicately."   —Brad Leithauser, *The New York Times Book Review*

"Miss Moore has made a great triumph by building an art out of a lifetime of trust in small, real virtues."   —Stanley Kunitz

"One of the very few modern poets whom I can read on any day and in any mood . . . Those who believe as I do that what any poem says should be true and that, in our noisy, overcrowded age, a quiet and intimate poetic speech is the only genuine way of saying it, will find exactly what they are looking for."   —W. H. Auden

"There is so much life concentrated into, objectified on, these hard, tender, serious pages, there is so much wit and truth and moral imagination inhabiting this small space, that we are surprised at possibility, and marvel all over again at the conditions of human making and being."   —Randall Jarrell

"Marianne Moore is the inventor of a new kind of English poem, one that is able to fix the splendor and variety of prose in very compressed spaces."   —Robert Lowell

"More than any modern poet, she gives us the feeling that life is softly exploding around us, within easy reach."   —John Ashbery

The Poems of
MARIANNE
MOORE

Edited by

GRACE SCHULMAN

PENGUIN BOOKS

It's not a Herod's oath that cannot change.

—Marianne Moore

PENGUIN BOOKS
Published by the Penguin Group
Penguin Group (USA) Inc., 375 Hudson Street, New York, New York 10014, U.S.A.
Penguin Books Canada Ltd, 10 Alcorn Avenue, Toronto, Ontario, Canada M4V 3B2
    (a division of Pearson Penguin Canada Inc.)
Penguin Books Ltd, 80 Strand, London WC2R 0RL, England
Penguin Ireland, 25 St Stephen's Green, Dublin 2, Ireland (a division of Penguin Books Ltd)
Penguin Group (Australia), 250 Camberwell Road, Camberwell, Victoria 3124, Australia
    (a division of Pearson Australia Group Pty Ltd)
Penguin Books India Pvt Ltd, 11 Community Centre, Panchsheel Park, New Delhi – 110 017, India
Penguin Group (NZ) cnr Airborne and Rosedale Roads, Albany, Auckland 1310, New Zealand
    (a division of Pearson New Zealand Ltd)
Penguin Books (South Africa) (Pty) Ltd, 24 Sturdee Avenue, Rosebank, Johannesburg 2196, South Africa

Penguin Books Ltd, Registered Offices:
80 Strand, London WC2R 0RL, England

First published in the United States of America by Viking Penguin,
    a member of Penguin Group (USA) Inc. 2003
Published in Penguin Books 2005

10 9 8 7 6 5 4 3 2 1

Copyright © Marianne Craig Moore, Literary Executor of the Estate of Marianne Moore, 2003
Introduction and notes copyright © Grace Schulman, 2003
All rights reserved

The following selections are reprinted from *The Collected Poems of Marianne Moore* (Scribner): "Novices,"
"Bowls," "Marriage," "Silence," "Sea Unicorns and Land Unicorns," "An Octopus," "An Egyptian Pulled Glass
Bottle in the Shape of a Fish," "To a Snail," " 'Nothing Will Cure the Sick Lion but to Eat an Ape,' " "Peter," "The
Monkey Puzzle," "The Steeple-Jack," "The Hero," "No Swan So Fine," "The Jerboa," "The Plumet Basilisk,"
"Camellia Sabina," "The Frigate Pelican," "The Buffalo," and "Nine Nectarines." Copyright © 1935 by Marianne
Moore; copyright renewed 1963 by Marianne Moore and T. S. Eliot. "Virginia Britannia," "Bird-Witted,"
"Smooth Gnarled Crape Myrtle," "Four Quartz Crystal Clocks," "What Are Years," "The Paper Nautilus," "Rig-
orists," "Light Is Speech," and "Spenser's Ireland." Copyright © 1941 by Marianne Moore; copyright renewed
1969 by Marianne Moore. "He 'Digesteth Harde Yron,' " "The Wood-Weasel," "In Distrust of Merits," "Never-
theless," "Elephants," "The Mind Is an Enchanting Thing," and "A Carriage from Sweden." Copyright © 1944
by Marianne Moore; copyright renewed 1972 by Marianne Moore. " 'Keeping Their World Large,' " "His Shield,"
"Propriety," "A Face," "Efforts of Affection," "Voracities and Verities Sometimes Are Interacting," "By Disposi-
tion of Angels," "Armor's Undermining Modesty," and "The Icosasphere." Copyright © 1951 by Marianne
Moore; copyright renewed 1979 by Lawrence Brinn and Louise Crane. Reprinted with permission of Scribner,
a division of Simon & Schuster, Inc.

THE LIBRARY OF CONGRESS HAS CATALOGED THE HARDCOVER EDITION AS FOLLOWS:
Moore, Marianne, 1887–1972.
    [Poems]
    The Poems of Marianne Moore / edited by Grace Schulman.
        p.   cm.
    Includes index.
    ISBN 0-670-03198-4 (hc.)
    ISBN 0 14 30.39083 (pbk.)
    I. Schulman, Grace. II. Title
PS3525.O5616A17 2003
811'.52—dc21   2003050159

Printed in the United States of America   *Designed by Carla Bolte*

ACKNOWLEDGMENTS

I wish to thank Patricia Willis, of the Beinecke Library at Yale, who has guided me since she was curator of the Marianne Moore Archive at the Rosenbach Museum and Library. I'm grateful to Evelyn Feldman, another former curator of the Moore Archive at the Rosenbach, to Bonnie Costello, for telling me of the trials that awaited me, and to James Fenton for his essay, "Becoming Marianne Moore," in which he calls for a truly complete edition arranged chronologically. I'm indebted to Patricia Willis, Elizabeth Macklin, Linda Leavell, and especially to Alfred Corn, for their wise suggestions, and I'm grateful to Margaret Holley, formerly of Bryn Mawr, for leading me through the early publications and for sharing sources with me. I'm grateful to Charles Berger and Yerra Sugarman, who helped me prepare the paperback edition, in which corrections have been made. I'm thankful to Michael Millman and Claire Hunsaker, both of Viking, and I marvel at the copy-editing skills of Kate Griggs and Miranda Ottewell. I'm beholden to Miss Moore's nieces, Sarah Eustis Moore and Marianne Craig Moore, for giving me encouragement, trust, and a free hand, and to Truman Eustis for his dedication. For their early encouragement of my work on Marianne Moore, I'm grateful to Andreas Brown and to Frances Steloff. When I was a graduate student working on a Moore dissertation, I walked into the Gotham Book Mart and asked for a copy of the Moore bibliography. At that time Andreas, who did not know me from any other customer, lent me his only copy of the rare Lohf and Sheehy bibliography, *The Achievement of Marianne Moore*, and suggested I photocopy it at once. Above all, I wish I could thank my parents, Marcella and Bernard Waldman, and their friends, Marion and Edward McKnight Kauffer, who brought me together with Marianne Moore in a friendship that was to last beyond her death.

CONTENTS

Little Magazines, 1915–1919

World War II and After, 1940–1956

The Magic Flute, 1956–1965

Late Poems, 1965–1972

Selections from *The Fables of La Fontaine*

INTRODUCTION

It is an oddity of American letters that no major poet is cherished more and known less than Marianne Moore (1887–1972). Her readers know only a part of what she wrote, for upwards of half of her poems, great ones among them, are not easily accessible. Some can be found only in early editions, many of them out of print; some that appeared in literary journals or pamphlets never saw book publication. The non-scholar cannot easily observe her development, since neither her *Complete Poems* (1967) nor her *Collected Poems* (1951) is arranged in chronological order. Instead, both follow the arrangement that T. S. Eliot suggested to her for the *Selected Poems* of 1935, which began with "The Steeple-Jack," a poem she wrote in the early 1930s. The sequence was current in its day but not in ours.

The need for this edition first came to me in the spring of 1967, during a conversation with Marianne Moore in her apartment on Ninth Street in Manhattan. When she told me she had reduced "Poetry," a poem of many stanzas, to a mere three lines, I expressed astonishment. "Three lines?" "Yes," she said calmly, and began to quote the version that was to appear in *Complete Poems:*

"POETRY

"I, too, dislike it: there are things that are important
　　　　　　beyond this fiddle."

Noticing my anguish, she paused and said,

"Then I prolonged it:

"Reading it, however, with a perfect contempt for it,
　　　　　　one discovers in
it after all, a place for the genuine."

Delivering each word slowly and deliberately, as she did in her late years, she said that Edwin Kennebeck, her editor at Viking, feared that the editor in chief, Marshall Best, would fall dead when he saw it. "But," she recounted having said to Kennebeck, "the rest of it seemed to be padding."

The epigraph to Marianne Moore's *Complete Poems* (1967) famously reads: "Omissions are not accidents." That book contains 102 poems, fewer than half of the lot that appear in this edition. It omits such major poems as "Old Tiger," "Roses Only," "Melanchthon," "Half Deity," and "Radical," not to mention the early poems, some of them published at Bryn Mawr where Moore was educated, others not published at all. Moreover, she changed some stanzaic versions to free ones, altering the structure of well-known poems such as "Peter," "Picking and Choosing," "England." Poems like "The Steeple-Jack" went through years of revision. Many readers, preferring the stanzaic versions, have favored her *Collected Poems* which, even so, excluded some wonderful poems of its time. In any case, assembled more than twenty years before she died, it misses all of the later work. She was to continue writing until the end of her life.

I first met Miss Moore when I was about fourteen, at the home of my parents' friends E. McKnight Kauffer and Marion Dorn. Edward Kauffer, called Ted, was an artist Moore was to list later, in a 1951 essay, as "one of the few real artists alive today," placing him in the company of Pablo Casals, Soledad, Hans Mardersteig, Alec Guinness, and the Lippizan horsemen. At that first meeting, I was struck by her humor, which ranged from a wry, deadpan wit to high comedy. I noticed her precision in bringing to the luncheon a bag of Chinese pears she had found, the first I had ever seen, each of them perfect. After presenting them, she looked playfully at Ted Kauffer, and fluttered a white handkerchief printed with tiny hearts. His eyes twinkled in amusement. Over lunch she told us that she had stained a blouse swallowing a red capsule and had afterward written a letter to the pharmaceutical company asking, "If the capsule contains healing medication, why not put the medication *inside* the capsule?"

Moore's passion for revision made itself known to me almost immediately. After our meeting, she sent my father a copy of a book she had inscribed for me, her *Nevertheless,* with textual insertions and deletions she had made in ink. For my birthday some years later, she inked changes in my copy of *Like a Bulwark,* and inscribed it "from her father," simply because he had purchased it and asked for her inscription. Once she wrote to him, "Next time if you *buy* my books instead of letting me provide them, you are going to have to take *money* for them." When I sent her my first poems, she wrote in reply, "The flawless typing shows the work to the *very best* advantage." Even one of the poems she avoided commenting on was encouraged, in a way: "What is not contained in that epigraph from *Hercules Furens*?" Knowing the extent of her honesty, I was pleased even more, years and poems later, when she wrote to me: "I wish Edward Kauffer could see that his ambition for you was not misplaced."

When occasions mattered, Marianne Moore was there. At my wedding to Jerome Schulman, in 1959, Marianne said to me, minutes after the service, "I like that rabbi, Dr. Bamberger. He gave you both the responsibility for your marriage." Days later, she wrote to my parents, "The marriage service itself *was* a sacrament—a consecration of those present could sufficiently dwell on it, —for love and dedication should govern every act of every one. Do they not! I hope to see my brother soon and tell him about Dr. Bamberger's conducting of the service."

Later, when I told her that I wanted to write a doctoral dissertation about her poetry, she replied with the wry wit I remembered from our first meeting. At first she said, "If this is *about* me, the least I can do is try to help." True to her word, we discussed the plan in her apartment, where a tall wooden clock solemnly bonged out the hours. The phone interrupted us. It was Monroe Wheeler, an editor and curator of the Museum of Modern Art, who was a friend of Marianne Moore, Ted Kauffer, and my father. "Yes," she said loudly. "I've been talking with Grace Waldman—Grace Schulman now. She is writing a dissertation about me." Silence, then: "No, she has an M.A. This is for a Ph.D."

On that afternoon, she expressed reservations: "Well, I don't know, Grace. I never got a Ph.D. And T. S. Eliot never had a Ph.D. And Ezra Pound never had one, either. And yet you persist." Often in the course of my project, she would say, as well as write, "How is your *work*?" meaning, I knew, my own poems. Still, all the while she did talk of her poetry, and she allowed me to tape-record at least one long conversation about her methods of composition. While those conversations amplified the poems for me, their high value was to our friendship, which they enabled to continue: In transcribing the tape, made on an old reel-to-reel, I learned every nuance of her then failing voice, for she suffered from aphasia after multiple strokes. Then, when she could no longer speak clearly to others of her thoughts, sometimes darting, sometimes meditative, I could understand her. She spoke in "light syllables" when she said, "Do I look well?" And in "heavy stresses" for "*How* is your *mother*?"

Once she said, "Can you hear me? I speak badly now. When Ezra Pound came, he could not say a word." I quoted those words in an early poem called "In the Country of Urgency, There Is a Language." "Urgency" refers to a line

Moore attributed to Ezra Pound and repeated often, changing the words each time. The epigraph to my poem reads: "Ezra Pound said never, NEVER to use any word you would not actually SAY in moments of utmost urgency." For me those late "conversations" about friends, art, and occasions, consisting of disembodied stresses and syllables, were of the "utmost urgency." I heard every one of them.

She spoke often of his aesthetic principles and of his guidance, even when I expressed doubts about his impact on her work. Once, at the British Museum, I saw a tapestry of what I thought were leopards spotted everywhere. I'd remembered that she had written to Pound, referring to a line in "Old Tiger," that "leopards are not spotted everywhere, but in the tapestries they are, and I liked the idea." When I returned to New York, I learned that she had been sick. I arrived at her apartment and found her lying in bed, her untied hair a white wheel on the pillow. I gave her a postcard photo of those spotted beasts, and suddenly she sat upright in bed. "Those are cheetahs, Grace!" she exclaimed, and lay down again.

In his later years, Ezra Pound did not "say a word"—that is, until Moore died. Their friendship had begun with an exchange of letters, in 1918–19, and they continued to correspond, although they did not meet until 1939, and conversed directly only a few times after that. When Marianne Moore died, in February 1972, Pound came out of his vast silence to recite her poem of 1940, "What Are Years," at a memorial service for her in Italy.

What is our innocence,
what is our guilt

he began, and continued to the end:

This is mortality,
this is eternity.

By coincidence, it had been the same poem I reached for, after a glance at the King James Bible, to have with me at her first memorial service in 1972. Her body was on view at Good Shepherd's Chapel of the First Presbyterian Church near Washington Square and near her home. What I know of that evening has been reconstructed, not remembered. I know that I sat beside Frances Steloff after my parents left the chapel; I know that I was glad to meet

Sarah Eustis ("Sallie") Moore, for her aunt Marianne had praised the devotion in late years of Sallie and her sister, Marianne's namesake, Marianne Craig ("Bee") Moore. And I think occasionally of how fitting it was that the church was one of two that Henry James had prized in *New York Revisited*. All I actually remember of those hours were the lines that echo still:

This is mortality
This is eternity

———

One of the books Marianne Moore gave me early on was an edition roughly the shape of an index card called *Omaggio a Marianne Moore* (1964), printed in Milan by Vanni Scheiwiller and translated into Italian by Mary de Rachewiltz. And in fact I had only my limited Italian to help me read "Old Tiger" and "Radical." Their original versions stand among the beautiful poems never included in any book, certainly not in the *Collected* or the *Complete*. Well, why not put the healing *inside* the capsule, I thought, wishing to read them in a book and remembering her rebuke to the pharmaceutical company.

As I consider it now, the exclusion of those poems seems out of keeping with her customary allegiance to the work done. I recall a freezing afternoon in the early 1960s, when we rode in a taxi across the Brooklyn Bridge on the way to a matinee. On the Manhattan side, we were intrigued to see a man in tattered black pants standing by what was apparently a painted canvas burning in a metal trash can, its purple, green, and orange flames leaping in air. "Would you stop here, please," Moore said, sitting forward. When the driver had pulled over awkwardly to a curb near the fire, she rolled down her window and leaned out, holding down a wide-brimmed hat to keep it from flapping off in the wind. "Don't burn your work," she commanded. Her voice was plangent. The man looked at her, bewildered. "No, don't ever burn your work," she called out again, as though talking as well to me, and to herself. After a pause, she asked the driver to move on. Remembering that ride, I realize now that we never found out just why he was burning the canvas, just as I've never known the actual reasons for her omissions. Still, at the very least, the memory is a sign.

———

When asked to prepare this edition, I couldn't imagine doing it. I was torn between wanting to follow my friend's last editorial wishes and the driving need to represent her work. I knew that readers desired the poems in full, and that a chronological edition would enable us to watch her grow. Even negative arguments had positive rejoinders. For example, she herself writes, in an early essay praising Wallace Stevens, "It is rude, perhaps, after attributing conscious artistry and a severely intentional method of procedure to an artist, to cite work that he has been careful to omit from his collected work." After that disclaimer, she explains that "one regrets" the exclusion of four poems and lists them. It would be even ruder, I thought, to cite well over one hundred poems, unpublished or uncollected or both, which the exacting artist saw fit to put aside. Nevertheless, as she herself knew, a regret for excluded poems can weigh heavily.

What overcame my hesitation was my sense of her predilection for change. That theme enlivens poems like "Spenser's Ireland," "Half Deity," and "To a Chameleon." She knew that change had a place in her life, as well. On one occasion, she alluded to her poem "Mercifully" with its image of a taproot, or the center of a plant that grows directly downward. "I think it's good to be positive," she said. "But I can't be. I never think that anything I say is unalterable. I'm always changing things. . . . I aspire to have a taproot, but I don't have one."

Indeed, what she has said is unalterable. The changes, though, are the lifeblood of her poems. As for the chronological ordering of the poems, it does in fact show her development through the years, and it does reveal the work's wholeness. "Art is exact perception" is the opening line of "Qui S'Excuse, S'Accuse," first published in 1910, in the poet's junior year at Bryn Mawr. The declaration is to become central, for seeing is at the heart of Moore's poetry. The speaker of "Old Tiger," a hitherto uncollected poem, declares:

> you
> see more than I see but even I
> see too much,

just as the observer of "Critics and Connoisseurs" has "seen this swan," and just as both of them join, later, "the watchful maker" of "The Paper Nautilus" and "the hero" who sees not just a sight but "the rock-crystal thing to see." Virtually all of Marianne Moore's poems between January 1921 and June 1953 contain direct references to obtaining knowledge by sight. Hers is emphatically an art of exact perception: to feel deeply is to see clearly, to peer beyond surfaces, and to explore permanent truths. The poet amasses facts, remarks, observations, details from guidebooks and manuals, in pursuit of answers to the mysteries of modern love, of nobility, of timeless values that she probes and probes again.

Moore's liking for poetic sequences—that long form used by her major contemporaries, Eliot, Pound, Stevens, and Williams—is another of the facets that had been veiled in the *Collected Poems* and the *Complete Poems*. Three of Moore's sequences, early and late, happen to have appeared in *Poetry*. Although sequences were to blossom in 1932–36, the first, "Pouters and Fantails," which consisted of five independent poems, appeared in *Poetry* as early as 1915. The sequence called "Part of a Novel, Part of a Poem, Part of a Play," comprising "The Steeple-Jack," "The Student," and "The Hero," came out there in 1932. "Imperious Ox, Imperial Dish" was the overall title she gave to "The Buffalo" and "Nine Nectarines" when *Poetry* published them in 1934. Two years later, a sequence called "The Old Dominion," made up of "Virginia Brittania," "Bird-Witted," the remarkable, hard-to-find, unjustly excluded "Half Deity," "Smooth Gnarled Crape Myrtle," and "The Pangolin," was published in England as part of a slim book, *The Pangolin and Other Verse*.

At times the sequence form amplifies concerns of individual lyrics. For example, in "Part of a Novel, Part of a Poem, Part of a Play," her notion of heroism emerges with resonance, after the hero has entered in different guise in each of the poems, the very word *hero* echoed by *ee* and *o* sounds throughout. In this edition I've shown "Pouters and Fantails" as it appeared in *Poetry*. Although I have shown other poems in their later, more finished, revisions, I have kept the order of how they once appeared in sequence form. Three sequences are given in their entirety among the variants in the Editor's Notes.

As to my choices of individual poems, I could not rely on any single edition for this project. The abundance of revisions, omissions, and late additions precluded reliance on any one volume or even on one period in Moore's work. Wherever possible, and where versions did not vary excessively, I used the *Complete Poems* (1967). These represent the author's wishes at the time, and were checked for accuracy in Patricia Willis's 1981 version of that book. Moore's late revisions sometimes went back to earlier versions, as with "Critics and Connoisseurs" and "The Steeple-Jack." In many cases, I used versions that I liked from earlier editions and/or literary journals, aware that she changed her work continually. I went to earlier appearances also for the excluded and the altered. Versions from *Observations* (1924) and *Collected Poems* (1951) appear often in this edition. After having cut "Poetry" to three lines,

Marianne Moore agreed to keep an earlier version in her notes, so that it will save "the serious reader from looking up these things as they were." In that case I reversed the process, placing an earlier version in the body of the text and the 1967 cut in the Editor's Notes, along with other variants.

Because of the vast difference in early and late versions, I treated "Sun," which went through sixty years of revision, as a separate poem from "Fear Is Hope." Otherwise, for the most part, I selected only one version for each poem. In the end, I chose what I loved best by a method I can only describe as "conscientious inconsistency."

———

To read a poem by Marianne Moore is to be aware of exactitude. It is to know that the writer has looked at a subject—a cliff, a sea animal, an ostrich—from all sides, and has examined the person looking at it as well. This method can be found from her very early poems, some of them published in Bryn Mawr journals. For Marianne Moore, seeing an object meant speaking of its various aspects on many levels of discourse. Her poetics of inquiry begins with a conversational style, and with a manner of argumentation found in poems such as "To the Soul of Progress" ("To Military Progress," 1915). "I began writing in response to adverse ideas," she told me once, and quoted from memory her early poem "Progress" (c. 1907) whose title she changed later to "I May, I Might, I Must." To insure an unimpeded flow from one line to another, we find her dropping capital letters at the beginnings of lines as early as in "To William Butler Yeats on Tagore" (1915). The conversations develop into dialectical arguments, as in "Critics and Connoisseurs," 1916, and "Old Tiger," c. 1918, a beautiful poem published only in two small journals after its Italian debut, and from there on to complex inner arguments, as in "No Swan So Fine" (1932) and "The Paper Nautilus" (1939). The discourse moves. It propels the poems forward and turns our attention to their progress from beginning to end. It constitutes her form for engagement with larger issues.

Under the poet's inquiring gaze are the mystery of modern love ("Marriage"), the proliferation of sights and sounds that crowd the senses ("Those Various Scalpels"), the vast, puzzling structure of the urban metropolis ("People's Surroundings"), and the unity that each person strives for in a life that urges disruption. Beyond that, she ventures to apprehend permanent truths that are seen by the eye of the mind.

A recurrent theme of Moore's poetry is the mind's tendency to pivot from one vivid figure to another. Her vision of a shifting reality captures an age whose leading philosophers have questioned objective reality. "What is more precise than precision? Illusion," asserts the speaker of "Armor's Undermining Modesty," expressing the early-twentieth-century view that what we perceive to be real is not actual, and that optical illusion is the rule, rather than the exception.

The poet's images of change enact that process of the mind encountering what is real. Not standard myths, such as Ariel or Daphne, but objects from the world around her are portrayed in shifting states, moving even as they are perceived. Images of water, fire and rock—those classic elements of metamorphosis—abound in her poetry, often accompanied by moments of change. Other images are dialectical in that they move and are moved, act and are acted upon, see and are seen ("enchanting"/"enchanted," "enslaver"/"enslaved"), thereby enacting the struggle of consciousness toward illumination.

In this edition there are many hitherto excluded poems of change. Early examples are "Ennui," "Fish," "Artificers and the Alchemist," "To a Stiff-winged Grasshopper," "Sun, Moon, and Stars." "Half Deity," a major poem of metamorphosis, was dropped after its appearance in *What Are Years*.

Late in her life, in 1967, Marianne Moore told me that the sound of the verse was more important to her than its visual pattern. She remarked that "it ought to be continuous," and that she had always wanted her verse to sound "unstrained and natural, as though I were talking to you." At the time she told me of her distaste for the commonplace that she wrote in syllabic verse, in which the line lengths of a repeated stanza pattern are determined by the numbers of syllables, rather than stresses. "Syllabics? Oh, I repudiate that." All the same, she added, "I like to see symmetry on the page, I will confess."

At the time, her statement confirmed my way of reading her poems for sound *and* visual pattern. In preparing this edition, though, I have found myself applauding the balletic turns of the visual patterns, especially those that were created in the poet's earlier years. And fortunately the present margins, wider than some previous printings, allow the longer stanzaic lines their space, thus enabling us to see stanzaic patterns the author intended. Even here, space restrictions make some "turnover lines" unavoidable, but the desired syllabic stanzaic structures are recognized in, for example, "Dock Rats" and "England."

"With what unfreckled integrity it has all been done," W. H. Auden wrote, praising her craft. That appraisal can apply many times over to a probing, courageous morality, rare in an artist of her time, indeed of any time. Moore was a feminist when she studied at Bryn Mawr, a socialist when she taught at the Carlisle Indian School, and by religious belief a lifelong Presbyterian. Major and minor poems reveal principles that she won not by following fixed rules but by a continuous self-examination. She deplored human greed that failed to spare "the harmless solitaire / or great auk in its grandeur." She was a supporter of Irish rebellion ("Sojourn in the Whale") but was otherwise against war, and especially offended by fighting for a world that lacked moral insight. "Sun, Moon, and Stars," a hitherto unpublished poem, has her questioning the use of force: "Is impotence more virtuous than might, or less / In worth? Which is of greater consequence?" Several of the early unprinted poems join "To Military Progress" in deploring warmongering, there in the image of "minute men" who "seek their prize / Till the evening sky's / Red." And a poem of 1943, published only in the *New Republic*, is a plea to

> save us from the captivity
> of surfeit; save us from complacency.
>
> Life must stop stifling life with life.
> It must. Alas that we must put
> an end to death by death.
> We're begging; we are begging for
> news to the prisoner that he may
> come out of his dungeon at last.
> He's seen destruction and would see
> deliverance. Turn sighing into breath.

Other poems reveal, though in the bare, sometimes jolting appellations characteristic of Moore, her firm stand on racial equality and elevation of the oppressed. The Labors of Hercules in the poem of that title include convincing "snake-charming controversialists"

> that one keeps on knowing
> "that the Negro is not brutal,
> that the Jew is not greedy,
> that the Oriental is not immoral,
> that the German is not a Hun."

In "Virginia Brittania" she writes again with disarming bareness, but with adoration, of "the Negro, / inadvertent ally and best enemy of / tyranny." Reproaching imperialists for practicing brutality, she avows: "The redskin with the deer- / fur crown, famous for his cruelty, is not all brawn / and animality." And it is a black man, one she calls a "decorous, frock-coated Negro" who emerges as "the hero" in the poem of that name, possessing a "sense of human dignity / and reverence for mystery." The moral precepts that appear throughout her poems and, in fact, her prose, have for this reader a plangent resonance in "Blessed Is the Man"

> who does not sit in the seat of the scoffer—
>> the man who does not denigrate, depreciate, denunciate;
>>> who is not "characteristically intemperate,"
> who does not "excuse, retreat, equivocate; and will be heard."

Her moral stature, though, is inseparable from the poetry's aesthetic triumph. In this regard, I believe the permanence of Marianne Moore's poetry is in its depiction of a dramatic struggle between the poet's mind and the world. Objects and animals embody the mind's tenacious, life-giving power that

> tears off the veil, tears
>> the temptation, the
> mist the heart wears,
>>>> from its eyes—if the heart
>>>> has a face . . .

In each of the poems, the mind, engaged with an object or animal, moves forward to a fresh idea. In "The Paper Nautilus," the speaker, contemplating the sea animal taking care of her eggs, works through to the idea of love as "the only fortress / strong enough to trust to." The notion is at once parallel and antithetical to the "entrapped writers" and the "authorities" at the outset of the poem, since we find in each statement about the nautilus a reference to those limited people. In that way, the mind, exploring everything about an object, has seen beyond it to the world.

Moore's poetics is rooted in the native "instinct to amass and reiterate" that she ascribed to her countryman in an essay, "Henry James as a Characteristic American." Although her approach to subject matter changed throughout her career, she chose essentially the same kinds of material, which included elephants she had seen in a lecture-film on Ceylon, an icosasphere she had read about in the *New York Times*, a lyrebird she had seen in an engraving by Thomas Bewick, an exhibit of sixteenth-century Persian treasures. Her poetry carries forward an American tradition in its use of what surrounds us, and in its insistence on the poet's freedom to contemplate any subject without a diminishment of energy: being American was for her, as she wrote it was for Henry James, "intrinsically and actively ample, . . . reaching westward, southward, anywhere, everywhere," with a mind "incapable of the shut door in any direction."

In Marianne Moore's poetry, creativity rises from the subtle dialectic between freedom and repression. We learn of the struggle for freedom from the ostrich, in "He 'Digesteth Harde Yron'"; from Hercules, who was "hindered to succeed" in "The Paper Nautilus"; from the salamander in "His Shield" who knows that freedom is "the power of relinquishing / what one would keep."

Paradoxically, such freedom is built on the very limitations life imposes. Just as the poet's fascination with worldly things is generated by her perception of life's boundaries, her concept of freedom is that of the liberty wrung from a struggle with constraint. In an essay called "Idiosyncrasy and Technique," she wrote of the artistic process, "Creative secrets, are they secrets? Impassioned interest in life, that burns its bridges behind it and will not contemplate defeat, is one, I would say."

And her meditative poem, "What Are Years," deals with a restricted freedom that is, paradoxically, the source of creative energy. That aesthetic is, I believe, at the heart of the poetry of Marianne Moore:

> He
> sees and is glad, who
>   accedes to mortality
> and in his imprisonment rises
> upon himself as
> the sea in a chasm, struggling to be
> free and unable to be,
>   in its surrendering
>   finds its continuing.

PRELUDE

DECEMBER 25, 1895

Dear St. Nicklus;
This Christmas morn
you do adorn
Bring Warner a horn
And me a doll
That is all.
December 25th 1895.

Horn.

Doll.

Dear St. Nicklus;

This Christmas morn
You do adorn
Bring Warner a horn
And me a doll
That is all.

EARLY POEMS

1907-1913

Under a Patched Sail

"Oh, we'll drink once more
when the wind's off shore,"
We'll drink from the good old jar,
And then to port,
For the time grows short.
Come lad—to the days that are!

hornpipe?

To Come After a Sonnet

A very awkward sketch, 'tis true;
But since it is a sketch of you,
And then because I made it, too,
I like it here and there; —do you?

To My Cup-Bearer

A lady or a tiger lily,
Can you tell me which,
I see her when I wake at night,
Incanting, like a witch.
Her eye is dark, her vestment rich,
Embroidered with a silver stitch,
A lady or a tiger lily,
Slave, come tell me which?

The Sentimentalist

Sometimes in a rough beam sea,
When the waves are running high,
I gaze about for a sight of the land,
Then sing, glancing up at the sky,
"Here's to the girl I love,
And I wish that she were nigh,
If drinking beer would bring her here
I'd drink the ship's hold dry."

He Made This Screen

not of silver nor of coral,
but of weatherbeaten laurel.

Here, he introduced a sea
uniform like tapestry;

here, a fig-tree; there, a face;
there, a dragon circling space—

designating here, a bower;
there, a pointed passion-flower.

Ennui

He often expressed
A curious wish,
To be interchangeably
Man and fish;
To nibble the bait
Off the hook,
Said he,
And then slip away
Like a ghost
In the sea.

A Red Flower

Emotion,
Cast upon the pot,
Will make it
Overflow, or not,
According
As you can refrain
From fingering
The leaves again.

A Jelly-Fish

Visible, invisible,
A fluctuating charm,
An amber-colored amethyst
Inhabits it; your arm
Approaches, and
It opens and
It closes;
You have meant
To catch it,
And it shrivels;
You abandon
Your intent—
It opens, and it
Closes and you
Reach for it—
The blue
Surrounding it
Grows cloudy, and
It floats away
From you.

proposit

Observation

Progress

If you will tell me why the fen
Appears impassable, I then
Will tell you why I think that I
Can get across it, if I try.

A Fish

No heart was planted in my body.
   God knows how that came to be.
But in vouchsafing me that loss, He
   Has vouchsafed me courtesy.

surprisingly
Emblematic

My Lantern

The banners unfurled by the warden
Float
Up high in the air and sink down; the
Moat
Is black as a plume on a casque; my
Light,
Like a patch of high light on a flask, makes
Night
A gibbering goblin that bars the way—
So noisy, familiar, and safe by day.

Tunica Pallio Proprior

My coat is nearer than my cloak;
Inside
My coat is an integument of pride.

My Senses Do Not Deceive Me

Like the light of a candle
   Blown suddenly out,
I witness illusion,
   And subsequent doubt.
Like a drop in the bucket
   And liquid as flame,
Is the proof of enjoyment
   Compared with the name.

Qui S'Excuse, S'Accuse

Art is exact perception;
If the outcome is deception
Then I think the fault must lie
Partly with the critic's eye,
And no man who's done his part
Need apologize for art.

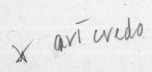

Elfride, Making Epigrams

Devices as slender as pennons float
Up high in the air and sink down; the moat
   Encases her head like a casque;
      Her light
   Sorties, like highlights on a flash,
      Requite
Men with torrents of toads from lips of lead
And then grind up her bones to make their bread.

A Talisman

Under a splintered mast,
torn from ship and cast
             near her hull,

a stumbling shepherd found
embedded in the ground,
             a sea-gull

of lapis lazuli,
a scarab of the sea,
             with wings spread—

curling its coral feet,
parting its beak to greet
             men long dead.

Leaves of a Magazine

They open of their own will to the place
Where Captain Kidd stands with averted face
And folded arms, as solid as an oak,
His loosely knotted sash and scarlet cloak
Encircling him, and flapping in the breeze
That lines the withered, undulating seas.
Upon the page across from him, a frame
Of knives lie point to point about the name
Of a dim verse fantastically made
In praise of him, —a ragged block of shade;
A block of shade, with blurs and puckers where
Admiring hands have often brought to bear
Their pressure on the picture and the rhyme
Of buccaneering in the olden time.

The Beast of Burden

I think the scourge was made for men
That have the power to rise again.

Because when scourged such beasts as I
Have no alternative. We die.

At death, we lose, man gains a soul.
We forfeit, he attains the goal.

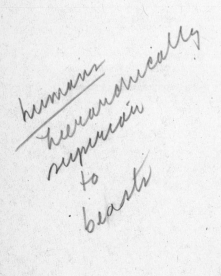

humans
hierarchically
superior
to
beasts

Things Are What They Seem

Literality [handwritten]

The cloud between
Perforce must mean
  Dissension.

The broken crock's
Condition mocks
  Prevention.

This Is the Way Toads Talk:

The spot upon my back that none would see there
Needs must be there—
   Undisguised:
Immaculate, the heart that God has newly
Claimed, as truly
   Lies despised

To Pierrot Returning to His Orchid

Spider, with the freckles of a clown
   And sumptuous contortions of a gnome,
      How came you by that one bright object in my room
      That you could fitly call your own—upon whose flame you
                seemed unconsciously to drift
And like a moth to settle down?
   The forest is your home.

I shall not evict you, spider, no.
   You strayed exotic from the pantomime,
      Your dog-flower carried by the stream to drown yourself,
      Like inland seaweed, in a pond of tough-stemmed lilies:
             You are here; apparently
Content to be my guest—*Say* so.
   It is Christmastime.

To Pharaoh's Baker Plucking Up Courage to Ask the Interpretation of His Dream, When a Favorable Interpretation Had Been Accorded the Dream of Pharaoh's Butler

Red flowers will not make red wine
Nor will the anodyne
   Of flattery quench thirst.
    Free men fare worst,
    When handed gold
   That smells of brass, when told
Lies will not breed disdain
Or doomed men perish on the plain.

Piningly

Yes, they looked piningly on her, she had professed
   An interest in each separate one
   Of them; she'd made them all drunk. "Babylon
      Was a golden cup." She called them the commonwealth—those
                              positive young men
        With the perforated morality. Old, without the
          Venerableness of experience, the sieve said to the needle,
                                  "You've
           A hole in your tail." They called her needle and she

Called them sieve. Each owned a horse that he had conjured
   Up by the drawing of a breath or
     The uncovering of a dish. Each wore
        The extravagant freedom that he had manufactured out of wealth as
         Modestly as he could, but even so, with more ado
           Than was becoming. They flamed through the streets in their
                            panoply like torches
          Taking their direction from the wind. One or two

Objected to ultra rigorous forms of self
   Advertisement; they discussed "commerce
  And the national destiny"—averse
        To the nightmare of anything like a fact. "They extended their
                            pampered
        Bodies on ivory and prated and purred to the sound
         Of the viol while poverty and overwork stared them in the face.
                                  Half
        Of them were raw; less than half of them had been browned

Till they were brittle uneatable cinders." They
   Had intellectualized it all.
   As the nucleus of their nation's fall,

They could not get away from themselves and so commemorated the
                                                                    feast.
    They were left like food: they were the inevitable mere
        Residue—scattered negligently. "They were left like crumbs
                                                    from a lion's
        Meal—a couple of shins and the bit of an ear."

Artificers and the Alchemist

(Symbolized by a snake swallowing its tail)

The things that they fashion,
When finished are passionless, cold—
Like the dust of his choosing
Transformed in the using to gold.

To You—of the World, Not in the World:

Butler! I regret that life should have
   Been so bitter to you
      Whose perceptions were so acute:
Damning your eyesight you saw much, and
   in your own lackluster intensive
      Fashion you were resolute.

Wisdom at Last

Sometimes cutting, but in this instance
   Silent—unique
      As one of the gold-and-silver products of the Greek
         Artificers—you are more than symmetrical.
            In your very cunningly
               Wrought
            Modesty,
          You are the
            Naught
          And the everything. When we
       Decline to pronounce, we are hypocritical
      Sometimes, but not when we decline in your presence, Greek
   Scimitar. Speak:
For in you wisdom finds furtherance.

To a Stiff-winged Grasshopper

As I unfolded its wings,
   In examining it for the first time,
      I forgot the war:
         I thought I had discovered something. Then I discovered
            That others, also, thought they had discovered something.
               We stood like the snake swallowing its tail, comprising a ring.

Superstition forges rings
   Of iron. A ring is the most extreme form
      Of symbol. Rings mar
         The symmetry of loyal regard: we philosophized:
            And said we could not have been acts in anyone's ring,
            Had it not been inevitable in the case of this thing.

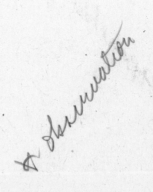

Emeralds

It arouses my indignation that they should be so rare,
   Yet I think I should be as willing to wear green
Sapphires as I should be willing to wear
Emeralds, the point of the thing's being, not to make people stare
    But to have to wear, what keeps life from becoming a parcel of
                           uniformities—
What prevents its deteriorating into a bugbear:
   To have what makes it start from its rut like the horse seen
Showing its might in the book of Job, where
The dramatist watches it leap like a locust into the air,
    And swerving neither to the right nor left, bore its way
      up into the heart of the breeze.

Sun, Moon, and Stars:

To look up at you calling you angels is unprofitable, yes—
If as I look, I am reminded to admire men's heartlessness
   And piercing pride, and platinum pretense.

Man's valor, man's submission—each has spiritual work. Then confess,
Sun, Moon, and Stars: Is impotence more virtuous than might, or less
   In worth? Which is of greater consequence?

Polyphonic Craftsman, Coated Like a Zebra,
Fleeing Like the Wild Ass, Mourning Like a Dove,

You are not a candle but the light that is yourself—
    Unseizable as moon and inescapable as sun;
    You are the transcendentalized criterion
        Of forthright action in a stolid universe.

Dissonance is in the air: you are the orchestra.
    Amusing animal, too bent upon your body's good
    To make the gaping multitude your picnic food—
        I shall not cavil at you for being perverse.

37

All of It, as Recorded

Down the village street, a lame boy
And the women leaned on
   The half-open doors and saw nothing.

Down the village street, a lame old man
And the women leaned on
   The half-open doors and saw nothing.

Down the village street, a bier
And the children saw it as the actor
   Sees the letter which he writes
   In the second act of the play.

"Am I a Brother to Dragons and a Companion to Owls?"

    I am exactly that: brusque, blind—
Unsocialized in deed, convinced in mind,
    Of my strict duty to mankind.

"And Shall Life Pass an Old Maid By?"

It would seem so, judging by neat
Delineations of the lady, in her zeal to meet
   Commiseration fitly, from beneath a dusty mask.
Convention's face misleads the artist's feet.

Bloody in youth, withered in age,
That powdered mask could not induce a more outrageous rage
   Were it a poisoned thing and yet, for all its emptiness,
It dares to print a profile on the page.

It copies to the life, some freak
Of sentiment in lavender sprigged silk; bids bloodhounds speak
   From picket gates, adjuring every lonely optimist
That he press on, and hastening, be meek;

Or it depicts an Amazon
Harsh voiced and candle-cheeked, a sort of blunderbuss, a Don
   Quixote, crating wildly where incisive action is
Required—exploded—with its luster gone.

Regard unprejudiced, the plate
Of pewter with the satin rim—more lustrous, more sedate
   When it's a grandmother's than when it's polished by old maids.
Old maids exist but they're precipitate.

How diagnose felicity?
It is an abstract thing, distributed impartially
   Between good, bad, all sorts—and is renounceable.
Who knows where it may be, or may not be?

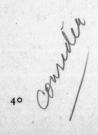

The Assassins

Gold is their god
  And blood their prophet;
Fear, their king,
  Their kingdom, Tophet.

Axiomatic

The sinful man
Who seeks to bury sin in sacred ground,
Has surely found
That fiends surround him.

The sinless man
Who dares to publish truth has surely found
Though sins abound,
None may confound him.

Reprobate Silver

Freighted with allusion "of the sort to which we are accustomed,"
Hand wrought slang—in the spirit of Cellini and after the manner of
                                                          Thor—

Like Panshin's horse, not permitted to be willful,
Trembling incessantly and champing the bit—
It is worthy of examination.
It is quite as much a matter of art as the careful
And a kind of Carthage by Flaubert.
It is like the castles in the air that manufacture themselves

Out of clouds before our eyes
When we are listening to a scientific explanation of things in which we are
                                                          not interested.

The fact that there is no justification for its existence
And that perhaps it had to be written
About what ought never to have been written at all.

The Candle-Stick Maker

Have I extinguishers to snuff out my benighted fellow men!
Blake and his flea! Dante exhumed again
And Bunyan in his den!
Art is my servant and she serves me when
   She ties my struggling body to my spirit. "Tell me what you need."

"How shall a king anticipate a watery disgrace?"
Immortal upstarts are a commonplace?
How shall a pillar face
A flood? How shall extinguishers encase
   Illumination with their bodies! That is what you said to me.

"Coral-and-Brown" Admiring Herself in the Mirror

As in a room
   Where silver hangings wall the golden past,
     She sees the shadows cast
Brocaded gloom:
   "Worlds rise that none have seen and none admire."
     Till touched by the same fire
That warped his loom.

"Crepe Hanger?" He

Said, "but the expression was not original with me.
   Shall I play," he said, "only play?"
"And sing," said we. "Ah," said he.

With limestone gates and ghosts abroad interiorly
   He had quartered reason in a
Porter's lodge of raillery.

pout of cracked (Halloween notation

To a Cantankerous Poet Ignoring His Compeers—
Thomas Hardy, Bernard Shaw, Joseph Conrad, Henry James

Pandora's bees,
Shaw's heliologies,
   Conrad's log book,
And James's odysseys
   Of intricate outlook—
You must account for these,
Who advertise the ease
    In which we sit.

Is Persian cloth
One thread with Persian sloth?
   Is gold dust bran?
Shall we see Ashtaroth
   Be made a Puritan?
Must every gorgeous moth
Be calico, and Thoth
    Be thanked for it?

The Fashion, Poor Lady, Behaving Like a Dungeon, Looking Like a Church

She winds the moat
Like curling fur about her throat.

Beneath the law,
She stands like an ecclesia.

Her sorrows flash
Through the portcullis of her lash,

While she makes hay
As famished men make holiday.

You are very pensive—
Hammering out in darkness
what will not bear the light of Day.

The sure
Measure of failure

Will bring
What you are doing,

To naught.
I'm not sure it ought

Not to
And neither are you.

Flints, Not Flowers

I sense your glory.
For things that I desire and have not got:
For things I have that I wish I had not,
   You compensate me,
      Stones. The moth shan't eat you up, rust shall not waste
      You. How far more cunningly than Keats has placed
   His toy, that poor hack
Flung you up as he walked round. Praise god, stones.
Initially God made that horse, his bones
      And lasting glory.

The Grass That Perisheth

"And now I commend you to God,"
said the Kaiser from his balcony.

They take things into their own hands,
    Their consuls have come back
From Heaven, when they go to war.
    Pride guards their bivouac—

A figure-head of silly men
    With knees of molten brass.
Their hopes go down like sinking ships;
    Their days are as the grass.

Guillemots

Merged with the wilting apex of the tide,
without colliding with the rock,
they came back multiplied.
They kept up with the water's glassy stride,
to the sea's edge encrusted with white grit,
advancing as one bird against the ocean's tilted side,
and carried back
from barnacles adhering by their heads—
minute marine steam dredges with large mouths,
their base of operations designated by the sun,
mouths shut but living every one,
their jaws swung out and made voracious in the thin
translucent ferment of the sea as it comes in.

He Did Mend It. His Body Filled a Substantial Interstice

God did make this man,
A complicated pattern of beautiful design—to span
   A fissure in the earth.
Could he have contemplated such a plan,
     The subsequent experiment?

The experiment?
Dined with Ezekiel and with Isaiah. He was content,
   Indeed exuberant
To do so, and when he had dined he went
     Home resolved to do God's bidding.

If all the body
were the ear, where were the hearing! The earth's continuity
   Is requisite, and when
Blake found that he could mend the landscape, he
     Did it. He glorified the ground.

"I Like a Horse but I Have a Fellow Feeling for a Mule"

I like the mule: his sides are thin.
He takes his ease in no man's inn.
When contrarieties are thick
About his mind's eye, he will kick;
Men bewail their false position;
Closing with the mule's tradition.
He skirts the treeless precipice.
The former groan at that and this:
Though steeped in incredulity,
He treads on "nothing" safely; he
Erects his body as a hedge
Between their bodies and the edge.

I Tell You No Lie

Your face is a gospel, to read now and again
And place above the faces of the rest of men.

You are Elijah sojourning to God when you
Set out to illustrate a point. You waved and grew.

Like the "good will of Him that dwelleth in the bush"
When the flames sprang upward from the quivering push

And flush of scarlet on the thorn. A statuette—
A terminal—occurs to me, well, you are yet

More fine. You are not marble, you are not a stone,
You are that bush of thorns round which the flames have grown.

Ichabod

"Conditions continually change. What is good
enough today may become obsolete tomorrow. One
of the attributes of the progressive educator is
   a willingness to investigate."

Without intending to be rude,
You smother him with platitude;
   Curb your insistence—

When astigmatic Ichabod,
Attached to his outmoded rod,
   Resists resistance.

Change

Inheritance

Erect as she,
Like deity
  Sin stood—

In beauty's guise,
Supremely wise
  And good—

Enticing Eve,
Who could perceive
  No snare

In eyes like those
At which she chose
  To stare.

Strong men may smile
At Satan's guile,
  And yet

Sin stamped disgrace
On Adam's face.
  Regret

Sprang up too late.
Eve and her mate
  Looked down,

Bowed by the curse
That could reverse
  God's frown.

The serpent shook
Beneath God's look
  Then said

To mitigate
His own dark weight
  Of woe

"Her seed," God said
"Shall bruise your head."
  Then he

Lit like a gem
Flashed woe at them,
  To be.

"It Makes No Difference to Balbus Whether He Drinks Wine or Water"

Mixed metaphors are not necessarily.
A bird's eye view or a back seat,
the *acta diurna* or the *New York Times*—
one cannot say under parts, heads and titles,
what one's provender should be; the leaves are disturbed
and the branches let down fruit; is all.
Perfumed jelly and water-melon seeds
on the Pearl River, or cinnamon-buns,
Columbia River salmon and ginger ale
on the Erie Canal; it is the same thing.
One associates the love of beauty
with a wish to see it exemplified.
If "the disorderly order of the veins in the marble"
does not disturb you, it is not necessary to say so.
It is impossible to find anyone who will tell you the truth,
who does not regard the published fact as a surrender;
but if you are not interested in art,
it is not necessary to say so.
"I could have been happy in Carthage
watching the elephants with Tyrian tassels
crushing marigolds as they moved along"
or, "You know things always disgust me
in the morning." In either case,
the inference is plain.

Kay Nielson in *Cinderella*

The eye, the slipper,
    but particularly the eye

Kay Nielson's cinder-wench's disembodied glance:
"Nothing will cure the sick lion but to eat an ape."

Omnis, amens, amens
omnis *amans* amens
    The lover raves.
    Where passion is
Capacities are slaves.

Kay Nielson's Little Green Patch in the Midst of the Forest

"If there is a heaven upon earth, it
  is this, it
  is this, it
    is this."
     Trees? Is it this?
       It is not trees
      That the protagonist of the piece sees.
        As always is the case.
     It is not this:
       It is the essence of a place
        That is not here.

A heaven of air? With horses to ride,
  Dogs to slip,
  Dogs to slip,
    Dogs to
    Slip—and swords to—
      Draw? Yes. The great
      Material gorgeousness of man's state.
       When supernatural
  Good elects to
    Be more than a fiction in all
      That's known as fact.

A Lady with Pearls, to a Blood Red Rook from Turkey, Who Has Depicted Her with Pathos in Surly Monotone

To hang one's ivory fingers like a string,
About the head of any hooded thing.
  Is indefensible:
    Is it not, blood red bird?

Falcon, you should know without your being told,
That ornament, like armament, is cold
  And barely sensible
    When deaf to that one word

That fashioned you, as Insolence has man's wrist—
"Audacity"—Am I a dogmatist,
  Incomprehensible
    And worthless to be heard?

Light Through a Keyhole

As if an eye should wink
With Midas' touch, a chink
  Of gold crept through
  The double-bolted door;

As if a dog should think
His master's thoughts and link
  The occult with
  His fund of canine lore.

Like Bertram Dobell, You Achieve Distinction by Disclaiming It

You are the most modest man I know;
    But if you are the butt of compliment
        You are expert to parry it with reticence.
We speak of our houses, of our "shells"—
    And joke about our self-protectiveness.
        The barrier of the lips is the best defense.

Majestic Haystack

Majestic Haystack, Empress of my life,
   Your ample waist
Just fits the gown I fancy for my wife,
   And suits my taste;
Yet there you stand, flatfooted, square and deep,
An unresponsive elephantine heap,
Coquetting with the stars while I'm asleep—
   O cruel stack—
Coy, silent monster, matron of the fields,
   I sing to you;
And all the fondest love that summer yields
   I bring to you
Yet there you squat, immense in your disdain,
Heedless of all the tears of streaming rain
All eyes drip over you—your breathless swain;
   O stony stack!
Stupendous maiden, sweetest when oblong,
   Does inner flame
Now smolder in thy soul to hear my song
   Repeat thy name?
Or does thy huge and ponderous heart object
To the advances of my passion and reject
My love because it's airy and elect?
   O wily stack!

You've spurned my love as though I were a worm,
But next September when I see thy form
I'll woo her with an equinoctial storm
   I have that knack!

Man's Feet Are a Sensational Device

Rest assured that netting butterflies,
   Flying from mice,
      And crushing spiders,
         Is portentous cowardice.
The field of moral choice affords man's
   Feet crackling ice
      To tread, and feet are
         A sensational device.

Patriotic Sentiment and the Maker

Once stout with gold,
   They meet their doom—
      His work and he. The threads that glimmered past
      Have tarnished in a last
   Brocaded gloom.
      (The WEFT—that none have seen and none desire
      Till touched by the same fire,
   That warped his loom
Whose bell has tolled.)

As Has Been Said

before, some speak of things we know as new;
    and you, of things unknown as things forgot,

the calligraphic coral of fruit dyed
    inside as by infusion of the rind,

or the couplet, say, that chanced to be prose,
    compromises a natural signature—

a mathematician's parenthesis,
    or is it a phase of the autograph?

There is a dedication qualitied
    indeed; at the opposite pole from the miser's

escutcheon, three vises hard-screwed—
    intruding on the accident of pleasure,

known if at all to sensibility
    which would not for the world intrude.

Rencontre

(Head of an animal full-face; heraldic)

With dots and acrostics as his ally,
one need not be shy—
perhaps use heraldry;

though the point of a point, say eye to eye
is a mystery
fraught with a quandary.

Rodin's *Penseur*

The woman, the shepherd, the father:
   The coin, the sheep, and the son:
The union of triple sorrow
   Expressed in the face of one.

Suaviter in Modo

"Oh, Gordon, how naughty!
   Now don't look so haughty—
That's Uncle's pet pipe you have got in your hand.
   If you go on smoking,
   We'll soon have you choking.
We'll then have to bury you under the sand."

Said Gordon to Nellie,
   "Go home and cook jelly,
And don't interfere so with me and my pipe!
   Or else go and garden,
   First begging my pardon.
And see if the plums have begun to get ripe."

Be more like Joanna,
   Dear Gordon, in mannah—
More bland, so that Nellie will not see your pipe,
   And cut short your smoking
   And possible choking.
Don't ask her to see if the plums have got ripe.

Long, long years ago
   Lived this Joanna;
Sweet was her face, also
   Sweet was her mannah.
Reading as she went to church—
   This was her mannah,
The very birdies on their perch
   Sang to Joanna.

To See It Is to Know That Mendelssohn Would Never Do:

The Times, *commenting on Norman Wilkinson's settings in the Granville Barker
production of* A Midsummer Night's Dream

Newspaper comment, that stiff-jawed,
   Black bodied puppet show, here
      Stands erect, upon the wings of verity:
      It will not clatter, flouted, to the earth.
Its gestures print conviction on
   My mind. The want of clothes here
      Makes the man. The scantness of the melody
      Smooths creases straight and seals the fellow's worth.

To Worldly Wisemen Recommending the Town of Carnal Policy as a Substitute for the Celestial City

Poor thing,
What are you doing?

The sure
Measure of failure

Looms high
As the bright fire-fly

Of Death.
Farewell, day breaketh.

God Bless You, Sir

With portcullis guarded by you,
enchanter in the world's sometimes prosaic garden,
need I stir? No.
Since you are the master,
could I rhyme *or* with *Sir*? Yes, yes, our prime enchanter
much more than prime "amuser."

We All Know It

That silence is best: that action and re-
Action are equal: that control, discipline, and
Liberation are bywords when spoken by an appraiser, that the
    Accidental sometimes achieves perfection, loath though we may be to
                          admit it:

And that the realm of art is the realm in
Which to look for "fishbones in the throat of the gang." Pin-
Pricks and the unstereotyped embarrassment being the contin-
    Ual diet of artists. And in spite of it all, poets ask us just what it

Is in them that we cannot subscribe to:
People overbear till told to stop: no matter through
What sobering process they have gone, some inquire if emotion, true
    And stimulated are not the same thing: promoters request us to take
                        our oath

That appearances are not cosmic: mis-
Fits in the world of achievement want to know what bus-
Iness people have to reserve judgment about undertakings. It is
    A strange idea that one must say what one thinks in order to be
                        understood.

Experimental

74

Why That Question:

"What is the difference between prose and poetry"
    If it is one?
On so much pleasantness? If the world is right about the

Thing, it is entitled to a place on some feature
    Of inquiry and there may
Be a difference, only no one says so who is sure:

                    .

Because it is the people who know, who say nothing
    Against whose principles it
Is, to be interested in what is uninteresting.

You Are Very Pensive—Hammering Out in Darkness
What Will Not Bear the Light of Day

The sure
Measure of failure

Will bring
What you are doing

To naught.
I'm not sure it ought

Not to
And neither are you.

LITTLE MAGAZINES

1915–1919

Ezra Pound:

"'Frae bank to bank, frae wood to wood I rin.'"

The rinning that you do,
Is not so new
   As it is admirable.
     "Vigor informs your
   SS Shape" and ardor knits it.

Good Meditatio
And poor Li Po;
   And that page of *Blast*, on which
     Small boats ply to and
 Fro in bee lines. Bless *Blast*.

To a Man Working His Way Through the Crowd

To Gordon Craig: Your lynx's eye
Has found the men most fit to try
    To serve you. Ingenious creatures follow in your wake.

Your speech is like Ezekiel's;
You make one feel that wrath unspells
    Some mysteries—some of the cabals of the vision.

The most propulsive thing you say
Is that one need not know the way
    To be arriving. That foreword smacks of retrospect.

Undoubtedly you overbear.
But one must do that to come where
    There is a space, a fit gymnasium for action.

To Military Progress

You use your mind
Like a millstone to grind
    Chaff.

You polish it
And with your warped wit
    Laugh

At your torso,
Prostrate where the crow—
    Falls

On such faint hearts
As its God imparts—
    Calls,

And claps its wings
Till the tumult brings
    More

Black minute-men
To revive again,
    War

At little cost.
They cry for the lost
    Head

And seek their prize
Till the evening sky's
    Red.

That Harp You Play So Well

O David, if I had
Your power, I should be glad—
    In harping, with the sling,
    In patient reasoning!

Blake, Homer, Job, and you,
Have made old wine-skins new.
    Your energies have wrought
    Stout continents of thought.

But, David, if the heart
Be brass, what boots the art
    Of exorcising wrong,
    Of harping to a song?

The sceptre and the ring
And every royal thing
    Will fail. Grief's lustiness
    Must cure that harp's distress.

To an Intra-Mural Rat

You make me think of many men
Once met, to be forgot again;
  Or merely resurrected
In a parenthesis of wit,
That found them hastening through it
  Too brisk to be inspected.

Counseil to a Bachelor

Elizabethan Trencher Motto—Bodleian Library

If thou bee younge, then marie not yett;
If thou bee olde, then no wyfe gett;
For younge mens' wyves will not bee taught,
And olde mens' wyves bee good for naught.

Appellate Jurisdiction

Fragments of sin are a part of me,
New brooms shall sweep clean the heart of me
    Shall they? Shall they?

When this light life shall have passed away,
God shall redeem me, a castaway.
    Shall He? Shall He?

The Wizard in Words

"When I am dead,"
The wizard said,
    "I'll think upon the narrow way
    And this Dante,
        And know that he was right
        And he'll delight
            In my remorse,
            Of course."
"When I am dead,"
The student said,
        "I shall have grown so tolerant,
        I'll find I can't
        Laugh at your sorry plight
        Or take delight
            In your chagrin,
            Merlin."

To William Butler Yeats on Tagore

It is made clear by the phrase,
even the mood—by virtue of which he says

the thing he thinks—that it pays,
to cut gems even in these conscience-less days;

but the jewel that always
outshines ordinary jewels, is your praise.

The North Wind to a Dutiful Beast Midway Between the Dial and the Foot of a Garden Clock

Why clamber up the pedestal?
   Steal from me half an hour and be made
     Rich. Climb
       Down and bask,
        Little lizard.
        In the blizzard,
      Who shall ask
     The time?
   Be persuaded. Do not be afraid;
Your conscientious feet sha'n't fall.

Isaiah, Jeremiah, Ezekiel, Daniel

Bloodshed and Strife Are Not of God

What is war
For;
Is it not a sore
   On this life's body?

Yes? Although
So
Long as men will go
   To battle fighting

With gun-shot,
What
Argument will not
   Fail of a hearing!

To a Strategist

You brilliant Jew,
You bright particular chameleon, you
   Regild a shabby fence.

They understood
Your stripes and particolored mind, who could
   Begrudge you prominence

And call you cold!
But when has prejudice been glad to hold
   A lizard in its hand—

A subtle thing?
To sense fed on a fine imagining,
   Sound sense is contraband.

Injudicious Gardening

If yellow betokens infidelity,
   I am an infidel.
     I could not bear a yellow rose ill will
     Because books said that yellow boded ill,
   White promised well;

However, your particular possession—
   The sense of privacy
     In what you did—deflects from your estate
     Offending eyes, and will not tolerate
   Effrontery.

To a Prize Bird

You suit me well; for you can make me laugh,
Nor are you blinded by the chaff
   That every wind sends spinning from the rick.

You know to think, and what you think you speak
With much of Samson's pride and bleak
   Finality; and none dare bid you stop.

Pride sits you well, so strut, colossal bird.
No barnyard makes you look absurd;
   Your brazen claws are staunch against defeat.

Diligence Is to Magic as Progress Is to Flight

With an elephant to ride upon—"with rings on her fingers and bells
                                                              on her toes,"
   she shall outdistance calamity anywhere she goes.
Speed is not in her mind inseparable from carpets. Locomotion arose
   in the shape of an elephant; she clambered up and chose
to travel laboriously. So far as magic carpets are concerned, she knows
   that although the semblance of speed may attach to scarecrows
of aesthetic procedure, the substance of it is embodied in such of those
   tough-grained animals as have outstripped man's whim to suppose
them ephemera, and have earned that fruit of their ability to endure blows
   which dubs them prosaic necessities—not curios.

To a Steam Roller

The illustration
is nothing to you without the application.
    You lack half wit. You crush all the particles down
        into close conformity, and then walk back and forth on them.

Sparkling chips of rock
are crushed down to the level of the parent block.
    Were not "impersonal judgment in aesthetic
        matters, a metaphysical impossibility," you

might fairly achieve
it. As for butterflies, I can hardly conceive
    of one's attending upon you, but to question
        the congruence of the complement is vain, if it exists.

[handwritten annotations:]

a judge

pleasant + interference
levels

Rational

exact fit.
as if the other is
a butterfly.

Experimental

Haughty
Knowitall

To Statecraft Embalmed

There is nothing to be said for you. Guard
Your secret. Conceal it under your "hard
   Plumage," necromancer.
      O
Bird, whose tents were "awnings of Egyptian
Yarn," shall Justice' faint zigzag inscription—
   Leaning like a dancer—
      Show
The pulse of its once vivid sovereignty?
You say not, and transmigrating from the
   Sarcophagus, you wind
      Snow
Silence round us and with moribund talk,
Half limping and half ladified, you stalk
   About. Ibis, we find
      No
Virtue in you—alive and yet so dumb,
Discreet behavior is not now the sum
   Of statesmanlike good sense.
      Though
It were the incarnation of dead grace?
As if a death mask ever could replace
   Life's faulty excellence!
      Slow
To remark the steep, too strict proportion
Of your throne, you'll see the wrenched distortion
   Of suicidal dreams
      Go
Staggering toward itself and with its bill
Attack its own identity, until
   Foe seems friend and friend seems
      Foe.

Experimental

93

To a Friend in the Making

You wild, uncooked young fellow!
   The swinkèd hind will stumble home
      Not looking at the tasks he scorned to shirk.
   Impelled to respite by rough hands,
The labored ox will bellow;
      While you stand there agape before your handiwork.

Not all good men are mellow.
   You savor of a walnut rind,
      Of oak leaves, or plucked mullein on the brae.
   And yet with all your clumsiness,
You give me pleasure, fellow;
      Your candor compensates me for my old bouquet.

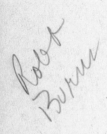

Blake

I wonder if you feel as you look at us,
As if you were seeing yourself in a mirror at the end
    Of a long corridor—walking frail-ly.
I am sure that we feel as we look at you,
As if we were ambiguous and all but improbable
    Reflections of the sun—shining pale-ly.

George Moore

In speaking of "aspiration,"
From the recesses of a pen more dolorous than blackness,
Were you presenting us with one more form of imperturbable French
drollery,
Or was it self-directed banter?
Habitual ennui
Took from you your invisible, hot helmet of anaemia
While you were filling your little glass from the decanter
Of a transparent-murky, would-be-truthful "hobohemia"—
And then facetiously
Went off with it? Your soul's supplanter,
The spirit of good narrative, flatters you, convinced that in reporting
briefly
One choice incident, you have known beauty other than of stys, on
Which to fix your admiration.

The Past Is the Present

If external action is effete
   and rhyme is outmoded,
     I shall revert to you
   Habakkuk, as when in a Bible class
     the teacher was speaking of unrhymed verse.
He said—and I think I repeat his exact words,
     "Hebrew poetry is prose
   with a sort of heightened consciousness." Ecstasy
                        affords
   the occasion and expediency determines the form.

Masks

"Loon" . . . "goose" . . . and "vulture" , . .
Thus, from the kings of water and of air,
Men pluck three catchwords for their empty lips.
Mock them in turn, wise, dumb triumvirate!
You, gander, with stout heart tooled like your wings of steel,
What coward knows your soul?
"Egyptian vultures, clean as cherubim,
All ivory and jet," sons of the burning sun,
What creatures call you "foul"?
And you, nature's own child,
You most precocious water bird,
That shouts exultantly among lone lakes,
You, foremost in the madman's alphabet—
Laugh in superb contempt at folly's catalogue!

Diogenes

Day's calumnies,
Midnight's translucencies,
    Pride's open book
Of closed humilities—
    With its inflated look;
Shall contrarieties
  As feasible as these
            Confound my wit?

Is Persian cloth
One thread with Persian sloth?
    Is gold dust bran?
Though spotted Ashtaroth
    Is not a Puritan,
Must every gorgeous moth
Be calico, and Thoth
            Be thanked for it?

Sun

Hope and Fear accost him

"No man may him hyde
From Deth holow-eyed";
For us, this inconvenient truth does not suffice.
You are not male or female, but a plan
deep-set within the heart of man.
Splendid with splendor hid you come, from your Arab abode,
a fiery topaz smothered in the hand of a great prince who rode
before you, Sun—whom you outran,
piercing his caravan.

O Sun, you shall stay
with us; holiday,
consuming wrath, be wound in a device
of Moorish gorgeousness, round glasses spun
to flame as hemispheres of one
great hour-glass dwindling to a stem. Consume hostility;
employ your weapon in this meeting-place of surging enmity!
Insurgent feet shall not outrun
multiplied flames, O Sun.

"He Wrote the History Book"

There! You shed a ray
   of whimsicality on a mask of profundity so
      terrific, that I have been dumbfounded by
it oftener than I care to say.
         The book? Titles are chaff.

Authentically
   brief and full of energy, you contribute to your father's
      legibility and are sufficiently
synthetic. Thank you for showing me
        your father's autograph.

To a Chameleon

Hid by the august foliage and fruit of the grape vine,
  twine
    your anatomy
      round the pruned and polished stem,
        Chameleon.
        Fire laid upon
      an emerald as long as
    the Dark King's massy
  one,
could not snap the spectrum up for food as you have done.

Is Your Town Nineveh?

Why so desolate?
   in phantasmagoria about fishes,
      what disgusts you? Could
         not all personal upheaval in
            the name of freedom, be tabooed?

Is it Nineveh
   and are you Jonah
      in the sweltering east wind of your wishes?
         I, myself, have stood
            there by the aquarium, looking
               At the Statue of Liberty.

You Are Fire Eaters

Not a mere blowing flame—
A clinking ash, I feel—with shame,
   At malendeavor in your service.

But as Jehoshaphat said on that occasion in
     Old Testament history,

"The battle is not mine,"
And strategy laid down—in fine
   Surrender, may be conquest.

Pedantic Literalist

Prince Rupert's drop, paper muslin ghost,
   white torch—"with power to say unkind
things with kindness, and the most
     irritating things in the midst of love and
       tears," you invite destruction.

You are like the meditative man
   with the perfunctory heart; its
carved cordiality ran
     to and fro at first like an inlaid and royal
       immutable production;

then afterward "neglected to be
   painful, deluding him with
loitering formality,"
     "doing its duty as if it did it not,"
       presenting an obstruction

to the motive that it served. What stood
   erect in you has withered. A
little "palm-tree of turned wood"
     informs your once spontaneous core in its
       immutable production.

Critics and Connoisseurs

There is a great amount of poetry in unconscious
    fastidiousness. Certain Ming
        products, imperial floor-coverings of coach-
wheel yellow, are well enough in their way but I have seen something
that I like better—a
        mere childish attempt to make an imperfectly ballasted animal stand up,
        similar determination to make a pup
            eat his meat from the plate.

I remember a swan under the willows in Oxford,
    with flamingo-colored, maple-
        leaflike feet. It reconnoitered like a battle-
ship. Disbelief and conscious fastidiousness were
    ingredients in its
        disinclination to move. Finally its hardihood was
            not proof against its
        proclivity to more fully appraise such bits
            of food as the stream

bore counter to it; it made away with what I gave it
    to eat. I have seen this swan and
        I have seen you; I have seen ambition without
understanding in a variety of forms. Happening to stand
    by an ant-hill, I have
        seen a fastidious ant carrying a stick north, south,
            east, west, till it turned on
        itself, struck out from the flower-bed into the lawn,
            and returned to the point

from which it had started. Then abandoning the stick as
    useless and overtaxing its
        jaws with a particle of whitewash—pill-like but
heavy—it again went through the same course of procedure.
            What is

there in being able
　　to say that one has dominated the stream in an attitude
　　　　　　　　　　　　　　　　　　　of self-defense;
　　in proving that one has had the experience
　　　of carrying a stick?

Experimental

In This Age of Hard Trying, Nonchalance Is Good and

"really, it is not the
   business of the gods to bake clay pots." They did not
     do it in this instance. A few
       revolved upon the axes of their worth
   as if excessive popularity might be a pot;

they did not venture the
   profession of humility. The polished wedge
     that might have split the firmament
       was dumb. At last it threw itself away
   and falling down, conferred on some poor fool, a privilege.

"Taller by the length of
   a conversation of five hundred years than all
     the others," there was one, whose tales
       of what could never have been actual—
   were better than the haggish, uncompanionable drawl

of certitude; his by-
   play was more terrible in its effectiveness
     than the fiercest frontal attack.
       The staff, the bag, the feigned inconsequence
   of manner, best bespeak that weapon, self-protectiveness.

To Be Liked by You Would Be a Calamity

"Attack is more piquant than concord," but when
   You tell me frankly that you would like to feel
     My flesh beneath your feet,
       I'm all abroad; I can but put my weapon up, and
         Bow you out.
Gesticulation—it is half the language.
   Let unsheathed gesticulation be the steel
     Your courtesy must meet,
       Since in your hearing words are mute, which to my senses
        Are a shout.

Feed Me, Also, River God

Lest by diminished vitality and abated
   vigilance, I become food for crocodiles—for that quicksand
   of gluttony which is legion. It is there, close at hand—
     on either side
     of me. You remember the Israelites who said in pride

and stoutness of heart: "The bricks are fallen down, we will
   build with hewn stone, the sycamores are cut down, we will
   change to cedars?" I am not ambitious to dress stones, to
     renew forts, nor to match
     my value in action, against their ability to catch

up with arrested prosperity. I am not like
   them, indefatigable, but if you are a god, you will
   not discriminate against me. Yet—if you may fulfill
     none but prayers dressed
     as gifts, in return for your own gifts—disregard the request.

Apropos of Mice

Come in, Rat, and eat with me;
One must occasionally—
   If one would rate the rat at his true worth—
   Practice catholicity;

Cheeseparings and a porkrind
Stock my house—good of their kind,
   But were they not, you would oblige me? Is
   Plenty, multiplicity?

"She Trimmed the Candles
Like One Who Loves the Beautiful"

It was right that such light
  As there was in the room should burn before her. She
Made me think of Diana—monkeys and penguins and white

Bears and herons: of wood
  Covered ravines cut by waterfalls, of mountains
With streaks of white smoke across them, of knife blades set in good

African ivory
  Hafts: of "white and blue foxes on the confines of
The icy sea." But when she spoke of externality

She flouted it and called
  Good looks, mortality decked out with circumstance;
She said: You speak of death and are respectfully appalled.

Things that one can suffer
  Without the appearance of a surface scratch, put
Dying far away. Death is not unique in character:

Always overrated,
  It is a needful happening like lighting these—
Or like reiterating to the deaf what has been said.

In "Designing a Cloak to Cloak His Designs," You Wrested from Oblivion a Coat of Immortality for Your Own Use

Cowed by his uningenious will
Of dragon-like demeanor, till
   It left them orphans.

His foibles clustered underneath
Him, dominated by a wreath
   Of upright half notes.

Encumbered as he was with pride,
But for that coat he might have died
   So despicably

That kindness might have seemed unkind
Had not the garment been designed
   To serve two masters.

Holes Bored in a Workbag by the Scissors

A neat round hole in the bank of a creek
    Means a rat;
        That is to say, craft, industry, resourcefulness:
           While
These indicate the unfortunate, meek
    Habitat
        Of surgery thrust home to fabricate useless
           Voids.

The Just Man and

His pie. "I would be
Repossessed of all the
Superlatives that I have squandered.
That I might use them in praise of it."

The four and twenty
Birds were singing while he
Apportioned it off casually
And found in it nothing for himself.

Those Various Scalpels

Those
various sounds, consistently indistinct, like intermingled echoes
   struck from thin glasses successively at random—
      the inflection disguised: your hair, the tails of two
    fighting-cocks head to head in stone—
       like sculptured scimitars repeating the curve of your ears in reverse order:
                                      your eyes,
    flowers of ice and snow

sown by tearing winds on the the cordage of disabled ships: your raised hand
an ambiguous signature: your cheeks, those rosettes
   of blood on the stone floors of French châteaux,
with regard to which the guides are so affirmative—
      your other hand

a bundle of lances all alike, partly hid by emeralds from Persia
   and the fractional magnificence of Florentine
      goldwork—a collection of little objects—
sapphires set with emeralds, and pearls with a moonstone, made fine
   with enamel in gray, yellow, and dragonfly blue;
     a lemon, a pear

and three bunches of grapes, tied with silver: your dress, a magnificent square
cathedral tower of uniform
   and at the same time diverse appearance—a
species of vertical vineyard, rustling in the storm
   of conventional opinion—are they weapons or scalpels?
     Whetted to brilliance

by the hard majesty of that sophistication which is superior to opportunity,
these things are rich instruments with which to experiment.
   But why dissect destiny with instruments
    more highly specialized than the components of destiny itself?

Like a Bulrush

Or the spike
of a channel marker or the
moon, he superintended the demolition of his image in
the water by the wind; he did not strike

them at the
time as being different from
any other inhabitant of the water; it was as if he
were a seal in the combined livery

of bird plus
snake; it was as if he knew that
the penguins were not fish and as if in their bat blindness, they did not
realize that he was amphibious.

To the Peacock of France

In "taking charge of your possessions when you saw them" you became a
                                                                    golden jay.
Scaramouche said you charmed his charm away,
   but not his color? Yes, his color when you liked.
   Of chiseled setting and black-opalescent dye,
     you were the jewelry of sense;
     of sense, not license; you but trod the pace
     of liberty in market-place
      and court. Molière,
       the huggermugger repertory of your first adventure, is your own affair.

"Anchorites do not dwell in theatres," and peacocks do not flourish in a cell.
Why make distinctions? The results were well
   when you were on the boards; nor were your triumphs bought
  at horrifying sacrifice of stringency.
     You hated sham; you ranted up
     and down through the conventions of excess;
     nor did the King love you the less
      nor did the world,
       in whose chief interest and for whose spontaneous delight, your
                                                                    broad tail was unfurled.

Sojourn in the Whale

Trying to open locked doors with a sword, threading
   the points of needles, planting shade trees
   upside down; swallowed by the opaqueness of one whom the seas
love better than they love you, Ireland—

you have lived and lived on every kind of shortage.
   You have been compelled by hags to spin
   gold thread from straw and have heard men say:
"There is a feminine temperament in direct contrast to ours,

which makes her do these things. Circumscribed by a
   heritage of blindness and native
   incompetence, she will become wise and will be forced to give in.
Compelled by experience, she will turn back;

water seeks its own level";
   and you have smiled. "Water in motion is far
   from level." You have seen it, when obstacles happened to bar
the path, rise automatically.

Roses Only

You do not seem to realize that beauty is a liability rather than
an asset—that in view of the fact that spirit creates form we are justified
in supposing
that you must have brains. For you, a symbol of the unit, stiff and
sharp,
conscious of surpassing by dint of native superiority and liking for
everything
self-dependent, anything an

ambitious civilization might produce: for you, unaided, to attempt through sheer
reserve to confute presumptions resulting from observation is idle. You
cannot make us
think you a delightful happen-so. But rose, if you are brilliant, it
is not because your petals are the without-which-nothing of pre-eminence.
You would look, minus
thorns—like a what-is-this, a mere

peculiarity. They are not proof against a storm, the elements, or mildew
but what about the predatory hand? What is brilliance without
coordination? Guarding the
infinitesimal pieces of your mind, compelling audience to
the remark that it is better to be forgotten than to be remembered too
violently,
your thorns are the best part of you.

The Monkeys

winked too much and were afraid of snakes. The zebras, supreme in
their abnormality; the elephants with their fog-colored skin
    and strictly practical appendages
        were there, the small cats; and the parakeet—
            trivial and humdrum on examination, destroying
            bark and portions of the food it could not eat.

I recall their magnificence, now not more magnificent
than it is dim. It is difficult to recall the ornament,
    speech, and precise manner of what one might
        call the minor acquaintances twenty
            years back; but I shall not forget him—that Gilgamesh among
            the hairy carnivora—that cat with the

wedge-shaped, slate-gray marks on its forelegs and the resolute tail,
astringently remarking, "They have imposed on us with their pale
    half-fledged protestations, trembling about
        in inarticulate frenzy, saying
            it is not for us to understand art; finding it
            all so difficult, examining the thing

as if it were inconceivably arcanic, as symmet-
rically frigid as if it had been carved out of chrysoprase
    or marble—strict with tension, malignant
        in its power over us and deeper
            than the sea when it proffers flattery in exchange for hemp,
            rye, flax, horses, platinum, timber, and fur."

Melanchthon

Elephant

Openly, yes,
with the naturalness
   of the hippopotamus or the alligator
   when it climbs out on the bank to experience the

sun, I do these
things which I do, which please
   no one but myself. Now I breathe and now I am sub-
   merged; the blemishes stand up and shout when the object

in view is a
renaissance; shall I say
   the contrary? The sediment of the river which
   encrusts my joints makes me very gray, but I am used

to it, it may
remain there; do away
   with it and I am myself done away with, for the
   patina of circumstance can but enrich what was

there to begin
with. This elephant-skin
   which I inhabit, fibred over like the shell of
   the coconut, this piece of black glass through which no light

can filter—cut
into checkers by rut
   upon rut of unpreventable experience—
   is a manual for the peanut-tongued and the

hairy-toed. Black
but beautiful, my back
   is full of the history of power. Of power? What
   is powerful and what is not? My soul shall never

be cut into
by a wooden spear; through-
   out childhood to the present time, the unity of
   life and death has been expressed by the circumference

described by my
trunk; nevertheless I
   perceive feats of strength to be inexplicable after
   all; and I am on my guard; external poise, it

has its center
well nurtured—we know
   where—in pride; but spiritual poise, it has its center where?
   My ears are sensitized to more than the sound of

the wind. I see
and I hear, unlike the
   wandlike body of which one hears so much, which was made
   to see and not to see; to hear and not to hear;

that tree-trunk without
roots, accustomed to shout
   its own thoughts to itself like a shell, maintained intact
   by who knows what strange pressure of the atmosphere; that

spiritual
brother to the coral-
   plant, absorbed into which, the equable sapphire light
   becomes a nebulous green. The I of each is to

the I of each
a kind of fretful speech
   which sets a limit on itself; the elephant is
   black earth preceded by a tendril? Compared with those

phenomena
which vacillate like a

translucence of the atmosphere, the elephant is
that on which darts cannot strike decisively the first

time, a substance
needful as an instance
    of the indestructibility of matter; it
    has looked at electricity and at the earth-

quake and is still
here; the name means thick. Will
    depth be depth, thick skin be thick, to one who can see no
    beautiful element of unreason under it?

An Ardent Platonist

Prone to observe the self-evident fact: One cannot sweep the
Ocean dry, even when it comes against one's own door, but one can
                              withdraw from the occupancy
Of land which is not very high: a just observation. Regarding with

volition

Curious relish that python of selfishness, personal
Will—too heavy for the tree on which it rests—he dwelt in his hardness, on
                              the theological
Aspect of his proximity to it and on the mysteries of the

Creature's subsistence. The emotional shorthand of the East,
The telegraphic code of the West, the harmless innuendoes of the monkey—
                              as of the beast
Higher up, which resembles it—are but the language of commerce; he was

Right about it. He used to sit at the window and smoke and
The mosquitos would come in; he was absolutely fearless. Formidable? No;
                              to understand
One is not to find one formidable. A philosopher, he was but

An apple which has not begun to mellow; the ratio
Is there; to be philosophical is to be no longer mysterious; it is to be no
Longer privileged, to say what one thinks in order to be understood.

Reinforcements

The vestibule to experience is not to
    Be exalted into epic grandeur. These men are going
to their work with this idea, advancing like a school of fish through

still water—waiting to change the course or dismiss
    the idea of movement, till forced to. The words of the Greeks
ring in our ears, but they are vain in comparison with a sight like this.

The pulse of intention does not move so that one
    can see it, and moral machinery is not labeled, but
the future of time is determined by the power of volition.

volition
+ The
future
of time

The Fish

wade
through black jade.
   Of the crow-blue mussel-shells, one keeps
   adjusting the ash heaps;
     opening and shutting itself like

an
injured fan.
   The barnacles, which encrust the side
   of the wave cannot hide
     there, for the submerged shafts of the

sun,
split like spun
   glass, move themselves with spotlight swiftness
   into the crevices—
     in and out, illuminating

the
turquoise sea
   of bodies. The water drives a wedge
   of iron through the iron edge
     of the cliff; whereupon the stars,

pink
rice-grains, ink-
   bespattered jellyfish, crabs like green
   lilies, and submarine
     toadstools slide each on the other.

All
external
   marks of abuse are present on this
   defiant edifice—
     all the physical features of

ac-
cident—lack
   of cornice, dynamite grooves, burns, and
   hatchet strokes, these things stand
      out on it; the chasm side is

dead.
Repeated
   evidence has proved that it can live
   on what can not revive
      its youth. The sea grows old in it.

Callot-Drecol-Cheruit-Jenny-Doucet-Aviotte-Lady

With wrists like paper knives and feet like
The leaves of the willow—those strike
    You as being brutish and restrained (synonyms alas)

Who view a matter calmly; when you
See a light and mothlike want to
    Go in, this is to be said in favor of staying out—

There is danger in being appre-
Ciated: Compliments are free
    To all but are not synonymous with admiration.

The principle of cause and effect
Does not apply, where to expect
    It to, is the most reasonable thing in the world. And

What of it? "Without enemies one's
Courage flags"—that fund of reasons
    Which comes from the desperate temptation to let go all

Waves on the kitchen floor, Manhattan
Or Long Beach for example—can
    Hardly be recognized as being of a piece with those

At the bottom of a chasm and
Philosophy succeeding band
    Concert repeats is not philosophy but I shall go

On: logic is a thing I rely
Upon as I would hazard my
    Life on the sea's remaining crimson after a sunset:

The minarets of the amusement
Park: the slipcoverlike, striped tent
    Above the beverages; the skeleton caterpil-

Lar called a Chase Through the Clouds, with wire
Humps that have begun to acquire
    Rust like coffee grounds; and you despite the disparity—

Are indebted but somehow you
Revere it though you know it to
    Be nonsense—for personal momentum will upset it.

You Say You Said

"Few words are best."
   Not here. Discretion has been abandoned in this part of the world too
                                                lately
   For it to be admired. Disgust for it is like the
Equinox—all things in

One. Disgust is
   No psychologist and has not opportunity to be a hypocrite.
   It says to the saw-toothed bayonet and to the cue
Of blood behind the sub-

Marine—to the
   Poisoned comb, to the Kaiser of Germany and to the intolerant gate-
   Man at the exit from the eastbound express: "I hate
You less than you must hate

Yourselves: You have
   Accoutred me. 'Without enemies one's courage flags.' Your error has
                                          been timed
   To aid me, I am in debt to you for you have primed
Me against subterfuge."

Old Tiger

You are right about it; that wary,
presumptuous young baboon is nothing to you; and the chimpanzee?
   An exemplary hind leg hanging like a plummet at the end of a

string—the tufts of fur depressed like grass
on which something heavy has been lying—nominal ears of black glass—
   what is there to look at? And of the leopard, spotted underneath and on

its toes; of the American rattler,
his eyes on a level with the crown of his head and of the lesser
   varieties, fish, bats, greyhounds and other animals of one thickness,

the same may be said, they are nothing
to you and yet involuntarily you smile; as at the dozing,
   magisterial hauteur of the camel or the facial expression

of the parrot: you to whom a no
is never a no, loving to succeed where all others have failed, so
   constituted that opposition is pastime and struggle is meat, you

see more than I see but even I
see too much; the select many are all but one thing to avoid, my
   prodigy and yours—as well as those mentioned above, who cannot
                               commit

an act of self-destruction—the will
apparently having been made part of the constitution until
   it has become subsidiary, but observe: in that exposition

is their passion, concealment, yours, they
are human, you are inhuman and the mysterious look, the way
   in which they comport themselves and the conversation imported from the

birdhouse, are one version of culture.
You demur? To see, to realize with a prodigious leap is your
   version and that should be all there is of it. Possibly so, but when one

is duped by that which is pleasant, who
is to tell one that it is too much? Attempt to brush away the Foo
   dog and it is forthwith more than a dog, its tail superimposed on its

self in a complacent half spiral—
incidentally so witty. One may rave about the barren wall
   or rave about the painstaking workmanship, the admirable subject;

the little dishes, brown, mulberry
or sea green, are half human and waiving the matter of artistry,
   anything which cannot be reproduced is "divine." It is as with the

book—that commodity inclusive
of the idea, the art object, the exact spot in which to live,
   the favorite item of wearing apparel. You have "read Dante's Hell

till you are familiar with it"—till
the whole surface has become so polished as to afford no little
   seam or irregularity at which to catch. So here, with the wise few;

the shred of superior wisdom
has engaged them for such a length of time as somehow to have become
   a fixture, without rags or a superfluous dog's ear by which to seize

it and throw it away before it
is worn out. As for you—forming a sudden resolution to sit
   still—looking at them with that fixed, abstracted lizardlike expression of

the eye which is characteristic
of all accurate observers, you are there, old fellow, in the thick
   of the enlightenment along with the cultured, the profusely lettered,

the intentionally hirsute—made
just as ludicrous by self-appointedly sublime disgust, inlaid
   with wiry, jet black lines of objection. You, however, forbear when the

mechanism complains—scorning to
push. You know one thing, an inkling of which has not entered their minds; you
   know that it is not necessary to live in order to be alive.

Radical

Tapering
to a point, conserving everything,
   this carrot is predestined to be thick.
     The world is
      but a circumstance, a mis-
        erable corn patch for its feet. With ambition, im-
         agination, outgrowth,

nutriment,
with everything crammed belligerent-
   ly inside itself, its fibres breed mon-
     opoly—
      a tail-like, wedge-shaped engine with the
        secret of expansion, fused with intensive heat to
         the color of the set-

ting sun and
stiff. For the man in the straw hat, stand-
   ing still and turning to look back at it
     as much as
     to say, my happiest moment has
       been funereal in comparison with this, the condi-
        tions of life pre-

determined
slavery to be easy, inclined
   away from progress, and freedom, hard. For
     it? Dismiss
     agrarian lore; it tells him this:
       that which it is impossible to force, it is impossible
        to hinder.

Poetry

Marianne

I, too, dislike it: there are things that are important beyond all this fiddle.
  Reading it, however, with a perfect contempt for it, one discovers in
   it, after all, a place for the genuine.
    Hands that can grasp, eyes
    that can dilate, hair that can rise
     if it must, these things are important not because a

high-sounding interpretation can be put upon them but because they are
  useful. When they become so derivative as to become unintelligible,
  the same thing may be said for all of us, that we
    do not admire what
    we cannot understand: the bat
     holding on upside down or in quest of something to

eat, elephants pushing, a wild horse taking a roll, a tireless wolf under
  a tree, the immovable critic twitching his skin like a horse that feels a flea,
                    the base-
    ball fan, the statistician—
     nor is it valid
      to discriminate against "business documents and

school-books"; all these phenomena are important. One must make a
                       distinction
  however: when dragged into prominence by half poets, the result is not
                          poetry,
    nor till the poets among us can be
     "literalists of
     the imagination"—above
      insolence and triviality and can present

for inspection, "imaginary gardens with real toads in them," shall we have
  it. In the meantime, if you demand on the one hand,
  the raw material of poetry in
    all its rawness and
    that which is on the other hand
     genuine, you are interested in poetry.

In the Days of Prismatic Color

not in the days of Adam and Eve, but when Adam
   was alone; when there was no smoke and color was
fine, not with the refinement
   of early civilization art, but because
of its originality; with nothing to modify it but the

mist that went up, obliqueness was a variation
   of the perpendicular, plain to see and
to account for: it is no
   longer that; nor did the blue-red-yellow band
of incandescence that was color keep its stripe: it also is one of

those things into which much that is peculiar can be
   read; complexity is not a crime, but carry
it to the point of murkiness
   and nothing is plain. Complexity,
moreover, that has been committed to darkness, instead of

granting itself to be the pestilence that it is, moves all a-
   bout as if to bewilder us with the dismal
fallacy that insistence
   is the measure of achievement and that all
truth must be dark. Principally throat, sophistication is as it al-

ways has been—at the antipodes from the init-
   ial great truths. "Part of it was crawling, part of it
was about to crawl, the rest
   was torpid in its lair." In the short-legged, fit-
ful advance, the gurgling and all the minutiae—we have the classic

multitude of feet. To what purpose! Truth is no Apollo
   Belvedere, no formal thing. The wave may go over it if it likes.
Know that it will be there when it says,
   "I shall be there when the wave has gone by."

Dock Rats

There are human beings who seem to regard the place as craftily
    as we do—who seem to feel that it is a good place to come
      home to. On what a river; wide—twinkling like a chopped sea under some
        of the finest shipping in the

world: the square-rigged four-rigged four-master, the liner, the battleship like
                                      the two-
    thirds submerged section of an iceberg; the tug
    dipping and pushing, the bell striking as it comes; the steam yacht, lying
      like a new made arrow on the

stream; the ferry-boat—a head assigned, one to each compartment, making
    a row of chessmen set for play. When the wind is from the east,
    the smell is of apples, of hay; the aroma increased and decreased
      as the wind changes;

of rope, of mountain leaves for florists; as from the west,
    it is aromatic of salt. Occasionally a parakeet
    from Brazil arrives clasping and clawing; or a monkey—tail and feet
      in readiness for an over-

ture; all arms and tail; how delightful! There is the sea, moving the bulk-
    head with its horse strength; and the multiplicity of rudders
    and propellers; the signals, shrill, questioning, peremptory, diverse;
      the wharf cats and the barge dogs; it

is easy to overestimate the value of such things. One does
    not live in such a place from motives of expediency
    but because to one who has been accustomed to it, shipping is the
    most interesting thing in the world.

Picking and Choosing

Literature is a phase of life. If
   one is afraid of it, the situation is irremediable; if
one approaches it familiarly
   what one says of it is worthless. Words are constructive
when they are true; the opaque allusion—the simulated flight

upward—accomplishes nothing. Why cloud the fact
   that Shaw is self-conscious in the field of sentiment but is otherwise re-
warding; that James is all that has been
   said of him if feeling is profound? It is not Hardy
the distinguished novelist and Hardy the poet, but one man

"interpreting life through the medium of the
   emotions." If he must give an opinion, it is permissible that the
critic should know what he likes. Gordon
   Craig with his "this is I" and "this is mine," with his three
wise men, his "sad French greens" and his Chinese cherry—Gordon Craig, so

inclinational and unashamed—has carried
   the precept of being a good critic to the last extreme, and Burke is a
psychologist—of acute, raccoon-
   like curiosity. *Summa diligentia;*
to the humbug, whose name is so amusing—very young and very

rushed, Caesar crossed the Alps "on the top of a
   diligence." We are not daft about the meaning, but this familiarity
with wrong meanings puzzles one. Humming-
   bug, the candles are not wired for electricity.
Small dog, going over the lawn, nipping the linen and saying

that you have a badger—remember Xenophon;
   only the most rudimentary sort of behavior is necessary
to put us on the scent; "a right good
   salvo of barks," a few "strong wrinkles" puckering the
skin between the ears, are all we ask.

THE *DIAL* YEARS

1920–1925

England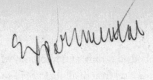

With its baby rivers and little towns, each with its abbey or its cathedral,
   with voices—one voice perhaps, echoing through the transept—the
criterion of suitability and convenience; and Italy with its equal
      shores—contriving an epicureanism from which the grossness has been

extracted: and Greece with its goat and its gourds, the nest of modified illusions:
   and France, the "chrysalis of the nocturnal butterfly" in
whose products, mystery of construction diverts one from what was
                                             originally one's
      object—substance at the core: and the East with its snails, its emotional

shorthand and jade cockroaches, its rock crystal and its imperturbability,
   all of museum quality: and America where there
is the little old ramshackle victoria in the south, where cigars are smoked on the
      street in the north; where there are no proof readers, no silkworms, no
                                             digressions;

the wild man's land; grassless, linksless, languageless country in which
                                          letters are written
   not in Spanish, not in Greek, not in Latin, not in shorthand,
but in plain American which cats and dogs can read! The letter *a* in psalm
                                          and calm, when
      pronounced with the sound of *a* in candle, is very noticeable, but

why should continents of misapprehension have to be accounted for by the
   fact? Does it follow that because there are poisonous toadstools
which resemble mushrooms, both are dangerous? In the case of
                              mettlesomeness which may be
      mistaken for appetite, of heat which may appear to be haste, no con-

clusions may be drawn. To have misapprehended the matter is to have confessed
   that one has not looked far enough. The sublimated wisdom
of China, Egyptian discernment, the cataclysmic torrent of emotion compressed
   in the verbs of the Hebrew language, the books of the man who is able

to say, "I envy nobody but him, and him only, who catches more fish than I do"—the flower and fruit of all that noted superi-
ority—should one not have stumbled upon it in America, must one imagine that it is not there? It has never been confined to one locality.

Lines on a Visit of Anne Carroll Moore to Hudson Park Branch

Before the shelves at Hudson Park
The brownies who appear at dark
For news of sport and picture screen,
And the good leprechaun in green—
One night assembled hand in hand
The modest number of the band,
Increasing till there was no space
That could accommodate a face
Or hand or pair of brownie feet.
The consternation was complete
Because a rumor gathered weight
That their great friend—a potentate
Among all brownies who could write
And read—would soon be lost to sight,
And all detected as they stood
By their pinocchio of wood
They vowed that each in turn a sentry
Hidden close beside the entry
Should keep watch at the front door
Until Miss Anne Carroll Moore
Should be at the Hudson once more.

When I Buy Pictures

or what is closer to the truth,
when I look at that of which I may regard myself as the imaginary possessor,
I fix upon what would give me pleasure in my average moments:
the satire upon curiosity in which no more is discernible
than the intensity of the mood;
or quite the opposite—the old thing, the medieval decorated hat-box,
in which there are hounds with waists diminishing like the waist of the
                                                                    hour-glass,
and deer and birds and seated people;
it may be no more than a square of parquetry; the literal biography perhaps,
in letters standing well apart upon a parchment-like expanse;
an artichoke in six varieties of blue; the snipe-legged hieroglyphic in three parts;
the silver fence protecting Adam's grave, or Michael taking Adam by the wrist.
Too stern an intellectual emphasis upon this quality or that detracts from
                                                                    one's enjoyment.
It must not wish to disarm anything; nor may the approved triumph easily
                                                                    be honored—
that which is great because something else is small.
It comes to this: of whatever sort it is,
it must be "lit with piercing glances into the life of things";
it must acknowledge the spiritual forces which have made it.

A Grave

Man looking into the sea,
taking the view from those who have as much right to it as you have to it
yourself,
it is human nature to stand in the middle of a thing,
but you cannot stand in the middle of this;
the sea has nothing to give but a well excavated grave.
The fins stand in a procession, each with an emerald turkey-foot at the top,
reserved as their contours, saying nothing;
repression, however, is not the most obvious characteristic of the sea;
the sea is a collector, quick to return a rapacious look.
There are others besides you who have worn that look—
whose expression is no longer a protest; the fish no longer investigate them
for their bones have not lasted:
men lower nets, unconscious of the fact that they are desecrating a grave,
and row quickly away—the blades of the oars
moving together like the feet of water-spiders as if there were no such thing
as death.
The wrinkles progress among themselves in a phalanx—beautiful under
networks of foam,
and fade breathlessly while the sea rustles in and out of the seaweed;
the birds swim through the air at top speed, emitting cat-calls as heretofore—
the tortoise-shell scourges about the feet of the cliffs, in motion beneath them;
and the ocean, under the pulsation of lighthouses and noise of bell-buoys,
advances as usual, looking as if it were not that ocean in which dropped
things are bound to sink—
in which if they turn and twist, it is neither with volition nor consciousness.

New York

the savage's romance,
accreted where we need the space for commerce—
the center of the wholesale fur trade,
starred with tepees of ermine and peopled with foxes,
the long guard-hairs waving two inches beyond the body of the pelt;
the ground dotted with deer-skins—white with white spots,
"as satin needlework in a single color may carry a varied pattern,"
and wilting eagle's-down compacted by the wind;
and picardels of beaver-skin; white ones alert with snow.
It is a far cry from the "queen full of jewels"
and the beau with the muff,
from the gilt coach shaped like a perfume-bottle,
to the conjunction of the Monongahela and the Allegheny,
and the scholastic philosophy of the wilderness.
It is not the dime-novel exterior,
Niagara Falls, the calico horses and the war-canoe;
it is not that "if the fur is not finer than such as one sees others wear,
one would rather be without it"—
that estimated in raw meat and berries, we could feed the universe;
it is not the atmosphere of ingenuity,
the otter, the beaver, the puma skins
without shooting-irons or dogs;
it is not the plunder,
but "accessibility to experience."

The Labors of Hercules

To popularize the mule, its neat exterior
expressing the principle of accommodation reduced to a minimum:
to persuade one of austere taste, proud in the possession of home, and a
                                        musician—
that the piano is a free field for etching; that his "charming tadpole notes"
belong to the past when one had time to play them:
to persuade those self-wrought Midases of brains
whose fourteen-carat ignorance aspires to rise in value, augurs disappointment,
that one must not borrow a long white beard and tie it on
and threaten with the scythe of time the casually curious:
to teach the bard with too elastic a selectiveness
that one detects creative power by its capacity to conquer one's detachment,
that while it may have more elasticity than logic
it flies along in a straight line like electricity,
depopulating areas that boast of their remoteness,
to prove to the high priests of caste
that snobbishness is a stupidity,
the best side out, of age-old toadyism,
kissing the feet of the man above,
kicking the face of the man below;
to teach the patron-saints-to-atheists
that we are sick of the earth,
sick of the pig-sty, wild geese and wild men;
to convince snake-charming controversialists
that one keeps on knowing
"that the Negro is not brutal,
that the Jew is not greedy,
that the Oriental is not immoral,
that the German is not a Hun."

Snakes, Mongooses, Snake-Charmers, and the Like

I have a friend who would give a price for those long fingers all of one length—
those hideous bird's claws, for that exotic asp and the mongoose—
products of the country in which everything is hard work, the country of the
                                                        grass-getter,
the torch-bearer, the dog-servant, the messenger-bearer, the holy-man.
Engrossed in this distinguished worm nearly as wild and as fierce as the day
                                                        it was caught,
he gazes as if incapable of looking at anything with a view to analysis.
"The slight snake rippling quickly through the grass,
the leisurely tortoise with its pied back,
the chameleon passing from twig to stone, from stone to straw,"
lit his imagination at one time; his admiration now converges upon this.
Thick, not heavy, it stands up from its traveling-basket,
the essentially Greek, the plastic animal all of a piece from nose to tail;
one is compelled to look at it as at the shadows of the Alps
imprisoning in their folds like flies in amber the rhythms of the skating-rink.
This animal to which from the earliest times, importance has attached,
fine as its worshipers have said—for what was it invented?
To show that when intelligence in its pure form
has embarked on a train of thought which is unproductive, it will come back?
We do not know; the only positive thing about it is its shape; but why protest?
The passion for setting people right is in itself an afflictive disease.
Distaste which takes no credit to itself is best.

People's Surroundings

They answer one's questions,
a deal table compact with the wall;
in this dried bone of arrangement
one's "natural promptness" is compressed, not crowded out;
one's style is not lost in such simplicity.

The palace furniture, so old-fashioned, so old-fashionable;
Sèvres china and the fireplace dogs—
bronze dromios with pointed ears, as obsolete as pugs;
one has one's preferences in the matter of bad furniture,
and this is not one's choice.

The vast indestructible necropolis
of composite Yawman-Erbe separable units;
the steel, the oak, the glass, the Poor Richard publications
containing the public secrets of efficiency
on paper so thin that "one thousand four hundred and twenty pages make
                                                          one inch,"
exclaiming, so to speak, "When you take my time, you take something I had
                                                          meant to use;"
the highway hid by fir-trees in rhododendrons twenty feet deep,
the peacocks, hand-forged gates, old Persian velvet,
roses outlined in pale black on an ivory ground,
the pierced iron shadows of the cedars,
Chinese carved glass, old Waterford, lettered ladies;
landscape gardening twisted into permanence;

straight lines over such great distances as one finds in Utah or in Texas,
where people do not have to be told
that a good brake is as important as a good motor;
where by means of extra sense-cells in the skin
they can, like trout, smell what is coming—
those cool sirs with the explicit sensory apparatus of common sense,
who know the exact distance between two points as the crow flies;
there is something attractive about a mind that moves in a straight line—

the municipal bat-roost of mosquito warfare;
the American string quartet;
these are questions more than answers,

and Bluebeard's Tower above the coral-reefs,
the magic mouse-trap closing on all points of the compass,
capping like petrified surf the furious azure of the bay,
where there is no dust, and life is like a lemon-leaf,
a green piece of tough translucent parchment,
where the crimson, the copper, and the Chinese vermilion of the poincianas
set fire to the masonry and turquoise blues refute the clock;
this dungeon with odd notions of hospitality,
with its "chessmen carved out of moonstones,"
its mocking-birds, fringed lilies, and hibiscus,
its black butterflies with blue half circles on their wings,
tan goats with onyx ears, its lizards glittering and without thickness,
like splashes of fire and silver on the pierced turquoise of the lattices

and the acacia-like lady shivering at the touch of a hand,
lost in a small collision of the orchids—
dyed quicksilver let fall,
to disappear like an obedient chameleon in fifty shades of mauve and amethyst.
Here where the mind of this establishment has come to the conclusion
that it would be impossible to revolve about oneself too much,
sophistication has, "like an escalator," "cut the nerve of progress."

In these non-committal, personal-impersonal expressions of appearance,
the eye knows what to skip;
the physiognomy of conduct must not reveal the skeleton;
"a setting must not have the air of being one,"
yet with X-ray-like inquisitive intensity upon it, the surfaces go back;
the interfering fringes of expression are but a stain on what stands out,

there is neither up nor down to it;
we see the exterior and the fundamental structure—
captains of armies, cooks, carpenters,
cutlers, gamesters, surgeons and armorers,
lapidaries, silkmen, glovers, fiddlers and ballad-singers,

sextons of churches, dyers of black cloth, hostlers and chimney-sweeps,
queens, countesses, ladies, emperors, travelers and mariners,
dukes, princes and gentlemen,
in their respective places—
camps, forges and battlefields,
conventions, oratories and wardrobes,
dens, deserts, railway stations, asylums and places where engines are made,
shops, prisons, brickyards and altars of churches—
in magnificent places clean and decent,
castles, palaces, dining-halls, theaters and imperial audience-chambers.

Novices

anatomize their work
in the sense in which Will Honeycomb was jilted by a duchess;
the little assumptions of the scared ego confusing the issue
so that they do not know "whether it is the buyer or the seller who gives the
money"—
an abstruse idea plain to none but the artist,
the only seller who buys, and holds on to the money.
Because one expresses oneself and entitles it wisdom, one is not a fool.
What an idea!
"Dracontine cockatrices, perfect and poisonous from the beginning,"
they present themselves as a contrast to sea-serpented regions
"unlit by the half-lights of more conscious art."

Acquiring at thirty what at sixty they will be trying to forget,
blind to the right word, deaf to satire
which like "the smell of the cypress strengthens the nerves of the brain,"
averse from the antique
with "that tinge of sadness about it which a reflective mind always feels,
it is so little and so much"—
they write the sort of thing that would in their judgment interest a lady;
curious to know if we do not adore each letter of the alphabet that goes to
make a word of it—
according to the Act of Congress, the sworn statement of the treasurer and
all the rest of it—
the counterpart to what we are:
stupid man; men are strong and no one pays any attention:
stupid woman; women have charm, and how annoying they can be.
Yes, "the authors are wonderful people, particularly those that write the most,"
the masters of all languages, the supertadpoles of expression.
Accustomed to the recurring phosphorescence of antiquity,
the "much noble vagueness and indefinite jargon" of Plato,
the lucid movements of the royal yacht upon the learned scenery of Egypt—
king, steward, and harper, seated amidships while the jade and
the rock crystal course about in solution,

their suavity surmounts the surf—
the willowy wit, the transparent equation of Isaiah, Jeremiah, Ezekiel, Daniel.
Bored by "the detailless perspective of the sea," reiterative and naive,
and its chaos of rocks—the stuffy remarks of the Hebrews—
the good and alive young men demonstrate the assertion
that it is not necessary to be associated with that which has annoyed one;
they have never made a statement which they found so easy to prove—
"split like a glass against a wall"
in this "precipitate of dazzling impressions,
the spontaneous unforced passion of the Hebrew language—
an abyss of verbs full of reverberations and tempestuous energy"
in which action perpetuates action and angle is at variance with angle
till submerged by the general action;
obscured by "fathomless suggestions of color,"
by incessantly panting lines of green, white with concussion,
in this drama of water against rocks—this "ocean of hurrying consonants"
with its "great livid stains like long slabs of green marble,"
its "flashing lances of perpendicular lightning" and "molten fires swallowed up,"
"with foam on its barriers,"
"crashing itself out in one long hiss of spray."

Experimental

*montage
collage*

153

Bowls

on the green
with lignum vitae balls and ivory markers,
the pins planted in wild duck formation,
and quickly dispersed—
by this survival of ancient punctilio
in the manner of Chinese lacquer-carving,
layer after layer exposed by certainty of touch and unhurried incision
so that only so much color shall be revealed as is necessary to the picture,
I learn that we are precisionists,
not citizens of Pompeii arrested in action
as a cross-section of one's correspondence would seem to imply.
Renouncing a policy of boorish indifference
to everything that has been said since the days of Matilda,
I shall purchase an etymological dictionary of modern English
that I may understand what is written,
and like the ant and the spider
returning from time to time to headquarters,
shall answer the question
"why do I like winter better than I like summer?"
and acknowledge that it does not make me sick
to look playwrights and poets and novelists straight in the face—
that I feel just the same;
and I shall write to the publisher of the magazine
which will "appear the first day of the month
and disappear before one has had time to buy it
unless one takes proper precaution,"
and make an effort to please—
since he who gives quickly gives twice
in nothing so much as in a letter.

Marriage

This institution,
perhaps one should say enterprise
out of respect for which
one says one need not change one's mind
about a thing one has believed in,
requiring public promises
of one's intention
to fulfill a private obligation:
I wonder what Adam and Eve
think of it by this time,
this fire-gilt steel
alive with goldenness;
how bright it shows—
"of circular traditions and impostures,
committing many spoils,"
requiring all one's criminal ingenuity
to avoid!
Psychology which explains everything
explains nothing,
and we are still in doubt.
Eve: beautiful woman—
I have seen her
when she was so handsome
she gave me a start,
able to write simultaneously
in three languages—
English, German, and French—
and talk in the meantime;
equally positive in demanding a commotion
and in stipulating quiet:
"*I* should like to be alone";
to which the visitor replies,
"I should like to be alone;
why not be alone together?"
Below the incandescent stars

155

below the incandescent fruit,
the strange experience of beauty;
its existence is too much;
it tears one to pieces
and each fresh wave of consciousness
is poison.
"See her, see her in this common world,"
the central flaw
in that first crystal-fine experiment,
this amalgamation which can never be more
than an interesting impossibility,
describing it
as "that strange paradise
unlike flesh, stones,
gold or stately buildings,
the choicest piece of my life:
the heart rising
in its estate of peace
as a boat rises
with the rising of the water";
constrained in speaking of the serpent—
shed snakeskin in the history of politeness
not to be returned to again—
that invaluable accident
exonerating Adam.
And he has beauty also;
it's distressing—the O thou
to whom from whom,
without whom nothing—Adam;
"something feline,
something colubrine"—how true!
a crouching mythological monster
in that Persian miniature of emerald mines,
raw silk—ivory white, snow white,
oyster white, and six others—
that paddock full of leopards and giraffes—
long lemon-yellow bodies

sown with trapezoids of blue.
Alive with words,
vibrating like a cymbal
touched before it has been struck,
he has prophesied correctly—
the industrious waterfall,
"the speedy stream
which violently bears all before it,
at one time silent as the air
and now powerful as the wind."
"Treading chasms
on the uncertain footing of a spear,"
forgetting that there is in woman
a quality of mind
which as an instinctive manifestation
is unsafe,
he goes on speaking
in a formal customary strain,
of "past states, the present state,
seals, promises,
the evil one suffered,
the good one enjoys,
hell, heaven,
everything convenient
to promote one's joy."
In him a state of mind
perceives what it was not
intended that he should;
"he experiences a solemn joy
in seeing that he has become an idol."
Plagued by the nightingale
in the new leaves,
with its silence—
not its silence but its silences,
he says of it:
"It clothes me with a shirt of fire."
"He dares not clap his hands

to make it go on
lest it should fly off;
if he does nothing, it will sleep;
if he cries out, it will not understand."
Unnerved by the nightingale
and dazzled by the apple,
impelled by "the illusion of a fire
effectual to extinguish fire,"
compared with which
the shining of the earth
is but deformity—a fire
"as high as deep
as bright as broad
as long as life itself,"
he stumbles over marriage,
"a very trivial object indeed"
to have destroyed the attitude
in which he stood—
the ease of the philosopher
unfathered by a woman.
Unhelpful Hymen!
a kind of overgrown cupid
reduced to insignificance
by the mechanical advertising
parading as involuntary comment,
by that experiment of Adam's
with ways out but no way in—
the ritual of marriage,
augmenting all its lavishness;
its fiddlehead ferns,
lotus flowers, opuntias, white dromedaries,
its hippopotamus—
nose and mouth combined
in one magnificent hopper—
its snake and the potent apple.
He tells us
that "for love that will

gaze an eagle blind,
that is with Hercules
climbing the trees
in the garden of the Hesperides,
from forty-five to seventy
is the best age,"
commending it
as a fine art, as an experiment,
a duty or as merely recreation.
One must not call him ruffian
nor friction a calamity—
the fight to be affectionate:
"no truth can be fully known
until it has been tried
by the tooth of disputation."
The blue panther with blue eyes,
entirely graceful—
one must give them the path—
the black obsidian Diana
who "darkeneth her countenance
as a bear doth,"
the spiked hand
that has an affection for one
and proves it to the bone,
impatient to assure you
that impatience is the mark of independence,
not of bondage.
"Married people often look that way"—
"seldom and cold, up and down,
mixed and malarial
with a good day and a bad."
We Occidentals are so unemotional,
self lost, the irony preserved
in "the Ahasuerus *tête-à-tête* banquet"
with its small orchids like snakes' tongues,
with its "good monster, lead the way,"
with little laughter

and munificence of humor
in that quixotic atmosphere of frankness
in which "four o'clock does not exist,
but at five o'clock
the ladies in their imperious humility
are ready to receive you";
in which experience attests
that men have power
and sometimes one is made to feel it.
He says, "What monarch would not blush
to have a wife
with hair like a shaving brush?"
The fact of woman
is "not the sound of the flute
but very poison."
She says, "Men are monopolists
of 'stars, garters, buttons
and other shining baubles'—
unfit to be the guardians
of another person's happiness."
He says, "These mummies
must be handled carefully—
'the crumbs from a lion's meal,
a couple of shins and the bit of an ear';
turn to the letter M
and you will find
that 'a wife is a coffin,'
that severe object
with the pleasing geometry
stipulating space not people,
refusing to be buried
and uniquely disappointing,
revengefully wrought in the attitude
of an adoring child
to a distinguished parent."
She says, "This butterfly,
this waterfly, this nomad

that has 'proposed
to settle on my hand for life'—
What can one do with it?
There must have been more time
in Shakespeare's day
to sit and watch a play.
You know so many artists who are fools."
He says, "You know so many fools
who are not artists."
The fact forgot
that "some have merely rights
while some have obligations,"
he loves himself so much,
he can permit himself
no rival in that love.
She loves herself so much,
she cannot see herself enough—
a statuette of ivory on ivory,
the logical last touch
to an expansive splendor
earned as wages for work done:
one is not rich but poor
when one can always seem so right.
What can one do for them—
these savages
condemned to disaffect
all those who are not visionaries
alert to undertake the silly task
of making people noble?
This model of petrine fidelity
who "leaves her peaceful husband
only because she has seen enough of him"—
that orator reminding you,
"I am yours to command."
"Everything to do with love is mystery;
it is more than a day's work
to investigate this science."

One sees that it is rare—
that striking grasp of opposites
opposed each to the other, not to unity,
which in cycloid inclusiveness
have dwarfed the demonstration
of Columbus with the egg—
a triumph of simplicity—
that charitive Euroclydon
of frightening disinterestedness
which the world hates,
admitting:

    "I am such a cow,
    if I had a sorrow
    I should feel it a long time;
    I am not one of those
    who have a great sorrow
    in the morning
    and a great joy at noon";

which says: "I have encountered it
among those unpretentious
protégés of wisdom,
where seeming to parade
as the debater and the Roman,
the statesmanship
of an archaic Daniel Webster
persists to their simplicity of temper
as the essence of the matter:

    'Liberty and union
    now and forever';

the Book on the writing-table;
the hand in the breast-pocket."

Silence

My father used to say,
"Superior people never make long visits,
have to be shown Longfellow's grave
or the glass flowers at Harvard.
Self-reliant like the cat—
that takes its prey to privacy,
the mouse's limp tail hanging like a shoelace from its mouth—
they sometimes enjoy solitude,
and can be robbed of speech
by speech which has delighted them.
The deepest feeling always shows itself in silence;
not in silence, but restraint."
Nor was he insincere in saying, "Make my house your inn."
Inns are not residences.

she never knew her dad actually

X

with their respective lions—
"mighty monoceroses with immeasured tayles"—
these are those very animals
described by the cartographers of 1539,
defiantly revolving
in such a way that
the long keel of white exhibited in tumbling
disperses giant weeds
and those sea snakes whose forms, looped in the foam, "disquiet shippers."
Knowing how a voyager obtained the horn of a sea unicorn
to give to Queen Elizabeth,
who thought it worth a hundred thousand pounds,
they persevere in swimming where they like,
finding the place where sea-lions live in herds,
strewn on the beach like stones with lesser stones—
and bears are white;
discovering Antarctica, its penguin kings and icy spires,
and Sir John Hawkins' Florida
"abounding in land unicorns and lions;
since where the one is,
its arch-enemy cannot be missing."
Thus personalities by nature much opposed,
can be combined in such a way
that when they do agree, their unanimity is great,
"in politics, in trade, law, sport, religion,
china-collecting, tennis, and church going."
You have remarked this fourfold combination of strange animals,
upon embroideries
enwrought with "polished garlands" of agreeing difference—
thorns, "myrtle rods, and shafts of bay,"
"cobwebs, and knotts, and mulberries"
of lapis-lazuli and pomegranate and malachite—
Britannia's sea unicorn with its rebellious child
now ostentatiously indigenous to the new English coast;
and its land lion oddly tolerant of those pacific counterparts to it,

the water lions of the west.
This is a strange fraternity—these sea lions and land lions,
land unicorns and sea unicorns:
the lion civilly rampant,
tame and concessive like the long-tailed bear of Ecuador—
the lion standing up against this screen of woven air
which is the forest:
the unicorn also, on its hind legs in reciprocity.
A puzzle to the hunters, is this haughtiest of beasts,
to be distinguished from those born without a horn,
in use like Saint Jerome's tame lion, as domestics;
rebelling proudly at the dogs
which are dismayed by the chain lightning
playing at them from its horn—
the dogs persistent in pursuit of it as if it could be caught,
"deriving agreeable terror" from its "moonbeam throat"
on fire like its white coat and unconsumed as if of salamander's skin.
So wary as to disappear for centuries and reappear,
yet never to be caught,
the unicorn has been preserved
by an unmatched device
wrought like the work of expert blacksmiths—
this animal of that one horn
throwing itself upon which head foremost from a cliff,
it walks away unharmed;
proficient in this feat which, like Herodotus,
I have not seen except in pictures.
Thus the strange animal with its miraculous elusiveness
has come to be unique,
"impossible to take alive,"
tamed only by a lady inoffensive like itself—
as curiously wild and gentle;
"as straight and slender as the crest,
or antlet of the one-beam'd beast."
Upon the printed page,
also by word of mouth,
we have a record of it all

and how, unfearful of deceit,
etched like an equine monster of an old celestial map,
beside a cloud or dress of Virgin-Mary blue,
improved "all over slightly with shakes of Venice gold,
and silver, and some O's,"
the unicorn, "with pavon high," approaches eagerly;
until engrossed by what appears of this strange enemy,
upon the map, "upon her lap,"
its "mild wild head doth lie."

An Octopus

of ice. Deceptively reserved and flat,
it lies "in grandeur and in mass"
beneath a sea of shifting snow-dunes;
dots of cyclamen-red and maroon on its clearly defined pseudo-podia
made of glass that will bend—a much needed invention—
comprising twenty-eight ice-fields from fifty to five hundred feet thick,
of unimagined delicacy.
"Picking periwinkles from the cracks"
or killing prey with the concentric crushing rigor of the python,
it hovers forward "spider fashion
on its arms" misleadingly like lace;
its "ghostly pallor changing
to the green metallic tinge of an anemone-starred pool."
The fir-trees, in "the magnitude of their root systems,"
rise aloof from these maneuvers "creepy to behold,"
austere specimens of our American royal families,
"each like the shadow of the one beside it.
The rock seems frail compared with their dark energy of life,"
its vermilion and onyx and manganese-blue interior expansiveness
left at the mercy of the weather;
"stained transversely by iron where the water drips down,"
recognized by its plants and its animals.
Completing a circle,
you have been deceived into thinking that you have progressed,
under the polite needles of the larches
"hung to filter, not to intercept the sunlight"—
met by tightly wattled spruce-twigs
"conformed to an edge like clipped cypress
as if no branch could penetrate the cold beyond its company";
and dumps of gold and silver ore enclosing The Goat's Mirror—
that lady-fingerlike depression in the shape of the left human foot,
which prejudices you in favor of itself
before you have had time to see the others;
its indigo, pea-green, blue-green, and turquoise,
from a hundred to two hundred feet deep,

"merging in irregular patches in the middle lake
where, like gusts of a storm
obliterating the shadows of the fir-trees, the wind makes lanes of ripples."
What spot could have merits of equal importance
for bears, elk, deer, wolves, goats, and ducks?
Pre-empted by their ancestors,
this is the property of the exacting porcupine,
and of the rat "slipping along to its burrow in the swamp
or pausing on high ground to smell the heather";
of "thoughtful beavers
making drains which seem the work of careful men with shovels,"
and of the bears inspecting unexpectedly
ant-hills and berry-bushes.
Composed of calcium gems and alabaster pillars,
topaz, tourmaline crystals and amethyst quartz,
their den is somewhere else, concealed in the confusion
of "blue forests thrown together with marble and jasper and agate
as if whole quarries had been dynamited."
And farther up, in stag-at-bay position
as a scintillating fragment of these terrible stalagmites,
stands the goat,
its eye fixed on the waterfall which never seems to fall—
an endless skein swayed by the wind,
immune to force of gravity in the perspective of the peaks.
A special antelope
acclimated to "grottoes from which issue penetrating draughts
which make you wonder why you came,"
it stands its ground
on cliffs the color of the clouds, of petrified white vapor—
black feet, eyes, nose, and horns, engraved on dazzling ice-fields,
the ermine body on the crystal peak;
the sun kindling its shoulders to maximum heat like acetylene, dyeing them
white—
upon this antique pedestal,
"a mountain with those graceful lines which prove it a volcano,"
its top a complete cone like Fujiyama's
till an explosion blew it off.

Distinguished by a beauty
of which "the visitor dare never fully speak at home
for fear of being stoned as an impostor,"
Big Snow Mountain is the home of a diversity of creatures:
those who "have lived in hotels
but who now live in camps—who prefer to";
the mountain guide evolving from the trapper,
"in two pairs of trousers, the outer one older,
wearing slowly away from the feet to the knees";
"the nine-striped chipmunk
running with unmammal-like agility along a log";
the water ouzel
with "its passion for rapids and high-pressured falls,"
building under the arch of some tiny Niagara;
the white-tailed ptarmigan "in winter solid white,
feeding on heather-bells and alpine buckwheat";
and the eleven eagles of the west,
"fond of the spring fragrance and the winter colors,"
used to the unegoistic action of the glaciers
and "several hours of frost every midsummer night."
"They make a nice appearance, don't they,"
happy seeing nothing?
Perched on treacherous lava and pumice—
those unadjusted chimney-pots and cleavers
which stipulate "names and addresses of persons to notify
in case of disaster"—
they hear the roar of ice and supervise the water
winding slowly through the cliffs,
the road "climbing like the thread
which forms the groove around a snail-shell,
doubling back and forth until where snow begins, it ends."
No "deliberate wide-eyed wistfulness" is here
among the boulders sunk in ripples and white water
where "when you hear the best wild music of the forest
it is sure to be a marmot,"
the victim on some slight observatory,
of "a struggle between curiosity and caution,"

inquiring what has scared it:
a stone from the moraine descending in leaps,
another marmot, or the spotted ponies with glass eyes,
brought up on frosty grass and flowers
and rapid draughts of ice-water.
Instructed, none knows how, to climb the mountain,
by businessmen who require for recreation
three hundred and sixty-five holidays in the year,
these conspicuously spotted little horses are peculiar;
hard to discern among the birch-trees, ferns, and lily-pads,
avalanche lilies, Indian paint-brushes,
bears' ears and kittentails,
and miniature cavalcades of chlorophylless fungi
magnified in profile on the moss-beds like moonstones in the water;
the cavalcade of calico competing
with the original American menagerie of styles
among the white flowers of the rhododendron surmounting rigid leaves
upon which moisture works its alchemy,
transmuting verdure into onyx.

"Like happy souls in Hell," enjoying mental difficulties, the Greeks
amused themselves with delicate behavior
because it was "so noble and so fair";
not practiced in adapting their intelligence
to eagle-traps and snow-shoes,
to alpenstocks and other toys contrived by those
"alive to the advantage of invigorating pleasures."
Bows, arrows, oars, and paddles, for which trees provide the wood,
in new countries more eloquent than elsewhere—
augmenting the assertion that, essentially humane,
"the forest affords wood for dwellings and by its beauty
stimulates the moral vigor of its citizens."
The Greeks liked smoothness, distrusting what was back
of what could not be clearly seen,
resolving with benevolent conclusiveness,
"Complexities which still will be complexities
as long as the world lasts";

ascribing what we clumsily call happiness,
to "an accident or a quality,
a spiritual substance or the soul itself,
an act, a disposition, or a habit,
or a habit infused, to which the soul has been persuaded,
or something distinct from a habit, a power"—
such power as Adam had and we are still devoid of.
"Emotionally sensitive, their hearts were hard";
their wisdom was remote
from that of these odd oracles of cool official sarcasm,
upon this game preserve
where "guns, nets, seines, traps and explosives,
hired vehicles, gambling and intoxicants are prohibited;
disobedient persons being summarily removed
and not allowed to return without permission in writing."
It is self-evident
that it is frightful to have everything afraid of one;
that one must do as one is told
and eat rice, prunes, dates, raisins, hardtack, and tomatoes
if one would "conquer the main peak of Mount Tacoma,"
this fossil flower concise without a shiver,
intact when it is cut,
damned for its sacrosanct remoteness—
like Henry James "damned by the public for decorum";
not decorum, but restraint;
it is the love of doing hard things
that rebuffed and wore them out—a public out of sympathy with neatness.
Neatness of finish! Neatness of finish!
Relentless accuracy is the nature of this octopus
with its capacity for fact.
"Creeping slowly as with meditated stealth,
its arms seeming to approach from all directions,"
it receives one under winds that "tear the snow to bits
and hurl it like a sandblast
shearing off twigs and loose bark from the trees."
Is "tree" the word for these things
"flat on the ground like vines"?

some "bent in a half-circle with branches on one side
suggesting dust-brushes, not trees;
some finding strength in union, forming little stunted groves,
their flattened mats of branches shrunk in trying to escape"
from the hard mountain "planed by ice and polished by the wind"—
the white volcano with no weather side;
the lightning flashing at its base,
rain falling in the valleys, and snow falling on the peak—
this glassy octopus symmetrically pointed,
its claw cut by the avalanche
"with a sound like the crack of a rifle,
in a curtain of powdered snow launched like a waterfall."

An Egyptian Pulled Glass Bottle in the Shape of a Fish

Here we have thirst
And patience, from the first,
    And art, as in a wave held up for us to see
    In its essential perpendicularity;

Not brittle but
Intense—the spectrum, that
    Spectacular and nimble animal the fish,
    Whose scales turn aside the sun's sword by their polish.

To a Snail

If "compression is the first grace of style,"
you have it. Contractility is a virtue
as modesty is a virtue.
It is not the acquisition of any one thing
that is able to adorn,
or the incidental quality that occurs
as a concomitant of something well said,
that we value in style,
but the principle that is hid:
in the absence of feet, "a method of conclusions";
"a knowledge of principles,"
in the curious phenomenon of your occipital horn.

"The Bricks Are Fallen Down, We Will Build with Hewn Stones. The Sycamores Are Cut Down, We Will Change to Cedars"

In what sense shall we be able to
   secure to ourselves peace and do as they did—
  who, when they were not able to rid
     themselves of war, cast out fear?
       They did not say: "We shall not be brought
       into subjection by the naughtiness of the sea;
though we have 'defeated ourselves with
   false balances' and laid weapons in the scale,
  glory shall spring from in-glory; hail,
     flood, earthquake, and famine shall
       not intimidate us nor shake the
       foundations of our inalienable energy."

"Nothing Will Cure the Sick Lion but to Eat an Ape"

Perceiving that in the masked ball
attitude, there is a hollowness
that beauty's light momentum can't redeem;
   since disproportionate satisfaction anywhere
   lacks a proportionate air,

he let us know without offense
by his hands' denunciatory
upheaval, that he despised the fashion
   of curing us with an ape—making it his care
   to smother us with fresh air.

Peter

a Black T White cat *sleep*

Strong and slippery, built for the midnight grass-party confronted by four cats,
  he sleeps his time away—the detached first claw on his foreleg which
                                          corresponds
    to the thumb, retracted to its tip; the small tuft of fronds
      or katydid legs above each eye, still numbering the units in each group;
        the shadbones regularly set about his mouth, to droop or rise—

in unison like the porcupine's quills—motionless. He lets himself be flat-
  tened out by gravity, as it were a piece of seaweed tamed and weakened by
    exposure to the sun; compelled when extended, to lie
      stationary. Sleep is the result of his delusion that one must do as
        well as one can for oneself; sleep—epitome of what is to

him as to the average person, the end of life. Demonstrate on him how
  the lady caught the dangerous southern snake, placing a forked stick on either
    side of its innocuous neck; one need not try to stir
      him up; his prune shaped head and alligator eyes are not a party to the
        joke. Lifted and handled, he may be dangled like an eel or set

up on the forearm like a mouse; his eyes bisected by pupils of a pin's
  width, are flickeringly exhibited, then covered up. May be? I should say,
    might have been; when he has been got the better of in a
      dream—as in a fight with nature or with cats—we all know it.
                                        Profound sleep is
        not, with him, a fixed illusion. Springing about with froglike ac-

curacy, emitting jerky cries when taken in the hand, he is himself
  again; to sit caged by the rungs of a domestic chair would be unprofit-
    able—human. What is the good of hypocrisy? It
      is permissible to choose one's employment, to abandon the wire nail, the
        roly-poly, when it shows signs of being no longer a pleas-

ure, to score the adjacent magazine with a double line of strokes. He can
  talk, but insolently says nothing. What of it? When one is frank, one's very
    presence is a compliment. It is clear that he can see

the virtue of naturalness, that he is one of those who do not regard
the published fact as a surrender. As for the disposition

invariably to affront, an animal with claws wants to have to use
them; that eel-like extension of trunk into tail is not an accident. To
leap, to lengthen out, divide the air—to purloin, to pursue,
to tell the hen: fly over the fence, go in the wrong way—in your perturba-
tion—this is life; to do less would be nothing but dishonesty.

The Monkey Puzzle

A kind of monkey or pine-lemur
not of interest to the monkey,
in a kind of Flaubert's Carthage, it defies one—
this "Paduan cat with lizard," this "tiger in a bamboo thicket."
"An interwoven somewhat," it will not come out.
Ignore the Foo dog and it is forthwith more than a dog,
its tail superimposed upon itself in a complacent half spiral,
this pine-tree—this pine-tiger—is a tiger, not a dog.
It knows that if a nomad may have dignity,
Gibraltar has had more—
that "it is better to be lonely than unhappy."
A conifer contrived in imitation of the glyptic work of jade and hard-stone
cutters,

a true curio in this bypath of curio-collecting,
it is worth its weight in gold, but no one takes it
from these woods in which society's not knowing is colossal,
the lion's ferocious chrysanthemum head seeming kind by comparison.
This porcupine-quilled, complicated starkness—
this is beauty—"a certain proportion in the skeleton which gives the best
results."

One is at a loss, however, to know why it should be here,
in this morose part of the earth—
to account for its origin at all;
but we prove, we do not explain our birth.

A Fool, a Foul Thing, a Distressful Lunatic

With webs of cool
   Chain mail and his stout heart, is not the gander
   Mocked, and ignorantly designated, yet,
To play the fool?
     "Egyptian vultures clean as cherubim,
     All ivory and jet," are they most foul?
And nature's child,
   That most precocious water bird, the loon—why
   Is he foremost in the madman's alphabet;
Why is he styled
In folly's catalogue, distressful lunatic?

Loon

LYRICS AND SEQUENCES

1926–1940

The Steeple-Jack

Dürer would have seen a reason for living
　　in a town like this, with eight stranded whales
to look at; with the sweet sea air coming into your house
on a fine day, from water etched
　　with waves as formal as the scales
on a fish.

One by one, in two's, in three's, the seagulls keep
　　flying back and forth over the town clock,
or sailing around the lighthouse without moving the wings—
rising steadily with a slight
　　quiver of the body—or flock
mewing where

a sea the purple of the peacock's neck is
　　paled to greenish azure as Dürer changed
the pine green of the Tyrol to peacock blue and guinea
grey. You can see a twenty-five-
　　pound lobster and fish-nets arranged
to dry. The

whirlwind fife-and-drum of the storm bends the salt
　　marsh grass, disturbs stars in the sky and the
star on the steeple; it is a privilege to see so
much confusion.

　　　　　　A steeple-jack in red, has let
　　a rope down as a spider spins a thread;
he might be part of a novel, but on the sidewalk a
sign says C. J. Poole, Steeple-jack,
　　in black and white; and one in red
and white says

Danger. The church portico has four fluted
　　columns, each a single piece of stone, made

modester by white-wash. This would be a fit haven for
waifs, children, animals, prisoners,
    and presidents who have repaid
sin-driven

senators by not thinking about them. One
    sees a school-house, a post-office in a
store, fish-houses, hen-houses, a three-masted schooner on
the stocks. The hero, the student,
    the steeple-jack, each in his way,
is at home.

It scarcely could be dangerous to be living
    in a town like this, of simple people,
who have a steeple-jack placing danger signs by the church
while he is gilding the solid-
    pointed star, which on a steeple
stands for hope.

The Student

"In America," began
the lecturer, "everyone must have a
degree. The French do not think that
all can have it, they don't say everyone
    must go to college." We
incline to feel, here,
    that although it may be unnecessary

to know fifteen languages,
one degree is not too much. With us, a
school—like the singing tree of which
the leaves were mouths that sang in concert—
    is both a tree of knowledge
and of liberty,—
    seen in the unanimity of college

mottoes, *lux et veritas,*
Christo et ecclesiae, sapiet
felici. It may be that we
have not knowledge, just opinions, that we
    are undergraduates,
not students; we know
    we have been told with smiles, by expatriates

of whom we had asked "When will
your experiment be finished?" "Science
is never finished." Secluded
from domestic strife, Jack Bookworm led a
    college life, says Goldsmith;
and here also as
    in France or Oxford, study is beset with

dangers—with bookworms, mildews,
and complaisancies. But someone in New
England has known enough to say

that the student is patience personified,
    a variety
of hero, "patient
    of neglect and of reproach,"—who can "hold by

himself." You can't beat hens to
make them lay. Wolf's wool is the best of wool,
but it cannot be sheared, because
the wolf will not comply. With knowledge as
    with wolf's surliness,
the student studies
    voluntarily, refusing to be less

than individual. He
"gives his opinion and then rests upon it";
he renders service when there is
no reward, and is too reclusive for
    some things to seem to touch
him, not because he
    has no feeling but because he has so much.

The Hero

Where there is personal liking we go.
   Where the ground is sour; where there are
   weeds of beanstalk height,
   snakes' hypodermic teeth, or
   the wind brings the "scarebabe voice"
   from the neglected yew set with
   the semi-precious cat's eyes of the owl—
awake, asleep, "raised ears extended to fine points," and so
on—love won't grow.

We do not like some things and the hero
   doesn't; deviating head-stones
   and uncertainty;
   going where one does not wish
   to go; suffering and not
   saying so; standing and listening where something
   is hiding. The hero shrinks
as what it is flies out on muffled wings, with twin yellow
eyes—to and fro—

with quavering water-whistle note, low,
   high, in basso-falsetto chirps
   until the skin creeps.
   Jacob when a-dying, asked
   Joseph: Who are these? and blessed
   both sons, the younger most, vexing Joseph. And
   Joseph was vexing to some.
Cincinnatus was; Regulus; and some of our fellow
men have been, though

devout, like Pilgrim having to go slow
   to find his roll; tired but hopeful—
   hope not being hope
   until all ground for hope has
   vanished; and lenient, looking

upon a fellow creature's error with the
    feelings of a mother—a
woman or a cat. The decorous frock-coated Negro
by the grotto

answers the fearless sightseeing hobo
    who asks the man she's with, what's this,
    what's that, where's Martha
    buried, "Gen-ral Washington
    there; his lady, here"; speaking
    as if in a play—not seeing her; with a
    sense of human dignity
and reverence for mystery, standing like the shadow
of the willow.

Moses would not be grandson to Pharaoh.
    It is not what I eat that is
    my natural meat,
    the hero says. He's not out
    seeing a sight but the rock
    crystal thing to see—the startling El Greco
    brimming with inner light—that
covets nothing that it has let go. This then you may know
as the hero.

No Swan So Fine

"No water so still as the
    dead fountains of Versailles." No swan,
with swart blind look askance
and gondoliering legs, so fine
    as the chintz china one with fawn-
brown eyes and toothed gold
collar on to show whose bird it was.

Lodged in the Louis Fifteenth
    candelabrum-tree of cockscomb-
tinted buttons, dahlias,
sea-urchins, and everlastings,
    it perches on the branching foam
of polished sculptured
flowers—at ease and tall. The king is dead.

The Jerboa

Too Much

Find This fountain

A Roman had an
artist, a freedman,
   contrive a cone—pine-cone
   or fir-cone—with holes for a fountain. Placed on
      the prison of St. Angelo, this cone
      of the Pompeys, which is known

now as the Popes', passed
for art. A huge cast
   bronze, dwarfing the peacock
   statue in the garden of the Vatican,
      it looks like a work of art made to give
      to a Pompey, or native

of Thebes. Others could
build, and understood
   making colossi and
   how to use slaves, and kept crocodiles and put
      baboons on the necks of giraffes to pick
      fruit, and used serpent magic.

They had their men tie
hippopotami
   and bring out dappled dog-
   cats to course antelopes, dikdik, and ibex;
      or used small eagles. They looked on as theirs,
      impalas and onagers,

the wild ostrich herd
with hard feet and bird
   necks rearing in back in the
   dust like a serpent preparing to strike, cranes,
      mongooses, storks, anoas, Nile geese;
      and there were gardens for these—

combining planes, dates,
limes, and pomegranates,
   in avenues—with square
   pools of pink flowers, tame fish, and small frogs. Besides
      yarns dyed with indigo, and red cotton,
      they had a flax which they spun

into fine linen
cordage for yachtsmen.
   These people liked small things;
   they gave to boys little paired playthings such as
      nests of eggs, ichneumon and snake, paddle
      and raft, badger and camel;

and made toys for them-
selves: the royal totem;
   and toilet-boxes marked
   with the contents. Lords and ladies put goose-grease
      paint in round bone boxes—the pivoting
      lid incised with a duck-wing

or reverted duck-
head; kept in a buck
   or rhinoceros horn,
   the ground horn; and locust oil in stone locusts.
   . It was a picture with a fine distance;
      of drought, and of assistance

in time, from the Nile
rising slowly, while
   the pig-tailed monkey on
   slab-bands, with arched-up slack-slung gait, and the brown
      dandy looked at the jasmine two-leafed twig
      and bud, cactus-pads, and fig.

Dwarfs here and there lent
to an evident
   poetry of frog-grays,

duck-egg greens, and eggplant blues a fantasy
and a verisimilitude that were
right to those with, everywhere,

power over the poor.
The bees' food is your
food. Those who tended flower-
beds and stables were like the king's cane in the
form of a hand, or the folding bedroom
made for his mother of whom

he was fond. Princes
clad in queens' dresses,
calla or petunia
white, that trembled at the edge, and queens in a
king's underskirt or fine-twilled thread like silk-
worm gut, as bee-man and milk-

maid, kept divine cows
and bees; limestone brows,
and gold-foil wings. They made
basalt serpents and portraits of beetles; the
king gave his name to them and he was named
for them. He feared snakes, and tamed

Pharaoh's rat, the rust-
backed mongoose. No bust
of it was made, but there
was pleasure for the rat. Its restlessness was
its excellence; it was praised for its wit;
and the jerboa, like it,

a small desert rat,
and not famous, that
lives without water, has
happiness. Abroad seeking food, or at home
in its burrow, the Sahara field-mouse
has a shining silver house

of sand. O rest and
joy, the boundless sand,
   the stupendous sand-spout,
   no water, no palm-trees, no ivory bed,
      tiny cactus; but one would not be he
      who has nothing but plenty.

Abundance

Africanus meant
the conqueror sent
   from Rome. It should mean the
   untouched: the sand-brown jumping rat—free-born; and
      the blacks, that choice race with an elegance
      ignored by one's ignorance.

Part terrestrial,
and part celestial,
   Jacob saw, cudgel staff
   in claw-hand—steps of air and air angels; his
      friends were the stones. The translucent mistake
      of the desert does not make

hardship for one who
can rest and then do
   the opposite—launching
as if on wings, from its match-thin hind legs, in
      daytime or at night; with the tail as a weight,
      undulated out by speed, straight.

Looked at by daylight,
the underside's white,
   though the fur on the back
   is buff-brown like the breast of the fawn-breasted
      bower bird. It hops like the fawn-breast, but has
      chipmunk contours—perceived as

it turns its bird head—
the nap directed
  neatly back and blending
  with the ear which reiterates the slimness
    of the body. The fine hairs on the tail,
    repeating the other pale

markings, lengthen until
at the tip they fill
  out in a tuft—black and
  white; strange detail of the simplified creature,
    fish-shaped and silvered to steel by the force
    of the large desert moon. Course

the jerboa, or
plunder its food store,
  and you will be cursed. It
  honors the sand by assuming its color;
    closed upper paws seeming one with the fur
    in its flight from a danger.

By fifths and sevenths,
in leaps of two lengths,
  like the uneven notes
  of the Bedouin flute, it stops its gleaning
    on little wheel castors, and makes fern-seed
    foot-prints with kangaroo speed.

Its leaps should be set
to the flageolet;
  pillar body erect
  on a three-cornered smooth-working Chippendale
    claw—propped on hind legs, and tail as third toe,
    between leaps to its burrow.

To Peace

Word that trembles with the glory
  Of self-conquest, mend, control.
Thirst for quickening compassion,
  Grow till craving make us whole.

Power of God, alive with glory,
  Unself-love as majesty,
Make us one, submerging hatred;
  Peace of heaven, make us free.

peace

The Plumet Basilisk

In Costa Rica

In blazing driftwood
    the green keeps showing at the same place;
as, intermittently, the fire-opal shows blue and green.
    In Costa Rica the true Chinese lizard face
is found, of the amphibious falling dragon, the living fire-work.

He leaps and meets his
    likeness in the stream and, king with king,
helped by his three-part plume along the back, runs on two legs,
    tail dragging; faints upon the air; then with a spring
dives to the stream-bed, hiding as the chieftain with gold body hid in

Guatavita Lake.
    He runs, he flies, he swims, to get to
his basilica— "the ruler of Rivers, Lakes, and Seas,
    invisible or visible," with clouds to do
as bid—and can be "long or short, and also coarse or fine at pleasure."

The Malay Dragon

We have ours; and they
    have theirs. Ours has a skin feather crest;
theirs has wings out from the waist which is snuff-brown or sallow.
    Ours falls from trees on water; theirs is the smallest
dragon that knows how to dive head-first from a tree-top to something dry.

Floating on spread ribs,
    the boat-like body settles on the
clamshell-tinted spray sprung from the nutmeg tree—minute legs
    trailing half akimbo—the true divinity
of Malay. Among unfragrant orchids, on the unnutritious nut-

tree, *Myristica*
   fragans, the harmless god spreads ribs that
do not raise a hood. This is the serpent-dove peculiar
   to the East; that lives as the butterfly or bat
can, in a brood, conferring wings on what it grasps, as the air-plant does.

The Tuatera

Elsewhere, sea lizards—
   congregated so there is not room
to step, with tails laid criss-cross, alligator-style, among
   birds toddling in and out—are innocent of whom
they neighbor. Bird-reptile social life is pleasing. The tuatera

will tolerate a
   petrel in its den, and lays ten eggs
or nine—the number laid by dragons since "a true dragon
   has nine sons." The frilled lizard, the kind with no legs,
and the three-horned chameleon are non-serious ones that take to flight

if you do not. In
   Copenhagen the principal door
of the bourse is roofed by two pairs of dragons standing on
   their heads—twirled by the architect—so that the four
green tails conspiring upright symbolize four-fold security.

In Costa Rica

Now, where sapotans drop
   their nuts out on the stream, there is, as
I have said, one of the quickest lizards in the world—the
   basilisk—that feeds on leaves and berries and has
shade from palm-vines, ferns, and peperomias; or lies basking on a

horizontal branch
   from which sour-grass and orchids sprout. If
beset, he lets go, smites the water, and runs on it—a thing
   difficult for fingered feet. But when captured—stiff
and somewhat heavy, like fresh putty on the hand—he is no longer

the slight lizard that
   can stand in a receding flattened
S—small, long and vertically serpentine or sagging,
   span the bushes in a fox's bridge. Vines suspend
the weight of his faint shadow fixed on silk.

As by a Chinese brush, eight green
bands are painted on
   the tail—as piano keys are barred
by five black stripes across the white. This octave of faulty
   decorum hides the extraordinary lizard
till night-fall, which is for man the basilisk whose look will kill; but is

for lizards men can
   kill, the welcome dark—with galloped
ground-bass of the military drum, the squeak of bag-pipes
   and of bats. Hollow whistled monkey-notes disrupt
the castanets. Taps from the back of the bow sound odd on last year's gourd,
or when they touch the
   kettledrums—at which (for there's no light),
a scared frog, screaming like a bird, leaps out from weeds in which
   it could have hid, with curves of the meteorite,

      wide water-bug strokes,
   in jerks which express
   a regal and excellent awkwardness,

      the basilisk portrays
   mythology's wish
   to be interchangeably man and fish—

traveling rapidly upward, as
spider-clawed fingers can twang the
bass strings of the harp, and with steps
as articulate, make their way
back to retirement on strings that
vibrate till the claws are spread flat.

    Among tightened wires,
minute noises swell
and change, as in the woods' acoustic shell

they will with trees as avenues of steel to veil

as from black opal emerald opal emerald—
scale which Swinburne called in prose, the
noiseless music that hangs about
the serpent when it stirs or springs.

No anonymous
    nightingale sings in a swamp, fed on
sound from porcupine-quilled palm-trees
    that rattle like the rain. This is our Tower-of-London
jewel that the Spaniards failed to see, among the feather capes

and hawk's-head moths and black-chinned
    humming-birds; the innocent, rare, gold-
defending dragon that as you look begins to be a
    nervous naked sword on little feet, with three-fold
separate flame above the hilt, inhabiting

    fire eating into air. Thus nested
in the phosphorescent alligator that copies each
    digression of the shape, he pants and settles—head
up and eyes black as the molested bird's, with look of whetted fierceness,

in what is merely
    breathing and recoiling from the hand.

Thinking himself hid among the yet unfound jade ax-heads,
    silver jaguars and bats, and amethysts and
polished iron, gold in a ten-ton chain, and pearls the size of pigeon-eggs,

he is alive there
    in his basilisk cocoon beneath
the one living green; his quicksilver ferocity
    quenched in the rustle of his fall into the sheath
which is the shattering sudden splash that marks his temporary loss.

Camellia Sabina

    and the Bordeaux plum
from Marmande (France) in parenthesis with
A. G. on the base of the jar—Alexis Godilot—
unevenly blown beside a bubble that
is green when held up to the light; they
are a fine duet; the screw-top
    for this graft-grown briar-black bloom
on black-thorn pigeon's-blood,
    is, like Certosa, sealed with foil. Appropriate custom.

    And they keep under
glass also, camellias catalogued by
lines across the leaf. The French are a cruel race—willing
to squeeze the diner's cucumber or broil a
meal on vine-shoots. Gloria mundi
with a leaf two inches, nine lines
    broad, they have; and the smaller,
Camellia Sabina
    with amanita-white petals; there are several of her

    pale pinwheels, and pale
stripe that looks as if on a mushroom the
sliver from a beet-root carved into a rose were laid. "Dry
the windows with a cloth fastened to a staff.
In the camellia-house there must be
no smoke from the stove, or dew on
    the windows, lest the plants ail,"
the amateur is told;
    "mistakes are irreparable and nothing will avail."

    A scentless nosegay
is thus formed in the midst of the bouquet
from bottles, casks and corks, for sixty-four million red wines
and twenty million white, which Bordeaux merchants
and lawyers "have spent a great deal of

trouble" to select, from what was
      and what was not Bordeaux. A
food-grape, however—"born
      of nature and of art"—is true ground for the grape-holiday.

      The food of a wild
mouse in some countries is wild parsnip- or sunflower- or
morning-glory-seed, with an occasional
grape. Underneath the vines of the Bolzano
grape of Italy, the Prince of Tails
might stroll. Does yonder mouse with a
      grape in its hand and its child
in its mouth not portray
      the Spanish fleece suspended by the neck? In that well-piled

      larder above your
head, the picture of what you will eat is
looked at from the end of the avenue. The wire cage is
locked, but by bending down and studying the
roof, it is possible to see the
pantomime of Persian thought: the
      gilded, too tight undemure
coat of gems unruined
      by the rain—each small pebble of jade that refused to mature,

      plucked delicately
off. Off jewelry not meant to keep Tom
Thumb, the cavalry cadet, on his Italian upland
meadow-mouse, from looking at the grapes beneath
the interrupted light from them, and
dashing round the *concours hippique*
      of the tent, in flurry
of eels, scallops, serpents,
      and other shadows from the blue of the green canopy.

The wine-cellar? No.
It accomplishes nothing and makes the
soul heavy. The gleaning is more than the vintage, though the
history *de la Vigne et du Vin* has placed
mirabelle in the *bibliothèque*
unique depuis seventeen-ninety-seven.
    (Close the window,
says the Abbé Berlèse,
    for Sabina born under glass.) O generous Bolzano!

The Frigate Pelican

Rapidly cruising or lying on the air there is a bird
   that realizes Rasselas's friend's project
    of wings uniting levity with strength. This
      hell-diver, frigate-bird, hurricane-
bird, unless swift is the proper word
     for him, the storm omen when
    he flies close to the waves, should be seen
     fishing, although oftener
     he appears to prefer

to take, on the wing, from industrious crude-winged species,
   the fish they have caught, and is seldom successless.
    A marvel of grace, no matter how fast his
     victim may fly or how often may
turn. The others with similar ease,
    slowly rising once more,
     move out of the top
     of the circle and stop

and blow back, allowing the wind to reverse their direction—
   unlike the more stalwart swan that can ferry the
   woodcutter's two children home. Make hay; keep
    the shop; I have one sheep; were a less
limber animal's mottoes. This one
    finds sticks for the swan's-down-dress
    of his child to rest upon and would
     not know Gretel from Hänsel.
     As impassioned Handel—

meant for a lawyer and a masculine German domestic
   career—clandestinely studied the harpsichord
   and never was known to have fallen in love,
    the unconfiding frigate-bird hides
in the height and in the majestic
   display of his art. He glides

a hundred feet or quivers about
    as charred paper behaves—full
      of feints; and an eagle

of vigilance . . . *Festina lente*. Be gay
   civilly? How so? "If I do well I am blessed
   whether any bless me or not, and if I do
      ill I am cursed." We watch the moon rise
on the Susquehanna. In his way,
   this most romantic bird flies
to a more mundane place, the mangrove
      swamp to sleep. He wastes the moon.
      But he, and others, soon

rise from the bough and though flying, are able to foil the tired
    moment of danger that lays on heart and lungs the
    weight of the python that crushes to powder.

The Buffalo

    Black in blazonry means
prudence; and niger, unpropitious. Might
hematite-
    black, compactly incurved horns on bison,
      have significance? The
  soot-brown tail-tuft on
    a kind of lion-

    tail; what would that express?
And John Steuart Curry's Ajax pulling
grass—no ring
    in his nose—two birds standing on the back?

        • • •

    The modern
ox does not look like the Augsburg ox's
portrait. Yes,
    the great extinct wild aurochs was a beast
      to paint, with stripe and six-
  foot horn-spread—decreased
      to Siamese-cat-

    brown Swiss size or zebu-
shape, with white plush dewlap and warm-blooded
hump; to red-
    skinned Hereford or to piebald Holstein. Yet
      some would say the sparse-haired
  buffalo has met
      human notions best—

    unlike the elephant,
both jewel and jeweller in the hairs
that he wears—
    no white-nosed Vermont ox yoked with its twin

        to haul the maple-sap,
    up to their knees in
            snow; no freakishly

        Over-Drove Ox drawn by
    Rowlandson, but the Indian buffalo,
    albino-
        footed, standing in a mud-lake with a
            day's work to do. No white
        Christian heathen, way-
                laid by the Buddha,

        serves him so well as the
    buffalo—as mettlesome as if check-
    reined—free neck
        stretching out, and snake tail in a half-twist
            on the flank; nor will so
        cheerfully assist
                the Sage sitting with

        feet at the same side, to
    dismount at the shrine; nor are there any
    ivory
        tusks like those two horns which when a tiger
            coughs, are lowered fiercely
        and convert the fur
                to harmless rubbish.

        The Indian buffalo,
    led by bare-leggèd herd-boys to a hay
    hut where they
        stable it, need not fear comparison
            with bison, with the twins,
        indeed with any
                of ox ancestry.

Nine Nectarines

Arranged by two's as peaches are,
at intervals that all may live—
eight and a single one, on twigs that
grew the year before—they look like
a derivative;
although not uncommonly
the opposite is seen—
nine peaches on a nectarine.
Fuzzless through slender crescent leaves
of green or blue or
both, in the Chinese style, the four

pairs' half-moon leaf-mosaic turns
out to the sun the sprinkled blush
of puce-American-Beauty pink
applied to bees-wax gray by the
uninquiring brush
of mercantile bookbinding.
Like the peach *Yu*, the red-
cheeked peach which cannot aid the dead,
but eaten in time prevents death,
the Italian
peach-nut, Persian plum, Ispahan

secluded wall-grown nectarine,
as wild spontaneous fruit was
found in China first. But was it wild?
Prudent de Candolle would not say.
One perceives no flaws
in this emblematic group
of nine, with leaf window
unquilted by *curculio*
which someone once depicted on
this much-mended plate
or in the also accurate

            unantlered moose or Iceland horse
or ass asleep against the old
        thick, low-leaning nectarine that is the
        color of the shrub-tree's brownish flower.

                        . . .

A Chinese "understands
the spirit of the wilderness"
        and the nectarine-loving kylin
        of pony appearance—the long-
tailed or the tailless
        small cinnamon-brown, common
camel-haired unicorn
with antelope feet and no horn,
        here enameled on porcelain.
                It was a Chinese
                who imagined this masterpiece.

Pigeons

Older than the ancient Greeks, than
Solomon, the pigeon family is a
ramifying one, a
banyan of banyans; to begin
with, bluish slate,
    but with ability. Modesty cannot dull
    the lustre of the pigeon
    swift and sure, coming quickest and
straightest just after a storm. The great
    lame war hero Cher Ami, the
    Lost Battalion's gallant bird; and
    Mocker with one eye
        destroyed, delivering his despatch
    to his superiors; and Sergeant Dunn,
    civilian pigeon who flew eight
    hundred sixty-eight miles
    in four days and six hours;
        and destined to hatch
    in France, Spike, veteran of
    the division in which Mocker
        served—exceptional messenger,
    "Rarely was confidence misplaced" a newspaper
    says. Dastardly comment
        inexactly phrased, as used of Her-
    mes, Ariel, or Leander—
    pigeons of the past. Neither was confidence
    misplaced in the Javan-
    Sumatran birds the Dutch had had
brought from Baghdad.
    Mysterious animal with a magnetic
    feel by which he traces back-
        ward his transportation outward,
even in a fog at sea, though glad
    to be tossed near enough the loft
    or coop to get back the same day.

"Home on time without
   his message." What matter since he has
got back. Migrating always in the same
direction, bringing all letters
to the same address, see-
ing better homes than his,
   he is not Theudas
boasting himself to be some-
body, this anonymous post-
   man who, as soon as he could fly,
was carrying valentines and messages of
state; or soberer news—
   "So please write me and believe that I
am yours very truly;" fine words
those. An instrument, not just an instinctive
individual, this
dove, that lifts his right foot over
the alighting-
   board to rejoin his ungainly pin-clad dark-skinned
brood as domestic turtle-
doves might; two. Invariably
two. The turtle, a not exciting
bird—in Britain shy, detected
by its constantly heard coo, with-
out a song but not
   without a voice—does well to stay far
out of sight; but the Pelew pigeon with
black head, metallic wasp-lustred
grass-green breast and purple
legs and feet, need not; nor
   need the Nicobar,
novel, narrow-feathered dove.
And one should see the Papuan
   fan crests with six-sided scale which
coats the foot; "not much is known about these splendid
birds" hid in unimag-

inably weak lead-colored ostrich—
plumes a third of an inch long, and
needle-fine cat-whisker-fibred battleship-
gray lace. The Samoan
tooth-billed pigeon fortunately
survives also—
saved from destruction by no longer feeding on
the ground, a bird with short legs
and heavy bill, remarkable
because related to the dodo
Didus ineptus; man's remorse
enshrines it now, abundant still
in sixteen-one. "A
little bigger than our swans, these birds
want wings and lay but one egg" the traveler
said— "defenceless unsuspicious
things, with a cry like the
cry of a Gosling." *Il*
dóudo (the words
mean simple one)—extinct as
the Solitaires which having "raised
their young one do not disunite."
A new pigeon cannot compensate, but we have
it. With neat-cered eye, long
face, trim form and posture, this delight-
ful bird outdoes the dashingly
black and white Dalmatian dog and map-freckled
pony that Indians dress
with feathers seriatim down
the mane and tail;—
a slender Cinderella deliberately
pied, so she on each side is
the same, an all-feather piebald,
cuckoo-marked on a titanic scale
taking perhaps sixteen birds to
show the whole design, as in chess

played with men and hors-
es. Yes, the thus medievally
two-colored sea-pie-patterned semi-swan-
necked magpie-pigeon, gamecock-legged
with long clawed toes, and all
extremes—head neck back tail
and feet—coal black, the
rest snow white, has a surpris-
ing modernness and fanciness
and stateliness and. . . . Yes indeed;
developed by and humbly dedicated to
the Gentlemen of the
Feather Club, this is a dainty breed.

Virginia Britannia

Pale sand edges England's Old
Dominion. The air is soft, warm, hot
above the cedar-dotted emerald shore
known to the red-bird, the red-coated musketeer,
the trumpet-flower, the cavalier,
the parson, and the wild parishioner. A deer-
track in a church-floor
brick, and a fine pavement tomb with engraved top, remain.
The now tremendous vine-encompassed hackberry,
starred with the ivy-flower,
shades the tall tower;
And a great sinner lyeth here under the sycamore.

A fritillary zigzags
toward the chancel-shaded resting-place
of this unusual man and sinner who
waits for a joyful resurrection. We-re-wo-
co-mo-co's fur crown could be no
odder than we were, with ostrich, Latin motto,
and small gold horse-shoe:
arms for an able sting-ray hampered pioneer—
painted as a Turk, it seems—continuously
exciting Captain Smith
who, patient with
his inferiors, was a pugnacious equal, and to

Powhatan as unflattering
as grateful. Rare Indian, crowned by
Christopher Newport! The Old Dominion has
all-green box-sculptured grounds.
An almost English green surrounds
them. Care has formed among un-English insect sounds,
the white wall-rose. As
thick as Daniel Boone's grape-vine, the stem has wide-spaced great
blunt alternating ostrich-skin warts that were thorns.

Care has formed walls of yew
        since Indians knew
the Fort Old Field and narrow tongue of land that Jamestown was.

  Observe the terse Virginian,
    the mettlesome gray one that drives the
owl from tree to tree and imitates the call
        of whippoorwill or lark or katydid—the lead-
        gray lead-legged mocking-bird with head
        held half away, and meditative eye as dead
as sculptured marble
    eye, alighting noiseless, musing in the semi-sun,
    standing on tall thin legs as if he did not see,
        conspicuous, alone,
        on the stone-
topped table with lead cupids grouped to form the pedestal.

  Narrow herring-bone-laid bricks,
    a dusty pink beside the dwarf box-
bordered pansies, share the ivy-arbor shade
        with cemetery lace settees, one at each side,
        and with the bird: box-bordered tide-
        water gigantic jet black pansies—splendor; pride—
not for a decade
    dressed, but for a day, in over-powering velvet; and
    gray-blue-Andalusian-cock-feather pale ones,
        ink-lined on the edge, fur-
        eyed, with ochre
on the cheek. The at first slow, saddle-horse quick cavalcade

  of buckeye-burnished jumpers
    and five-gaited mounts, the work-mule and
show-mule and witch-cross door and "strong sweet prison"
        are a part of what has come about—in the Black
        idiom—from "advancin' back-
        wards in a circle"; from taking the Potomac
cowbirdlike, and on

the Chickahominy establishing the Negro,
   inadvertent ally and best enemy of
      tyranny. Rare unscent-
      ed, provident-
ly hot, too sweet, inconsistent flower-bed! Old Dominion

   flowers are curious. Some wilt
   in daytime and some close at night. Some
have perfume; some have not. The scarlet much-quilled
      fruiting pomegranate, the African violet,
      fuchsia and camellia, none, yet
      the house-high glistening green magnolia's velvet-
textured flower is filled
   with anesthetic scent as inconsiderate as
   the gardenia's. Even the gardenia-sprig's
      dark vein on greener
      leaf when seen
against the light, has not near it more small bees than the frilled

   silk substanceless faint flower of
   the crape-myrtle has. Odd Pamunkey
princess, birdclaw-ear-ringed; with a pet raccoon
      from the Mattaponi (what a bear!). Feminine
      odd Indian young lady! Odd thin-
      gauze-and-taffeta-dressed English one! Terrapin
meat and crested spoon
   feed the mistress of French plum-and-turquoise-piped chaise-longue;
   of brass-knobbed slat front door, and everywhere open
      shaded house on Indian-
      named Virginian
streams in counties named for English lords. The rattlesnake soon

   said from our once dashingly
   undiffident first flag, "Don't tread on
me"—tactless symbol of a new republic.
      Priorities were cradled in this region not
      noted for humility; spot

that has high-singing frogs, cotton-mouth snakes and cot-
ton fields; a unique
    Lawrence pottery with loping wolf design; and too
    unvenomous terrapin in tepid greenness,
            idling near the sea-top;
            tobacco-crop
records on church walls; a Devil's Woodyard; and the one-brick-

    thick serpentine wall built by
    Jefferson. Like strangler figs choking
a banyan, not an explorer, no imperialist,
        not one of us, in taking what we
        pleased—in colonizing as the
        saying is—has been a synonym for mercy.
The redskin with the deer-
    fur crown, famous for his cruelty, is not all brawn
    and animality. The outdoor tea-table,
            the mandolin-shaped big
            and little fig,
the silkworm-mulberry, the French mull dress with the Madeira-

    vine-accompanied edge are,
    when compared with what the colonists
found here in tidewater Virginia, stark
        luxuries. The mere brown hedge-sparrow, with reckless
        ardor, unable to suppress
        his satisfaction in man's trustworthy nearness,
even in the dark
    flutes his ecstatic burst of joy—the caraway seed-
    spotted sparrow perched in the dew-drenched juniper
            beside the window-ledge;
            this little hedge-
sparrow that wakes up seven minutes sooner than the lark.

    The live oak's darkening filigree
    of undulating boughs, the etched
solidity of a cypress indivisible

from the now agèd English hackberry,
   become with lost identity,
   part of the ground, as sunset flames increasingly
against the leaf-chiseled
   blackening ridge of green; while clouds, expanding above
   the town's assertiveness, dwarf it, dwarf arrogance
         that can misunderstand
         importance; and
are to the child an intimation of what glory is.

Bird-Witted

With innocent wide penguin eyes, three
   large fledgling mocking-birds below
the pussy-willow tree,
   stand in a row,
wings touching, feebly solemn,
till they see
     their no longer larger
     mother bringing
something which will partially
feed one of them.

Toward the high-keyed intermittent squeak
   of broken carriage-springs, made by
the three similar, meek-
   coated bird's-eye
freckled forms she comes; and when
from the beak
     of one, the still living
     beetle has dropped
out, she picks it up and puts
it in again.

Standing in the shade till they have dressed
   their thickly filamented, pale
pussy-willow-surfaced
   coats, they spread tail
and wings, showing one by one,
the modest
     white stripe lengthwise on the
     tail and crosswise
underneath the wing, and the
accordion

is closed again. What delightful note
   with rapid unexpected flute-

sounds leaping from the throat
  of the astute
grown bird comes back to one from
the remote
    unenergetic sun-
    lit air before
the brood was here? How harsh
the bird's voice has become.

A piebald cat observing them,
  is slowly creeping toward the trim
trio on the tree-stem.
  Unused to him
the three make room—uneasy
new problem.
    A dangling foot that missed
    its grasp is raised
and finds the twig on which it
planned to perch. The

parent darting down, nerved by what chills
  the blood, and by hope rewarded—
of toil—since nothing fills
  squeaking unfed
mouths, wages deadly combat,
and half kills
    with bayonet beak and
    cruel wings, the
intellectual cautious-
ly c r e e p ing cat.

Half Deity

half worm. We all, infant and adult, have
   stopped to watch the butterfly, last of the
   elves, and learned to spare the wingless worm
      that hopefully ascends the tree. What zebra
   could surpass the zebra-
      striped swallow-tail of South America
on whose half-transparent wings crescents engrave

the silken edge with dragon's blood, weightless?
   They that have wings must not have weights. The north's
   yellower swallow-tail, with a pitch-
      fork-scalloped edge, has tails blunter at the tip.
   Flying with droverlike
      tenacity and weary from its trip,
one has lighted on the elm. Its yellowness

that almost counterfeits a leaf's has just
   now been observed. A nymph approaches, dressed
   in Wedgwood blue, tries to touch it and
      must follow to *micromalus,* the midget
   crab-tree, to a pear-tree,
      and from that, to the flowering pomegranate.
Defeated but encouraged by each new gust

of wind, forced by the summer sun to pant,
   she stands on rug-soft grass; though some are not
   permitted to gaze informally
      on majesty in such a manner as she
   is gazing here. The blind
      all-seeing butterfly, afraid of the
slight finger, floats as though it were ignorant

across the path, and choosing a flower's palm
   of air and stamens, settles; then pawing
   like a horse, turns round,—apostrophe-

tipped brown antennae porcupining out as
it arranges nervous
wings. Aware that curiosity has
been pursuing it, it cannot now be calm.

The butterfly's tobacco-brown unglazed
china eyes and furry countenance confront
the nymph's large eyes—gray eyes that now are
black, for she with controlled agitated glance
explores the insect's face
and all's a-quiver with significance.
It is Goya's scene of the tame magpie faced

by crouching cats. Butterflies do not need
home advice. As though the admiring nymph
were patent-leather cricket singing
loud or gnat-catching garden-toad, the swallow-
tail, bewitched and haughty,
springs away; flies where she cannot follow,
trampling the air as it trampled the flowers, feed-

ing where it pivots. Equine irascible
unwormlike unteachable butterfly-
zebra! Sometimes one is grateful to
a stranger for looking very nice; to the
friendly outspread hand. But
it flies, drunken with triviality
or guided by visions of strength, off until,

diminishing like wreckage on the sea,
rising and falling easily, it mounts
the swell and keeping its true course with
what swift majesty, indifferent to
her, is gone. Deaf to ap-
proval, magnet-nice as it fluttered through
airs now slack now fresh, it had strict ears when the

west wind spoke; for pleased by the butterfly's
   inconsequential ease, he held no net,
   did not regard the butterfly-bush
      as a trap, hid no decoy in half-shut
   palm since his is not a
      covetous hand. It was not Oberon, but ✓The Tempest
this quietest wind with piano replies,

the zephyr, whose detachment was enough
   to tempt the fiery tiger-horse to stand,
   eyes staring skyward and chest arching
      bravely out—historic metamorphoser
   and saintly animal
      in India, in Egypt, anywhere.
Their talk was as strange as my grandmother's muff. /

Smooth Gnarled Crape Myrtle

   A brass-green bird with grass-
green throat smooth as a nut springs from
    twig to twig askew, copying the
Chinese flower piece—businesslike atom
    in the stiff-leafed tree's blue-
    pink dregs-of-wine pyramids
    of mathematic
    circularity; one of a
    pair. A redbird with a hatchet
    crest lights straight, on a twig
    between the two, bending the
      peculiar
      bouquet down; and there are

    moths and lady-bugs,
a boot-jack firefly with black wings
    and a pink head. "The legendary white-
eared black bulbul that sings
    only in pure Sanskrit" should
    be here—"tame clever
    true nightingale." The cardinal-
    bird that is usually a
    pair looks somewhat odd, like
    "the ambassadorial
      Inverness
      worn by one who dresses

    in New York but dreams of
London." It was artifice saw,
    on a patch-box pigeon-egg, room for
fervent script, and wrote as with a bird's claw
    under the pair on the
    hyacinth-blue lid—"joined in
    friendship, crowned by love."
    As aspect may deceive; as the

elephant's columbine-tubed trunk
held waveringly out—
an at will heavy thing—is
   delicate.
   Art is unfortunate.

One may be a blameless
bachelor, and it is but a step
   to Congreve. A Rosalindless
redbird comes where people are, knowing they
   have not made a point of
   being where he is—this bird
which says not sings, "without
   loneliness I should be more
   lonely, so I keep it"—half in
Japanese. And what of
   our clasped hands that swear, "By Peace
     Plenty; as
     by Wisdom Peace." Alas!

Peace

The Pangolin

Another armored animal—scale
    lapping scale with spruce-cone regularity until they
form the uninterrupted central
   tail-row! This near artichoke with head and legs and grit-equipped gizzard,
   the night miniature artist engineer is,
      yes, Leonardo da Vinci's replica—
        impressive animal and toiler of whom we seldom hear.
      Armor seems extra. But for him,
      the closing ear-ridge—
        or bare ear lacking even this small
        eminence and similarly safe

contracting nose and eye apertures,
    impenetrably closable, are not;—a true ant-eater,
not cockroach-eater, who endures
   exhausting solitary trips through unfamiliar ground at night,
   returning before sunrise; stepping in the moonlight,
      on the moonlight peculiarly, that the outside
        edges of his hands may bear the weight and save the claws
      for digging. Serpentined about
      the tree, he draws
        away from danger unpugnaciously,
        with no sound but a harmless hiss; keeping

the fragile grace of the Thomas-
    of-Leighton Buzzard Westminster Abbey wrought-iron vine, or
rolls himself into a ball that has
   power to defy all effort to unroll it; strongly intailed, neat
  head for core, on neck not breaking off, with curled-in feet.
    Nevertheless he has sting-proof scales; and nest
      of rocks closed with earth from inside, which he can thus darken.
    Sun and moon and day and night and man and beast
    each with a splendor
      which man in all his vileness cannot
      set aside; each with an excellence!

"Fearful yet to be feared," the armored
    ant-eater met by the driver-ant does not turn back, but
engulfs what he can, the flattened sword-
    edged leafpoints on the tail and artichoke set leg- and body-plates
    quivering violently when it retaliates
        and swarms on him. Compact like the furled fringed frill
            on the hat-brim of Gargallo's hollow iron head of a
            matador, he will drop and will
            then walk away
                unhurt, although if unintruded on,
                he cautiously works down the tree, helped

by his tail. The giant-pangolin-
    tail, graceful tool, as prop or hand or broom or ax, tipped like
an elephant's trunk with special skin,
    is not lost on this ant- and stone-swallowing uninjurable
    artichoke which simpletons thought a living fable
        whom the stones had nourished, whereas ants had done
            so. Pangolins are not aggressive animals; between
            dusk and day they have the not unchain-like machine-like
                form and frictionless creep of a thing
                made graceful by adversities, con-

versities. To explain grace requires
    a curious hand. If that which is at all were not forever,
why would those who graced the spires
with animals and gathered there to rest, on cold luxurious
low stone seats—a monk and monk and monk—between the thus
        ingenious roof-supports, have slaved to confuse
            grace with a kindly manner, time in which to pay a debt,
            the cure for sins, a graceful use
            of what are yet
                approved stone mullions branching out across
                the perpendiculars? A sailboat

was the first machine. Pangolins, made
    for moving quietly also, are models of exactness,

on four legs; on hind feet plantigrade,
with certain postures of a man. Beneath sun and moon, man slaving
to make his life more sweet, leaves half the flowers worth having,
    needing to choose wisely how to use his strength;
      a paper-maker like the wasp; a tractor of foodstuffs,
    like the ant; spidering a length
    of web from bluffs
      above a stream; in fighting, mechanicked
      like the pangolin; capsizing in

disheartenment. Bedizened or stark
    naked, man, the self, the being we call human, writing-
master to this world, griffons a dark
  "Like does not like like that is obnoxious"; and writes error with four
  r's. Among animals, *one* has a sense of humor.
    Humor saves a few steps, it saves years. Unignorant,
      modest and unemotional, and all emotion,
    he has everlasting vigor,
    power to grow,
      though there are few creatures who can make one
      breathe faster and make one erecter.

• • •

Not afraid of anything is he,
    and then goes cowering forth, tread paced to meet an obstacle
at every step. Consistent with the
  formula—warm blood, no gills, two pairs of hands and a few hairs—that
  is a mammal; there he sits in his own habitat,
    serge-clad, strong-shod. The prey of fear, he, always
      curtailed, extinguished, thwarted by the dusk, work partly done,
    says to the alternating blaze,
  "Again the sun!
    anew each day; and new and new and new,
    that comes into and steadies my soul."

Walking-Sticks and Paper-Weights and Water Marks

Jointed against indecision,
the tree legs of the triskelion,
    meeting in the
middle between triangles, run
in unison,
    self-assisted. And yet, trudging
    on two legs that move contradictorily,
despite ghosts and witches, one
        does not fear to ask for beauty.

Stepped glass has been made in Ireland;
they still have blackthorn walking-sticks, and
    flax and linen
and paper-mills; and reprimand
you if you stand
    your stick on such and such a spot.
    You must keep to the path "on account of the
souls." And all can understand
        how centralizing loyalty

shapes matter as a die is hid
while used; and that such power, unavid
    since secure, can
mold an at first fluid solid
glass weight. Amid
    the wax the seal is safe. Also
    as the water mark's translucence clearly seen
can fascinate the vivid-
        ly white flower attracts one lightly

brushing against sceptre-headed
weeds and daisies swayed by wind. They said,
    "Do not scatter
your stick, on account of the dead."
The pathway led

into woods "where leafy trees meet
    overhead and noise of traffic is unknown"—
the mind exhilarated
    by life all round, so stirringly

alive. Fancy's rude root cudgel
with the bark left on, the woodbine smell-
    ing of the rain,
the very stones had life. Little
scars on churchbell-
    tongues, put there by the Devil's claws,
    and other forms of negativeness need but
be expressed and visible,
    to prove their unauthority.

Patience, with its superlatives,
firmness and loyalty and faith, gives
    intensive fruit.
As a device before it leaves
the wax, receives
    to give, and giving must itself
    receive, "difficulty is ordained to check
poltroons," and courage achieves
    despaired-of ends inversely,—

mute with power and strong with fear.
A bold outspoken gentleman, cheer-
    ful, plodding, to-
the-point, used to the atmosphere
of work, and there-
    fore author of the permanent,
says modestly, "This is my taste, it might not
be another man's." Sincere
    unforced unconscious honesty,

sine cera, can be furthest
from self-defensiveness and nearest;

as when a seal,
without haste, slowly is impressed,
and forms a nest
    on which the raised device reversed,
    shows round. It must have been an able workman,
humorous and self-possessed,
      a liker of solidity,

who gave this greenish Waterford
glass weight, with the summit curled down toward
    itself as the
    glass grew, the look of tempered sword-
steel; of three-ore'd
    fishscale-burnished antimony-
    lead-and-tin smoky water-drop type-metal
smoothness emery-armored
      against rust. Its subdued glossy

splendor leaps out at the eye as
the light does not shine even from glass
    air-twist canes, or
witchballs. This paperweight, in mass
a stone, surpass-
    ing it in tint, enlarges the
    fine chain-lines on the letter-flap weighted by
its hardened rain-drop surface.
      The paper-mold's similarly

at first unsolid blues, yellow-
whites and lavenders, when seen through, show
    leopards, eagles,
quills, acorns and anvils. "Stones grow,"
as volcano-
    sides and quartz-mines prove. "Plants feel? Men
    think." "Airmail is quick." "Save rags, bones, metals." Hopes
are harvest when deeds follow
      words postmarked "Dig for victory."

Postmark behests are clearer than
the water marks beneath,—than ox, swan,
    crane, or dolphin,
than eastern, open, jewelled, Span-
ish, Umbrian
    crown,—as symbols of endurance.
    And making the envelope secure, the sealed
wax reveals a pelican
        studying affectionately

the nest's three-in-one upturned tri-
form face. "For those we love, live and die"
    the motto reads.
The pelican's community
of throats, the high-
    way's trivia or crow's-foot where
    three roads meet, the fugue, the awl-leafed juniper's
whorls of three, objectify
        welded divisiveness. Of the

juniper that in balladry
has been kept green, the fugue's three times three
    reiterat-
ed chain of interactingly
linked harmony,
    says "On the first day of Christmas
    my true love he sent unto me, part of a
bough of a juniper-tree,"
        repeated to infinity.

See in the Midst of Fair Leaves

and much fruit, the swan—
   one line of the mathematician's
sign greater-than, drawn
   to an apex where the lake is
met by the weight on it; or an angel
standing in the sun, how well
   armed, how manly;

and promenading
   in sloughs of despond, a monster—
man when human nothing
   more, grown to immaturity,
punishing debtors, seeing his due—as
an arrow turned inward has
   no chance of peace.

WORLD WAR II AND AFTER

1940–1956

Four Quartz Crystal Clocks

There are four vibrators, the world's exactest clocks;
   and these quartz time-pieces that tell
time intervals to other clocks,
   these worksless clocks work well;
independently the same, kept in
   the 41° Bell
     Laboratory time

vault. Checked by a comparator with Arlington,
   punctualize the "radio,
cinéma," and "presse,"—a group the
   Giraudoux truth-bureau
of hoped-for accuracy has termed
   "instruments of truth." We know—
     as Jean Giraudoux says,

certain Arabs have not heard—that Napoleon
   is dead; that a quartz prism when
the temperature changes, feels
   the change and that the then
electrified alternate edges
   oppositely charged, threaten
     careful timing; so that

this water-clear crystal as the Greeks used to say,
   this "clear ice" must be kept at the
same coolness. Repetition, with
   the scientist, should be
synonymous with accuracy.
   The lemur-student can see
     that an aye-aye is not

an angwan-tíbo, potto, or loris. The sea-
   side burden should not embarrass

the bell-boy with the buoy-ball
   endeavoring to pass
hotel patronesses; nor could a
   practiced ear confuse the glass
      eyes for taxidermists

with eye-glasses from the optometrist. And as
   MEridian-7 one-two
one-two gives, each fifteenth second
   in the same voice, the new
data—"The time will be" so and so—
   you realize that "when you
      hear the signal," you'll be

hearing Jupiter or jour pater, the day god—
   the salvaged son of Father Time—
telling the cannibal Chronos
   (eater of his proxime
newborn progeny) that punctuality
      is not a crime.

What Are Years

What is our innocence,
what is our guilt? All are
    naked, none is safe. And whence
is courage: the unanswered question,
the resolute doubt,—
dumbly calling, deafly listening—that
in misfortune, even death,
        encourages others
        and in its defeat, stirs

    the soul to be strong? He
sees deep and is glad, who
    accedes to mortality
and in his imprisonment rises
upon himself as
the sea in a chasm, struggling to be
free and unable to be,
        in its surrendering
        finds its continuing.

    So he who strongly feels,
behaves. The very bird,
    grown taller as he sings, steels
his form straight up. Though he is captive,
his mighty singing
says, satisfaction is a lowly
thing, how pure a thing is joy.
        This is mortality,
        this is eternity.

The Paper Nautilus

For authorities whose hopes
are shaped by mercenaries?
    Writers entrapped by
    teatime fame and by
commuters' comforts? Not for these
    the paper nautilus
    constructs her thin glass shell.

Giving her perishable
souvenir of hope, a dull
    white outside and smooth-
    edged inner surface
glossy as the sea, the watchful
    maker of it guards it
    day and night; she scarcely

eats until the eggs are hatched.
Buried eight-fold in her eight
    arms, for she is in
    a sense a devil-
fish, her glass ram's-horn-cradled freight
    is hid but is not crushed;
    as Hercules, bitten

by a crab loyal to the hydra,
was hindered to succeed,
    the intensively
    watched eggs coming from
the shell free it when they are freed,—
    leaving its wasp-nest flaws
    of white on white, and close-

laid Ionic chiton-folds
like the lines in the mane of
    a Parthenon horse,
    round which the arms had
wound themselves as if they knew love
    is the only fortress
    strong enough to trust to.

Rigorists

    "We saw reindeer
browsing," a friend who'd been in Lapland said:
"finding their own food; they are adapted

    to scant *reino*
or pasture, yet they can run eleven
miles in fifty minutes; the feet spread when

    the snow is soft,
and act as snow-shoes. They are rigorists,
however handsomely cutwork artists

    of Lapland and
Siberia elaborate the trace
or saddle-girth with saw-tooth leather lace.

    One looked at us
with its firm face part brown, part white—a queen
of alpine flowers. Santa Claus' reindeer, seen

    at last, had gray-
brown fur, with a neck like edelweiss or
lion's foot—*leontopodium* more

    exactly." And
this candelabrum-headed ornament
for a place where ornaments are scarce, sent

    to Alaska,
was a gift preventing the extinction
of the Eskimo. The battle was won

    by a quiet man,
Sheldon Jackson, evangel to that race
whose reprieve he read in the reindeer's face.

Light Is Speech

One can say more of sunlight
   than of speech; but speech
   and light, each
aiding each—when French—
have not disgraced that still
unextirpated adjective.
Yes, light is speech. Free frank
impartial sunlight, moonlight,
starlight, lighthouse light,
   are language. The Creach'h
d'Ouessant light-
house on its defenseless dot of
rock is the descendant of Voltaire

whose flaming justice reached
   a man already harmed;
   of unarmed
Montaigne whose balance,
maintained despite the bandit's
hardness, lit remorse's saving
spark; of Émile Littré,
philology's determined,
ardent eight-volume
   Hippocrates-charmed
editor. A
man of fire, a scientist of
freedoms, was firm Maximilien

Paul Émile Littré. England
   guarded by the sea,
   we, with re-enforced Bartholdi's
Liberty holding up her
torch beside the port, hear France
demand, "Tell me the truth,
especially when it is

unpleasant." And we
cannot but reply,
"The word France means
enfranchisement; means one who can
'animate whoever thinks of her.'"

He "Digesteth Harde Yron"

Although the aepyornis
  or roc that lived in Madagascar and
the moa are extinct,
the camel-sparrow, linked
  with them in size—the large sparrow
Xenophon saw walking by a stream—was and is
a symbol of justice.

This bird watches his chicks with
  a maternal concentration—and he's
been mothering the eggs
at night six weeks—his legs
  their only weapon of defense.
He is swifter than a horse; he has a foot hard
as a hoof; the leopard

is not more suspicious. How
  could he, prized for plumes and eggs and young,
used even as a riding-beast, respect men
  hiding actor-like in ostrich skins, with the right hand
making the neck move as if alive
and from a bag the left hand strewing grain, that ostriches

might be decoyed and killed! Yes, this is he
whose plume was anciently
the plume of justice; he
  whose comic duckling head on its
great neck revolves with compass-needle nervousness
when he stands guard,

in S-like foragings as he is
preening the down on his leaden-skinned back.
The egg piously shown
as Leda's very own
  from which Castor and Pollux hatched,

was an ostrich-egg. And what could have been more fit
for the Chinese lawn it

    gazed on as a gift to an
    emperor who admired strange birds, than this
one, who builds his mud-made
nest in dust yet will wade
    in lake or sea till only the head shows.

        . . .

    Six hundred ostrich-brains served
    at one banquet, the ostrich-plume-tipped tent
and desert spear, jewel-
gorgeous ugly egg-shell
    goblets, eight pairs of ostriches
in harness, dramatize a meaning
always missed by the externalist.

    The power of the visible
    is the invisible, as even where
no tree of freedom grows,
so-called brute courage knows.
    Heroism is exhausting, yet
it contradicts a greed that did not wisely spare
the harmless solitaire

    or great auk in its grandeur;
    unsolicitude having swallowed up
all giant birds but an alert gargantuan
    little-winged, magnificently speedy running-bird.
This one remaining rebel
is the sparrow-camel.

Spenser's Ireland

has not altered; —
   a place as kind as it is green,
   the greenest place I've never seen.
Every name is a tune.
Denunciations do not affect
     the culprit; nor blows, but it
is torture to him to not be spoken to.
They're natural, —
     the coat, like Venus'
mantle lined with stars,
buttoned close at the neck, —the sleeves new from disuse.

If in Ireland
   they play the harp backward at need,
   and gather at midday the seed
of the fern, eluding
their "giants all covered with iron," might
     there be fern seed for unlearn-
ing obduracy and for reinstating
the enchantment?
     Hindered characters
seldom have mothers
in Irish stories, but they all have grandmothers.

It was Irish;
   a match not a marriage was made
   when my great great grandmother'd said
with native genius for
disunion, "Although your suitor be
     perfection, one objection
is enough; he is not
Irish." Outwitting
     the fairies, befriending the furies,
whoever again
and again says, "I'll never give in," never sees

that you're not free
    until you've been made captive by
    supreme belief, —credulity
you say? When large dainty
fingers tremblingly divide the wings
    of the fly for mid-July
with a needle and wrap it with peacock-tail,
or tie wool and
        buzzard's wing, their pride,
like the enchanter's,
is in care, not madness. Concurring hands divide

flax for damask
    that when bleached by Irish weather
    has the silvered chamois-leather
water-tightness of a
skin. Twisted torcs and gold new-moon-shaped
        lunulae aren't jewelry
like the purple-coral fuchsia-tree's. Eire—
the guillemot
        so neat and the hen
of the heath and the
linnet spinet-sweet—bespeak relentlessness? Then

they are to me
    like enchanted Earl Gerald who
    changed himself into a stag, to
a great green-eyed cat of
the mountain. Discommodity makes
        them invisible; they've dis-
appeared. The Irish say your trouble is their
trouble and your
        joy their joy? I wish
I could believe it; I'm troubled, I'm dissatisfied, I'm Irish.

The Wood-Weasel

emerges daintily, the skunk—
don't laugh—in sylvan black and white chipmunk
regalia. The inky thing
adaptively whited with glistening
goat-fur is wood-warden. In his
ermined well-cuttlefish-inked wool, he is
determination's totem. Out-
lawed? His sweet face and powerful feet go about
in chieftain's coat of Chilcat cloth.
He is his own protection from the moth,

noble little warrior. That
otter-skin on it, the living pole-cat,
smothers anything that stings. Well, —
this same weasel's playful and his weasel
associates are too. Only
Wood-weasels shall associate with me.

Pale Morning Moon, Dark Blue Black Sea,

    green cypresses all black against
    the sun's noon fire, liberty is
noble food. To divide
    it makes it more; more of it, not
    outstanding—futile word. When insight
    is not farsight, when grace would be
    outstanding without having been
indwelling, there is reason to have sighed.

    Boll - i - var, Bow - lee - var, I don't
    know what you call it but I know
he set them free. For the
    strengthenings of liberty, thought
    of in our minds, done with our fingers,
    hoped for in our lives, we're asking,
    save us from the captivity
of surfeit; save us from complacency.

    Life must stop stifling life with life.
    It must. Alas that we must put
an end to death by death.
    We're begging; we are begging for
    news to the prisoner that he may
    come out of his dungeon at last.
    He's seen destruction and would see
deliverance. Turn sighing into breath.

You, Your Horse

Gray like a mouse and minded like a dove,
   It could not be described as either one
      Thing or the other. It was thistledown
      Blown delicately through the town.

Under the stricture of its girth, the skin
   Was crowded in. A horselike creature, with
      Unhorselike feet, it trod with honied stroke
      The asphalt of the city's cloak.

You could not have gone faster had it been
   A wish, had you been perched up on a dream,
      "You—" who did, in fleeing that thoroughfare—
      Literally outride the air.

In Distrust of Merits

Strengthened to live, strengthened to die for
    medals and positioned victories?
They're fighting, fighting, fighting the blind
    man who thinks he sees,—
who cannot see that the enslaver is
enslaved; the hater, harmed. O shining O
        firm star, O tumultuous
            ocean lashed till small things go
        as they will, the mountainous
            wave makes us who look, know

depth. Lost at sea before they fought! O
    star of David, star of Bethlehem,
O black imperial lion
    of the Lord—emblem
of a risen world—be joined at last, be
joined. There is hate's crown beneath which all is
        death; there's love's without which none
            is king; the blessed deeds bless
        the halo. As contagion
            of sickness makes sickness,

contagion of trust can make trust. They're
    fighting in deserts and caves, one by
one, in battalions and squadrons;
    they're fighting that I
may yet recover from the disease, My
Self; some have it lightly; some will die. "Man's
        wolf to man" and we devour
            ourselves. The enemy could not
        have made a greater breach in our
        defenses. One pilot-

ing a blind man can escape him, but
    Job disheartened by false comfort knew

that nothing can be so defeating
     as a blind man who
can see. O alive who are dead, who are
proud not to see, O small dust of the earth
          that walks so arrogantly,
               trust begets power and faith is
          an affectionate thing. We
               vow, we make this promise

to the fighting—it's a promise—"We'll
     never hate black, white, red, yellow, Jew,
Gentile, Untouchable." We are
     not competent to
make our vows. With set jaw they are fighting,
fighting, fighting, —some we love whom we know,
          some we love but know not—that
               hearts may feel and not be numb.
          It cures me; or am I what
               I can't believe in? Some

in snow, some on crags, some in quicksands,
     little by little, much by much, they
are fighting fighting fighting that where
     there was death there may
be life. "When a man is prey to anger,
he is moved by outside things; when he holds
          his ground in patience patience
               patience, that is action or
          beauty," the soldier's defense
               and hardest armor for

the fight. The world's an orphan's home. Shall
     we never have peace without sorrow?
without pleas of the dying for
     help that won't come? O
quiet form upon the dust, I cannot
look and yet I must. If these great patient

             dyings—all these agonies
                     and wound bearings and bloodshed—
             can teach us how to live, these
                     dyings were not wasted.

Hate-hardened heart, O heart of iron,
       iron is iron till it is rust.
There never was a war that was
       not inward; I must
fight till I have conquered in myself what
causes war, but I would not believe it.
             I inwardly did nothing.
                     O Iscariot-like crime!
             Beauty is everlasting
                     and dust is for a time.

Nevertheless

you've seen a strawberry
     that's had a struggle; yet
     was, where the fragments met,

a hedgehog or a star-
     fish for the multitude
     of seeds. What better food

than apple-seeds—the fruit
     within the fruit—locked in
     like counter-curved twin

hazel-nuts? Frost that kills
     the little rubber-plant-
     leaves of *kok-saghyz*-stalks, can't

harm the roots; they still grow
     in frozen ground. Once where
     there was a prickly-pear-

leaf clinging to barbed wire,
     a root shot down to grow
     in earth two feet below;

as carrots form mandrakes
     or a ram's-horn root some-
     times. Victory won't come

to me unless I go
     to it; a grape-tendril
     ties a knot in knots till

knotted thirty times, —so
     the bound twig that's under-
     gone and over-gone, can't stir.

The weak overcomes its
     menace, the strong over-
     comes itself. What is there

like fortitude! What sap
     went through that little thread
     to make the cherry red!

Elephants

Uplifted and waved till immobilized
wistaria-like, the opposing opposed
mouse-gray twined proboscises' trunk formed by two
trunks, fights itself to a spiraled inter-nosed

deadlock of dyke-enforced massiveness. It's a
knock-down drag-out fight that asks no quarter? Just
a pastime, as when the trunk rains on itself
the pool it siphoned up; or when—since each must

provide his forty-pound bough dinner—he broke
the leafy branches. These templars of the Tooth,
these matched intensities, take master care of
master tools. One, sleeping with the calm of youth,

at full length in the half-dry sun-flecked stream-bed,
rests his hunting-horn-curled trunk on shallowed stone.
The sloping hollow of the sleeper's body
cradles the gently breathing eminence's prone

mahout, asleep like a lifeless six-foot
frog, so feather light the elephant's stiff
ear's unconscious of the crossed feet's weight. And the
defenseless human thing sleeps as sound as if

incised with hard wrinkles, embossed with wide ears,
invincibly tusked, made safe by magic hairs!
As if, as if, it is all ifs; we are at
much unease. But magic's masterpiece is theirs—

Houdini's serenity quelling his fears.
Elephant-ear-witnesses-to-be of hymns
and glorias, these ministrants all gray or
gray with white on legs or trunk, are a pilgrims'

pattern of revery not reverence—a
religious procession without any priests,
the centuries-old carefullest unrehearsed
play. Blessed by Buddha's Tooth, the obedient beasts

themselves as toothed temples blessing the street, see
the white elephant carry the cushion that
carries the casket that carries the Tooth.
Amenable to what, matched with him, are gnat

trustees, he does not step on them as the white-
canopied blue-cushioned Tooth is augustly
and slowly returned to the shrine. Though white is
the color of worship and of mourning, he

is not here to worship and he is too wise
to mourn—a life prisoner but reconciled.
With trunk tucked up compactly—the elephant's
sign of defeat—he resisted, but is the child

of reason now. His straight trunk seems to say: when
what we hoped for came to nothing, we revived.
As loss could not ever alter Socrates'
tranquillity, equanimity's contrived

by the elephant. With the Socrates of
animals as with Sophocles the Bee, on whose
tombstone a hive was incised, sweetness tinctures
his gravity. His held-up fore-leg for use

as a stair, to be climbed or descended with
the aid of his ear, expounds the brotherhood
of creatures to man the encroacher, by the
small word with the dot, meaning know—the verb bud.

These knowers "arouse the feeling that they are
allied to man" and can change roles with their trustees.

Hardship makes the soldier; then teachableness
makes him the philosopher—as Socrates,

prudently testing the suspicious thing, knew
the wisest is he who's not sure that he knows.
Who rides on a tiger can never dismount;
asleep on an elephant, that is repose.

The Mind Is an Enchanting Thing

is an enchanted thing
    like the glaze on a
katydid-wing
        subdivided by sun
        till the nettings are legion.
Like Gieseking playing Scarlatti;

like the apteryx-awl
    as a beak, or the
kiwi's rain-shawl
        of haired feathers, the mind,
        feeling its way as though blind,
walks along with its eyes on the ground.

It has memory's ear
    that can hear without
having to hear.
        Like the gyroscope's fall,
        truly unequivocal
because trued by regnant certainty,

it is a power of
    strong enchantment. It
is like the dove-
        neck animated by
        sun; it is memory's eye;
it's conscientious inconsistency.

It tears off the veil; tears
    the temptation, the
mist the heart wears,
        from its eyes—if the heart
        has a face; it takes apart
dejection. It's fire in the dove-neck's

iridescence; in the
    inconsistencies
of Scarlatti.

      Unconfusion submits
      its confusion to proof: it's
not a Herod's oath that cannot change.

A Carriage from Sweden

They say there is a sweeter air
    where it was made, than we have here;
    a Hamlet's castle atmosphere.
At all events there is in Brooklyn
something that makes me feel at home.

No one may see this put-away
    museum-piece, this country cart
    that inner happiness made art;
and yet, in this city of freckled
integrity it is a vein

of resined straightness from north-wind
    hardened Sweden's once-opposed-to-
    compromise archipelago
of rocks. Washington and Gustavus
Adolphus, forgive our decay.

Seats, dashboard and sides of smooth gourd-
    rind texture, a flowered step, swan-
    dart brake, and swirling crustacean-
tailed equine amphibious creatures
that garnish the axle-tree! What

a fine thing! What unannoying
    romance! And how beautiful, she
    with the natural stoop of the
snowy egret, gray-eyed and straight-haired,
for whom it should come to the door—

of whom it reminds me. The split
    pine fair hair, steady gannet-clear
    eyes and the pine-needled-path deer-
swift step; that is Sweden, land of the
free and the soil for a spruce-tree—

vertical though a seedling—all
        needles: from a green trunk, green shelf
        on shelf fanning out by itself.
The deft white-stockinged dance in thick-soled
shoes! Denmark's sanctuaried Jews!

The puzzle-jugs and hand-spun rugs,
        the root-legged kracken shaped like dogs,
        the hanging buttons and the frogs
that edge the Sunday jackets! Sweden,
you have a runner called the Deer, who

when he's won a race, likes to run
        more; you have the sun-right gable-
        ends due east and west, the table
spread as for a banquet; and the put-
in twin vest-pleats with a fish-fin

effect when you need none. Sweden,
        what makes the people dress that way
        and those who see you wish to stay?
The runner, not too tired to run more
at the end of the race? And that

cart, dolphin-graceful? A Dalén
        light-house, self-lit?—responsive and
        responsible. I understand;
it's not pine-needle-paths that give spring
when they're run on, it's a Sweden

of moated white castles—the bed
        of white flowers densely grown in an S
        meaning Sweden and stalwartness,
skill, and a surface that says
Made in Sweden: carts are my trade.

"Keeping Their World Large"

All too literally, their flesh and their spirit are our shield.
—New York Times, June 7, 1944

    I should like to see that country's tiles, bedrooms,
stone patios
        and ancient wells: Rinaldo
Caramonica's the cobbler's, Frank Sblendorio's
        and Dominick Angelastro's country—
        the grocer's, the iceman's, the dancer's—the
beautiful Miss Damiano's; wisdom's

    and all angels' Italy, this Christmas Day
this Christmas year.
        A noiseless piano, an
innocent war, the heart that can act against itself. Here,
        each unlike and all alike, could
        so many—stumbling, falling, multiplied
till bodies lay as ground to walk on—

    "If Christ and the apostles died in vain,
I'll die in vain with them"
        against this way of victory.
That forest of white crosses!
        My eyes won't close to it.
        All laid like animals for sacrifice—
like Isaac on the mount, were their own sacrifice.

    Marching to death, marching to life?
"Keeping their world large,"
        whose spirits and whose bodies
all too literally were our shield,
        are still our shield.

They fought the enemy,
we fight fat living and self-pity.
Shine, o shine,
unfalsifying sun, on this sick scene.

His Shield

The pin-swine or spine-swin
    (the edgehog miscalled hedgehog) with all his edges out,
  echidna and echinoderm in distressed-
pin-cushion thorn-fur coats, the spiny pig or porcupine,
    the rhino with horned snout—
  everything is battle-dressed.

Pig-fur won't do, I'll wrap
    myself in salamander-skin like Presbyter John.
  A lizard in the midst of flames, a firebrand
that is life, asbestos-eyed asbestos-eared, with tattooed nap
    and permanent pig on
  the instep; he can withstand

fire and won't drown. In his
    unconquerable country of unpompous gusto,
  gold was so common none considered it; greed
and flattery were unknown. Though rubies large as tennis-
    balls conjoined in streams so
  that the mountain seemed to bleed,

the inextinguishable
    salamander styled himself but presbyter. His shield
  was his humility. In Carpasian
linen coat, flanked by his household lion-cubs and sable
    retinue, he revealed
  a formula safer than

an armorer's: the power of relinquishing
    what one would keep; that is freedom. Become dinosaur-
  skulled, quilled or salamander-wooled, more ironshod
and javelin-dressed than a hedgehog battalion of steel, but be
    dull. Don't be envied or
  armed with a measuring-rod.

Propriety

is some such word
    as the chord
        Brahms had heard
        from a bird,
sung down near the root of the throat;
it's the little downy woodpecker
           spiraling a tree—
           up up up like mercury;

   a not long
   sparrow-song
       of hayseed
       magnitude—
a tuned reticence with rigor
from strength at the source. Propriety is
        Bach's Solfegietto—
        harmonica and basso.

   The fish-spine
   on firs, on
       somber trees
       by the sea's
walls of wave-worn rock—have it; and
a moonbow and Bach's cheerful firmness
        in a minor key.
        It's an owl-and-a-pussy-

   both-content
   agreement.
       Come, come. It's
       mixed with wits;
it's not a graceful sadness. It's
resistance with bent head, like foxtail
        millet's. Brahms and Bach,
        no; Bach and Brahms. To thank Bach

            for his song
          first is wrong.
                Pardon me;
              both are the
unintentional pansy-face
uncursed by self-inspection; blackened
            because born that way.

Advent

Written for the Christmas meeting of the Women's Federation

Comfort and Christmas glory for us all—
   With harp sounds in the air:
   Singing; yes, music everywhere.
Must the encircling hope be small?

Advent: the Advent-wreath,
   A hoop of green on which the candles stood,
   Had large ones for the Sundays.
The ever-circling wish, the evergreen,
   Meant that a day was coming.

   Must Advent mean
Some are content to have the circle small?

   "We are not wise or good."
Could not more ardent caring mean
   We may have brotherhood?
   It could. We know it could.

A Face

"I am not treacherous, callous, jealous, superstitious,
superciliuos, venomous, or absolutely hideous":
    studying and studying its expression,
    exasperated desperation
        though at no real impasse,
        would gladly break the mirror;

when love of order, ardor, uncircuitous simplicity
with an expression of inquiry, are all one needs to be!
    Certain faces, a few, one or two—or one
    face photographed by recollection—
        to my mind, to my sight,
        must remain a delight.

Efforts of Affection

Genesis tells us of Jubal and Jabal.
One handled the harp and one herded the cattle.

Unhackneyed Shakespeare's
"hay, sweet hay, which hath no fellow,"
Love's extraordinary-ordinary stubbornness
like La Fontaine's done
by each as if by each alone,
smiling and stemming distraction;
   how welcome:

vermin-proof and pilfer-proof integration
in which unself-righteousness humbles inspection.

"You know I'm not a saint!" Sainted obsession,
The bleeding-heart's—that strange rubber fern's attraction

puts perfume to shame.
Unsheared sprays of elephant-ears
do not make a selfish end look like a noble one.
Truly as the sun
can rot or mend, love can make one
bestial or make a beast a man.
   Thus wholeness—

wholesomeness? say efforts of affection—
attain integration too tough for infraction.

La Fontaine

At Rest in the Blast

Like a bulwark against fate,
    By the thrust of the blast
  Lead-saluted;
Saluted by lead?
As though flying
    Old Glory full mast.

Pent by power that holds it fast—
    A paradox . . . Hard-pressed,
  You take the blame
  And are inviolate—
    Down-cast but not cast

Down. Some bind by promises,
    But not the tempest-tossed—
  Borne by the might
  Of the storm to a height,
From destruction;
    At rest in the blast.

Like a Bulwark

Affirmed. Pent by power that holds it fast—
a paradox. Pent. Hard pressed,
   you take the blame and are inviolate.
     Abased at last?
     Not the tempest-tossed.
Compressed; firmed by the thrust of the blast
   till compact, like a bulwark against fate;
     lead-saluted,
      saluted by lead?
As though flying Old Glory full mast.

Voracities and Verities
Sometimes Are Interacting

    I don't like diamonds;
the emerald's "grass-lamp glow" is better;
    and unobtrusiveness is dazzling,
       upon occasion.
    Some kinds of gratitude are trying.

    Poets, don't make a fuss;
the elephant's "crooked trumpet" "doth write";
    and to a tiger-book I am reading—
       I think you know the one—
I am under obligation.

      One may be pardoned, yes I know
      one may, for love undying.

By Disposition of Angels

Messengers much like ourselves? Explain it.
Steadfastness the darkness makes explicit?
Something heard most clearly when not near it?
    Above particularities,
these unparticularities praise cannot violate.
   One has seen, in such steadiness never deflected,
   how by darkness a star is perfected.

Star that does not ask me if I see it?
Fir that would not wish me to uproot it?
Speech that does not ask me if I hear it?
    Mysteries expound mysteries.
Steadier than steady, star dazzling me, live and elate,
   no need to say, how like some we have known; too like her,
   too like him, and a-quiver forever.

Armor's Undermining Modesty

At first I thought a pest
must have alighted on my wrist.
It was a moth, almost an owl,
its wings were furred so well,
with backgammon-board wedges interlacing
on the wing—

like cloth of gold in a pattern
of scales with a hair-seal Persian
sheen. Once, self-determination
made an ax of a stone
and hacked things out with hairy paws. The consequence—our mis-set
alphabet.

Arise, for it is day.
Even gifted scholars lose their way
through faulty etymology.
No wonder we hate poetry,
and stars and harps and the new moon. If tributes cannot
be implicit,

give me diatribes and the fragrance of iodine,
the cork oak acorn grown in Spain;
the pale-ale-eyed impersonal look
which the sales-placard gives the bock beer buck.
What is more precise than precision? Illusion.
Knights we've known,

like those familiar
now unfamiliar knights who sought the Grail, were
ducs in Roman fashion
without the addition
of wreaths and silver rods, and armor gilded
or inlaid.

They did not let self bar
their usefulness to others who were
different. Though Mars is excessive
in being preventive,
heroes need not write an ordinall of attributes to enumerate
what they hate.

I should, I confess,
like to have a talk with one of them about excess,
and armor's undermining modesty
instead of innocent depravity.
A mirror-of-steel uninsistence should countenance
continence,

objectified and not by chance,
there in its frame of circumstance
of innocence and altitude
in an unhackneyed solitude.
There is the tarnish; and there, the imperish-
able wish.

The Stuttering Quagmires Speak

If "ennui is not surfeit but is hunger"
For a toy, precocious scent, or bit of coxcombry,
I am resigned to live and fight starvation
Hand to mouth. How shall a leap-frog idolize ennui?

The Icosasphere

"In Buckinghamshire hedgerows
   the birds nesting in the merged green density
      weave little bits of string and moths and feathers and thistledown,
         in parabolic concentric curves" and,
working for concavity, leave spherical feats of rare efficiency;
   whereas through lack of integration,

avid for someone's fortune,
   three were slain and ten committed perjury,
      six died, two killed themselves, and two paid fines for risks they'd run.
        But then there is the icosasphere
in which at last we have steel-cutting at its summit of economy,
   since twenty triangles conjoined can wrap one

ball or double-rounded shell
   with almost no waste, so geometrically
      neat, it's an icosahedron. Would the engineers making one,
        or Mr. J. O. Jackson, tell us
how the Egyptians could have set up seventy-eight-foot solid granite
                             vertically?

   We should like to know how that was done.

Pretiolae

The dutiful, the firemen of Hartford,
Are not without a reward—
A temple of Apollo on a velvet sword

And legend has it that small pretzels come,
Not from Reading but from Rome:
A suppliant's folded arms twisted by a thumb.

Quoting an Also Private Thought

Some speak of things we know, as new;
   And you, of things unknown as things forgot.

A similar coral invades the apple, dyed
   Inside as by infusion of the rind,

Or the poem that chanced to be prose,
   Disclosing the signature in an interior,

Mathematician's parenthesis—
   Astute device quite different from the autograph.

Somehow the accident of pleasure—a dedication qualified
   Indeed; at the opposite pole from the miser's

Escutcheon—three vices hard-screwed;
   Three padlocks clodhopping upon sensibility—

That devastating asset antipodal to pride,
   That would not for the world intrude.

We Call Them the Brave

who likely were reluctant to be brave.
Sitting by a slow fire on a waste
of snow, I would last about an hour.
Better not euphemize the grave.

In this fashionable town, endearments are the mode
though generals are appraised—not praised—
and one is not forced to walk about
where a muddy slough serves as a road.

"What are these shadows barely
visible, which radar fails to scan?"
ships "keeping distance on the gentle swell."
And "what is a free world ready

to do, for what it values most?"
bestow little discs the bereaved may touch?
forget it even when dead—
that congressionally honored ghost

mourned by a friend whose shoulder sags—
weeping on the shoulder of another
for another; with another sitting near,
filling out casualty tags.

What of it? We call them the brave
perhaps? Yes; what if the time should come
when no one will fight for anything
and there's nothing of worth to save.

Then the Ermine:

"rather dead than spotted"; and believe it
    despite reason to think not,
I saw a bat by daylight;
hard to credit

but I knew that I was right. It charmed me—
    wavering like a jack-in-
the-green, weaving about me
insecurely.

Instead of hammer-handed bravado
    strategy could have chosen
momentum with a motto:
Mutare sperno

vel timere—I don't change, am not craven;
    on what ground could one
say that I am hard to frighten?
Nothing's certain.

Fail, and Lavater's physiography
    has another admirer
of skill in obscurity—
now a novelty.

So let the *palisandre* settee express it,
    "ebony violet,"
Master Corbo in full dress,
and shepherdess,

an exhilarating hoarse crow-note
    or dignity with intimacy.

Foiled explosiveness is yet
a kind of prophet,

a perfecter, and so a concealer—
        with the power of implosion;
like violets by Dürer;
even darker.

Apparition of Splendor

Partaking of the miraculous
    since never known literally,
Dürer's rhinoceros
    might have startled us equally
    if black-and-white-spined elaborately.

Like another porcupine, or fern,
    the mouth in an arching egret
was too black to discern
    till exposed as a silhouette;
    but the double-embattled thistle of jet—

disadvantageous supposedly—
    has never shot a quill. Was it
some joyous fantasy,
    plain eider-eared exhibit
    of spines rooted in the sooty moss,

or "train supported by porcupines—
    a fairy's eleven yards long"?
as when the lightning shines
    on thistlefine spears, among
    prongs in lanes above lanes of a shorter prong,

"with the forest for nurse," also dark
    at the base—where needle-debris
springs and shows no footmark;
    the setting for a symmetry
    you must not touch unless you are a fairy.

Maine should be pleased that its animal
    is not a waverer, and rather
than fight, lets the primed quill fall.
    Shallow oppressor, intruder,
    insister, you have found a resister.

Tom Fool at Jamaica

Look at Jonah embarking from Joppa, deterred by
the whale; hard going for a statesman whom nothing could detain,
   although one who would not rather die than repent.
      Be infallible at your peril, for your system will fail,
and select as a model the schoolboy in Spain
   who at the age of six portrayed a mule and jockey
      who had pulled up for a snail.

   "There is submerged magnificence, as Victor Hugo
said." *Sentir avec ardeur;* that's it; magnetized by feeling.
   Tom Fool "makes an effort and makes it oftener
      than the rest"—out on April first, a day of some significance
in the ambiguous sense—the smiling
   Master Atkinson's choice, with that mark of a champion, the extra
      spurt when needed. Yes, yes. "Chance

   is a regrettable impurity"; like Tom Fool's
left white hind foot—an unconformity; though judging by
   results, a kind of cottontail to give him confidence.
      Up in the cupola comparing speeds, Fred Capossela keeps his head.
"It's tough," he said; "but I get 'em; and why shouldn't I?
   I'm relaxed, I'm confident, and I *don't bet.*" Sensational. He does not
      bet on his animated

valentines—his pink and black-striped, sashed or dotted silks.
Tom Fool is "a handy horse," with a chiseled foot. You've the beat
   of a dancer to a measure or harmonious rush
      of a porpoise at the prow where the racers all win easily—
like centaurs' legs in tune, as when kettledrums compete;
   nose rigid and suede nostrils spread, a light left hand on the rein, till
      well—this is a rhapsody.

Of course, speaking of champions, there was Fats Waller
with the feather touch, giraffe eyes, and that hand alighting in
   Ain't Misbehavin'! Ozzie Smith and Eubie Blake

ennoble the atmosphere; you recall the Lippizzaner;
the time Ted Atkinson charged by on Tiger Skin—
no pursuers in sight—cat-loping along. And you may have seen a monkey
on a greyhound. "But Tom Fool . . ."

The Web One Weaves of Italy

grows till it is not what but which,
blurred by too much. The very blasé alone could
    choose the contest or fair to which to go.
  The crossbow tournament at Gubbio?

For quiet excitement, canoe-ers
or peach fairs? or near Perugia, the mule-show;
    If not the Palio, slaying the Saracen.
  One salutes—on reviewing again

this modern *mythologica*
esopica— its nonchalances of the mind,
    that "fount by which enchanting gems are spilt."
  Are we not charmed by the result? —

quite different from what goes on
at the Sorbonne; but not entirely, since flowering
    in more than mere talent for spectacle.
  Because the heart is in it all is well.

The greater part of stanzas 1 and 2 is quoted from an article by Mitchell Goodman, "Festivals and Fairs for the Tourist in Italy," New York Times, April 18, 1954.

Rosemary

Beauty and Beauty's son and rosemary—
Venus and Love, her son, to speak plainly—
born of the sea supposedly
at Christmas each, in company,
braids a garland of festivity.
    Not always rosemary—

since the flight to Egypt, blooming differently.
With lancelike leaf, green but silver underneath,
its flowers—white originally—
turned blue. The herb of memory,
imitating the blue robe of Mary,
    is not too legendary

to flower both as symbol and as pungency.
Springing from stones beside the sea,
the height of Christ when thirty-three—
it feeds on dew and to the bee
"hath a dumb language"; is in reality
    a kind of Christmas-tree.

The Staff of Aesculapius

A symbol from the first, of mastery,
    experiments such as Hippocrates made
      and substituted for vague
    speculation stayed
        the ravages of a plague.

A "going on"; yes, *anastasis* is the word
    for research a virus has defied,
      and for the virologist
    with variables still untried—
        too impassioned to desist.

Suppose that research has hit on the right one
    and a killed vaccine is effective
      say temporarily—
    for even a year—although a live
        one could give lifelong immunity,

knowledge has been gained for another attack.
    Selective injury to cancer
      cells without injury to
    normal ones—another
        gain—looks like prophecy come true.

Now, after lung resection, the surgeon fills space.
    To sponge implanted, cells following
      fluid adhere and what
    was inert becomes living
        that was framework. Is it not

like the master-physician's Sumerian rod? —
    staff and effigy of the animal
      which by shedding its skin
    is a sign of renewal—
        the symbol of medicine.

The Sycamore

      Against a gun-metal sky
    I saw an albino giraffe. Without
      leaves to modify,
chamois-white as
said, although partly pied near the base,
    it towered where a chain of
        stepping-stones lay in a stream nearby;
        glamor to stir the envy

        of anything in motley—
    Hampshire pig, the living lucky-stone; or
      all-white butterfly.
A commonplace:
there's more than just one kind of grace.
    We don't like flowers that do
        not wilt; they must die, and nine
        she-camel-hairs aid memory.

      Worthy of Imami,
    the Persian—clinging to a stiffer stalk
      was a little dry
thing from the grass,
in the shape of a Maltese cross,
    retiringly formal
        as if to say: "And there was I
        like a field-mouse at Versailles."

THE MAGIC FLUTE

1956–1965

Style

    revives in Escudero's constant of the plumbline
axis of the hairfine moon—his counter-camber of the skater.
No more fanatical adjuster
        of the tilted hat
  than Escudero; of tempos others can't combine.
        And we—besides evolving
      the classic silhouette, Dick Button whittled slender—

  have an Iberian-American champion yet,
the deadly Etchebaster. Entranced, were you not, by Soledad?
black-clad solitude that is not sad;
       like a letter from
  Casals; or perhaps say literal alphabet—
        S soundholes in a 'cello
      set contradictorily; or should we call her

  la lagarta? or bamboos with fireflies a-glitter;
or glassy lake and the whorls which a vertical stroke brought about,
of the paddle half-turned coming out.
        As if bisecting
  a viper, she can dart down three times and recover
        without disaster, having
      been a bull-fighter. Well; she has a forgiver.

    Etchebaster's art, his catlike ease, his mousing pose,
his genius for anticipatory tactics, preclude envy
as the traditional unwavy
        Sandeman sailor
  is Escudero's; the guitar, Rosario's—
       wrist-rest for a dangling hand
      that's suddenly set humming fast fast fast and faster.

    There is no suitable simile. It is as though
the equidistant three tiny arcs of seeds in a banana
had been conjoined by Palestrina;

                    it is like the eyes,
        or say the face, of Palestrina by El Greco.
                O Escudero, Soledad,
            Rosario Escudero, Etchebaster!

Logic and "The Magic Flute"

Up winding stair,
    here, where, in what theater lost?
    was I seeing a ghost—
a reminder at least
        of a sunbeam or moonbeam
that has not a waist?
        By hasty hop
        or accomplished mishap,
the magic flute and harp
somehow confused themselves
        with China's precious wentletrap.

Near Life and Time
    in their peculiar catacomb,
    abalonean gloom
and an intrusive hum
        pervaded the mammoth cast's
small audience-room,
        Then out of doors,
        where interlacing pairs
of skaters raced from rink
to ramp, a demon roared
        as if down flights of marble stairs:

" 'What is love and
    shall I ever have it?' " The truth
    is simple. Banish sloth,
fetter-feigning uncouth
        fraud. Trapper Love with noble
noise, the magic sleuth,
        as bird-notes prove—
        first telecolor-trove—
illogically wove
what logic can't unweave:
        one need not shoulder, need not shove.

Blessed Is the Man

who does not sit in the seat of the scoffer—
    the man who does not denigrate, depreciate, denunciate;
      who is not "characteristically intemperate,"
who does not "excuse, retreat, equivocate; and will be heard."

(Ah, Giorgione! there are those who mongrelize
    and those who heighten anything they touch; although it may well be
      that if Giorgione's self-portrait were not said to be he,
it might not take my fancy. Blessed the geniuses who know

that egomania is not a duty.)
    "Diversity, controversy; tolerance"—in that "citadel
      of learning" we have a fort that ought to armor us well.
Blessed is the man who "takes the risk of a decision"—asks

himself the question: "Would it solve the problem"?
    Is it right as I see it? Is it in the best interests of all?"
      Alas. Ulysses' companions are now political—
living self-indulgently until the moral sense is drowned,

having lost all power of comparison,
    thinking license emancipates one, "slaves whom they themselves have
                                  bound."
      Brazen authors, downright soiled and downright spoiled, as if sound
and exceptional, are the old quasi-modish counterfeit,

mitin-proofing conscience against character.
    Affronted by "private lies and public shame," blessed is the author
      who favors what the supercilious do *not* favor—
who will not comply. Blessed, the unaccommodating man.

Blessed the man whose faith is different
    from possessiveness—of a kind not framed by "things which do appear"—
      who will not visualize defeat, too intent to cower;
whose illumined eye has seen the shaft that gilds the sultan's tower.

Values in Use

I attended school and I liked the place—
grass and little locust-leaf shadows like lace.

Writing was discussed. They said, "We create
values in the process of living, daren't await

their historic progress." Be abstract
and you'll wish you'd been specific; it's a fact.

What was I studying? Values in use,
"judged on their own ground." Am I still abstruse?

Walking along, a student said offhand,
" 'Relevant' and 'plausible' were words I understand."

A pleasing statement, anonymous friend.
Certainly the means must not defeat the end.

The middle way
of authorship

Hometown Piece for Messrs. Alston and Reese

To the tune:
"Li'l baby, don't say a word: Mama goin' to buy you a mockingbird.
Bird don't sing: Mama goin' to sell it and buy a brass ring."

"Millennium," yes; "pandemonium"!
Roy Campanella leaps high. Dodgerdom

crowned, had Johnny Podres on the mound.
Buzzie Bavasi and the Press gave ground;

the team slapped, mauled, and asked the Yankees' match,
"How did you feel when Sandy Amoros made the catch?"

"I said to myself"—pitcher for all innings—
"as I walked back to the mound I said, 'Everything's

getting better and better.'" (Zest: they've zest.
"Hope springs eternal in the Brooklyn breast."

And would the Dodger Band in 8, row 1, relax
if they saw the collector of income tax?

Ready with a tune if that should occur:
"Why Not Take All of Me—All of Me, Sir?")

Another series. Round-tripper Duke at bat,
"Four hundred feet from home-plate"; more like that.

A neat bunt, please; a cloud-breaker, a drive
like Jim Gilliam's great big one. Hope's alive.

Homered, flied out, fouled? Our "stylish stout"
so nimble Campanella will have him out.

A-squat in double-headers four hundred times a day,
he says that in a measure the pleasure is the pay:

catcher to pitcher, a nice easy throw
almost as if he'd just told it to go.

Willie Mays should be a Dodger. He should—
a lad for Roger Craig and Clem Labine to elude;

but you have an omen, pennant-winning Peewee,
on which we are looking surreptitiously.

Ralph Branca has Preacher Roe's number; recall?
And there's Don Bessent; he can really fire the ball.

As for Gil Hodges, in custody of first—
"He'll do it by himself." Now a specialist—versed

in an extension reach far into the box seats—
he lengthens up, leans and gloves the ball. He defeats

expectation by a whisker. The modest star,
irked by one misplay, is no hero by a hair;

in a strikeout slaughter when what could matter more,
he lines a homer to the signboard and has changed the score.

Then for his nineteenth season, a home run—
with four of six runs batted in—Carl Furillo's the big gun;

almost dehorned the foe—has fans dancing in delight.
Jake Pitler and his Playground "get a Night"—

Jake, that hearty man, made heartier by a barrier
who can bat as well as field—Don Demeter.

Shutting them out for nine innings—hitter too—
Carl Erskin leaves Cimoli nothing to do.

Take off the goat-horns, Dodgers, that egret
which two very fine base-stealers can offset.

You've got plenty: Jackie Robinson
and Campy and big Newk, and Dodgerdom again
watching everything you do. You won last year. Come on.

O to Be a Dragon

If I, like Solomon, . . .
could have my wish—
my wish . . . O to be a dragon,
a symbol of the power of Heaven—of silkworm
size or immense; at times invisible.
Felicitous phenomenon!

*link to
pre-oraudian
female culture
CtC (W) a sexton*

Enough: Jamestown, 1607–1957

Some in the *Godspeed,* the *Susan C.,*
others in the *Discovery,*

found their too earthly paradise,
a paradise in which hope dies,

found pests and pestilence instead,
the living outnumbered by the dead.

The same reward for best and worst
doomed communism, tried at first.

Three acres each, initiative,
six bushels paid back, they could live.

Captain Dale became kidnaper—
the master—lawless when the spur

was desperation, even though
his victim had let her victim go—

Captain John Smith. Poor Powhatan
was forced to make peace, embittered man.

Then teaching—insidious recourse—
enhancing Pocahontas, flowered of course

in marriage. John Rolfe fell in love
with her and she—in rank above

what she became—renounced her name
yet found her status not too tame.

The crested moss-rose casts a spell;
and bud of solid green as well;

old deep pink one with fragrant wings
imparting balsam scent that clings

where redbrown tanbark holds the sun—
path enticing beyond comparison.

Not to begin with. No select
artlessly perfect French effect

mattered at first. (Don't speak in rhyme
of maddened men in starving-time.)

Tested until so unnatural
that one became a cannibal.

Marriage, tobacco, and slavery,
initiated liberty

when the *Deliverance* brought seed
of that now controversial weed—

a blameless plant-Red-Ridinghood.
Blameless, but who knows what is good?

The victims of a search for gold
cast yellow soil into the hold.

With nothing but the feeble tower
to mark the site that did not flower,

could the most ardent have been sure
that they had done what would endure?

It was enough; it is enough
if present faith mend partial proof.

Melchior Vulpius

c. 1560–1615

a contrapuntalist—
                    composer of chorales
  and wedding-hymns to Latin words
  but best of all an anthem:
    "God be praised for conquering faith
    which feareth neither pain nor death."

We have to trust this art—
                    this mastery which none
  can understand. Yet someone has
  acquired it and is able to
    direct it. Mouse-skin-bellows'-breath
    expanding into rapture saith

"Hallelujah." Almost
                utmost absolutist
  and fugue-ist, Amen; slowly building
  from miniature thunder,
    crescendos antidoting death—
    love's signature cementing faith.

In the Public Garden

Boston has a festival—
    compositely for all—
and nearby, cupolas of learning
(crimson, blue, and gold) that
    have made education individual.

My first—an exceptional,
    an almost scriptural—
taxi-driver to Cambridge from Back Bay
said, as we went along, "They
    make some fine young men at Harvard." I recall

the summer when Faneuil Hall
    had its weathervane with gold ball
and grasshopper, gilded again by
a -leafer and -jack
    till it glittered. Spring can be a miracle

there—a more than usual
    bouquet of what is vernal—
"pear blossoms whiter than the clouds," pin-
oak leaves that barely show
    when other trees are making shade, besides small

fairy iris suitable
    for Dulcinea del
Toboso; O yes, and snowdrops
in the snow, that smell like
    violets. Despite secular bustle,

let me enter King's Chapel
    to hear them sing: "My work be praise while
others go and come. No more a stranger
or a guest but like a child
    at home." A chapel or a festival

means giving what is mutual,
    even if irrational:
black sturgeon-eggs—a camel
from Hamadan, Iran:
    a jewel, or, what is more unusual,

    silence—after a word-waterfall of the banal—
        as unattainable
as freedom. And what is freedom for?
For "self-discipline," as our
    hardest-working citizen has said—a school;

    it is for "freedom to toil"
        with a feel for the tool.
Those in the trans-shipment camp must have
a skill. With hope of freedom hanging
    by a thread—some gather medicinal

    herbs which they can sell.
        Ineligible if they ail.
            Well?

There are those who will talk for an hour
without telling you why they have
    come. And I? This is no madrigal—
        no medieval gradual.
    It is a grateful tale—
without that radiance which poets
are supposed to have—
    unofficial, unprofessional. But still one need not fail

    to wish poetry well
        where intellect is habitual
glad that the Muses have a home and swans—
that legend can be factual;
    happy that Art, admired in general,
        is always actually personal.

The Arctic Ox (or Goat)

Derived from "Golden Fleece of the Arctic," by John J. Teal, Jr., who rears musk oxen on his farm in Vermont, as set forth by him in the March 1958 issue of the Atlantic Monthly.

To wear the arctic fox
you have to kill it. Wear
   qiviut—the underwool of the arctic ox—
pulled off it like a sweater;
your coat is warm; your conscience, better.

I would like a suit of
qiviut, so light I did not
   know I had it on; and in the
course of time, another
since I had not had to murder

the "goat" that grew the fleece
that made the first. The musk ox
   has no musk and it is not an ox—
illiterate epithet.
Bury your nose in one when wet.

It smells of water, nothing else,
and browses goatlike on
   hind legs. Its great distinction
is not egocentric scent
but that it is intelligent.

Chinchillas, otters, water-rats,
and beavers, keep us warm
   but think! a "musk ox" grows six pounds
of *qiviut*; the cashmere ram,
three ounces—that is all—of pashm.

Lying in an exposed spot,
basking in the blizzard,
  these ponderosos could dominate
the rare-hairs market in Kashan and yet
you could not have a choicer pet.

They join you as you work;
love jumping in and out of holes,
  play in water with the children,
learn fast, know their names,
will open gates and invent games.

While not incapable
of courtship, they may find its
  servitude and flutter too much
like Procrustes' bed;
so some decide to stay unwed.

Camels are snobbish
and sheep, unintelligent;
  water buffaloes, neurasthenic—
even murderous.
Reindeer seem over-serious,

whereas these scarce *qivies*,
with golden fleece and winning ways,
  outstripping every fur-bearer—
there in Vermont quiet—
could demand Bold Ruler's diet:

Mountain Valley water,
dandelions, carrots, oats—
  encouraged as well by bed
made fresh three times a day—
to roll and revel in the hay.

Insatiable for willow
leaves alone, our goatlike
    qivi-curvi-capricornus
sheds down ideal for a nest.
Song-birds find *qiviut* best.

Suppose you had a bag
of it; you could spin a pound
    into a twenty-four-or-five-
mile thread—one, forty-ply—
that will not shrink in any dye.

If you fear that you are
reading an advertisement,
    you are. If we can't be cordial
to these creatures' fleece,
I think that we deserve to freeze.

Saint Nicholas,

might I, if you can find it, be given
a chameleon with tail
that curls like a watch spring; and vertical
on the body—including the face—pale
tiger-stripes, about seven;
(the melanin in the skin
having been shaded from the sun by thin
bars; the spinal dome
beaded along the ridge
as if it were platinum)?

If you can find no striped chameleon,
might I have a dress or suit—
I guess you have heard of it—of *qiviut*?
and to wear with it, a taslon shirt, the drip-dry fruit
of research second to none;
sewn, I hope, by Excello;
as for buttons to keep down the collar-points, no.
The shirt could be white—
and be "worn before six,"
either in daylight or at night.

But don't give me, if I can't have the dress,
a trip to Greenland, or grim
trip to the moon. The moon should come here. Let him
make the trip down, spread on my dark floor some dim
marvel, and if a success
that I stoop to pick up and wear,
I could ask nothing more. A thing yet more rare,
though, and different,
would be this: Hans von Marées'
St. Hubert, kneeling with head bent,

erect—in velvet and tense with restraint—
hand hanging down: the horse, free.
Not the original, of course. Give me
a postcard of the scene—huntsman and divinity—
   hunt-mad Hubert startled into a saint
     by a stag with a Figure entwined.
     But why tell you what you must have divined?
Saint Nicholas, O Santa Claus,
       would it not be the most
      prized gift that ever was!

For February 14th

      Saint Valentine,
although late, would "some interested law
impelled to plod in the poem's cause"
      be permitted a line?

      Might you have liked a stone
from a De Beers Consolidated Mine?
or badger-neat saber-thronged thistle
      of Palestine—the leaves alone

      down'd underneath,
worth a touch? or that mimosa-leafed vine
called an "alexander's armillary
      sphere" fanning out in a wreath?

      Or did the ark
preserve paradise-birds with jet-black plumes,
whose descendants might serve as presents?
      But questioning is the mark

      of a pest! Why think
only of animals in connection
with the ark or the wine Noah drank?
      but that the ark did not sink.

No Better Than "a Withered Daffodil"

Ben Jonson said he was? "O I could still
Like melting snow upon some craggy hill,
    Drop, drop, drop, drop."

I too until I saw that French brocade
blaze green as though some lizard in the shade
    became exact—

set off by replicas of violet—
like Sidney, leaning in his striped jacket
    against a lime—

a work of art. And I too seemed to be
an insouciant rester by a tree—
    no daffodil.

Combat Cultural

One likes to see a laggard rook's high
speed at sunset to outfly the dark,
    or a mount well schooled for a medal;
tucked up front legs for the barrier—
    or team of leapers turned aerial.

I recall a documentary
of Cossacks: a visual fugue, a mist
    of swords that seemed to sever
heads from bodies—feet stepping as though through
    harp-strings in a scherzo. However,

the quadrille of Old Russia for me:
with aimlessly drooping handkerchief
    snapped like the crack of a whip;
a deliriously spun-out-level
    frock-coat skirt, unswirled and a-droop

in remote promenade. Let me see . . .
Old Russia, I said? Cold Russia
    this time: the prize bunnyhug
platform-piece of experts in the
    trip-and-slug of wrestlers in a rug.

"Sacked" and ready for bed apparently—
with a jab, a kick, pinned to the wall,
    they work toward the edge and stick;
stagger off, and one is victim of a
    flipflop—leg having circled leg as thick.

"Some art, because of high quality,
is unlikely to command high sales";
    yes, yes; but here, oh no;
not with the frozen North's Nan-ai-ans
    of the sack in their tight touch-and-go.

These battlers, dressed identically—
just one person—may, by seeming twins,
    point a moral, should I confess;
we must cement the parts of any
    objective symbolic of *sagesse*.

Leonardo da Vinci's

Saint Jerome and his lion
    in that hermitage
of walls half gone,
    share sanctuary for a sage—
joint-frame for impassioned ingenious
    Jerome versed in language—
and for a lion like one on the skin of which
    Hercules' club made no impression.

The beast, received as a guest,
    although some monks fled—
with its paw dressed
    that a desert thorn had made red—
stayed as guard of the monastery ass . . .
    which vanished, having fed
its guard, Jerome assumed. The guest then, like an ass,
    was made to carry wood and did not resist,

but before long, recognized
    the ass and consigned
its terrorized
    thieves' whole camel-train to chagrined
Saint Jerome. The vindicated beast and
    saint somehow became twinned;
and now, since they behaved and also looked alike,
    their lionship seems officialized.

Pacific yet passionate—
    for if not both, how
could he be great?
    Jerome—reduced by what he'd been through—
with tapering waist no matter what he ate,
    left us the Vulgate. That in *Leo*
the Nile's rise grew food checking famine
    made lion's-mouth fountains appropriate,

        if not universally,
            at least not obscure.
        And here, though hardly a summary, astronomy
            or pale paint makes the golden pair
    in Leonardo da Vinci's sketch—seem
            sun-dyed. Blaze on, picture,
    saint, beast; and Lion Haile Selassie, with household
        lions as symbol of sovereignty.

Saint Valentine,

permitted to assist you, let me see . . .
   If those remembered by you
are to think of you and not me,
   it seems to me that the memento
   or compliment you bestow
should have a name beginning with "V,"

such as Vera, El Greco's only
   daughter (though it has never been
proved that he had one), her starchy
   veil, inside chiffon; the stone in her
   ring, like her eyes; one hand on
her snow-leopard wrap, the fur widely

dotted with black. It could be a vignette—
   a replica, framed oval—
bordered by a vine or vinelet.
   Or give a mere flower, said to mean the
   love of truth or truth of
love—in other words, a violet.

Verse—unabashedly bold—is appropriate;
   and always it should be as neat
as the most careful writer's "8."
   Any valentine that is *written*
Is as the *vendange* to the vine.
   Might verse not best confuse itself with fate?

Lines for Narrator

(Performance of L'Amfiparnaso, *the madrigal comedy by Orazio Vecchi, 1551–1605.)*

1

You are about to see in pleasant company,
    figures made famous by Italian Commedia:
    besides old Pantaloon, Pedrolina, and Hortensia,
some others—five scenes with plenty of variety—
    of life in Naples and Bologna—enacted in the city.
Our version's English, plain and simple. We wish it were
    delectable and witty like native Italian;
    please pity us and feel that now and then the words are pretty.

2

Although Hortensia loves anyone who sues—
ungrateful girl—she tells poor Pantaloon, infatuated,
    "Be off, my poor old goose, you're superannuated."

3

Isabella feigns true love for Captain Cardon,
    as obsessed a suitor and insatiate as any son of Spain
that, knife in wound, her death augmenting passion,
    may lend the final torture to his pain.

4

Francatrippa: "knock, knock, knock"—
has a diamond he must pawn.
The door won't open, has a lock.
   He knocks louder; Synagogue and Babel.
"Let me pawn it and be gone."

5

Blessed coincidence! With raptured glance,
   the impassed lovers pledge fidelity
   each vowing faithfulness to all eternity—
entranced by love's envisioned train of circumstance.

6

Consummate joy has made the awaited feast elate;
   while wedding-gifts abound, indoors—with some indeed, outside!
   alive and loud the songs of joy are multiplied
since the festive day has come which all have longed to celebrate.

Tell Me, Tell Me

      where might there be a refuge for me
        from egocentricity
and its propensity to bisect,
mis-state, misunderstand
      and obliterate continuity?
           Why, oh why, one ventures to ask, set
flatness on some cindery pinnacle
as if on Lord Nelson's revolving diamond rosette?

      It appeared: gem, burnished rarity
        and peak of delicacy—
in contrast with grievance touched off on
any ground—the absorbing
      geometry of a fantasy:
           a James, Miss Potter, Chinese
"passion for the particular," of a
tired man who yet, at dusk,
      cut a masterpiece of cerise—

      for no tailor-and-cutter jury—
        only a few mice to see,
who "breathed inconsistency and drank
contradiction," dazzled
      not by the sun but by "shadowy
          possibility." (I'm referring
to Henry James and Beatrix Potter's Tailor.)
I vow, rescued tailor
      of Gloucester, I am going

      to flee; by engineering strategy—
        the viper's traffic-knot—flee
to metaphysical newmown hay,
honeysuckle, or wood fragrance.
      Might one say or imply T. S. V. P.—
           Taisez-vous? "Please" does not make sense

to a refugee from verbal ferocity; I am
perplexed. Even so, "deference";
      yes, deference may be my defense.

A *précis*?
    In this told-backward biography
    of how the cat's mice when set free
by the tailor of Gloucester, finished
the Lord Mayor's cerise coat—
    the tailor's tale ended captivity
        in two senses. Besides having told
of a coat which made the tailor's fortune,
it rescued a reader
      from being driven mad by a scold.

Carnegie Hall: Rescued

"It spreads," the campaign—carried on
by long-distance telephone,
    with "Saint Diogenes
      supreme commander."
  At the fifty-ninth minute
      of the eleventh hour, a rescuer

makes room for Mr. Carnegie's
music hall, which by degrees
    became (becomes)
      our music stronghold
  (accented on the "né," as
      perhaps you don't have to be told).

Paderewski's "palladian
majesty" made it a fane;
    Tschaikovsky, of course,
      on the opening
  night, 1891;
      and Gilels, a master, playing.

With Andrew C. and Mr. R.,
"our spearhead, Mr. Star"—
    in music, Stern—
      has grown forensic,
  and by civic piety
      has saved our city panic;

rescuer of a music hall
menaced by the "cannibal
    of real estate"—bulldozing potentate,
      land-grabber, the human crab
  left cowering like a neonate.

As Venice "in defense of children"
has forbidden for the citizen,
      by "a tradition of
          noble behavior,
    dress too strangely shaped or scant,"
          posterity may impute error

to our demolishers of glory. Jean Cocteau's "Preface
to the Past" contains the phrase
      "When very young my dream
          was of pure glory."
    Must he say "was" of his "light
          dream," which confirms our glittering story?

They need their old brown home. Cellist,
violinist, pianist—
      used to unmusical
          impenetralia's
    massive masonry—have found
          reasons to return. Fantasias

of praise and rushings to the front
dog the performer. We hunt
      you down, Saint Diogenes—
          are thanking you for glittering,
    for rushing to the rescue
          as if you'd heard yourself performing.

Rescue with Yul Brynner

Appointed special consultant to the United Nations High Commissioner for Refugees, 1959–60.

   "Recital? 'Concert' is the word,"
and stunning, by the Budapest Symphony—
   displaced but not deterred—
listened to by me,
      though with detachment then,
        like a grasshopper that did not
       know it missed the mower, a pygmy citizen;
         a case, I'd say, of too slow a grower.
There were thirty million; there are thirteen still—
healthy to begin with, kept waiting till they're ill.
History judges. It will
salute Winnipeg's incredible
conditions: "Ill; no sponsor; and no kind of skill."
   Odd—a reporter with guitar—a puzzle.
   Mysterious Yul did not come to dazzle.

   Magic bird with multiple tongue—
five tongues—equipped for a crazy twelve-month tramp
   (a plod), he flew among
the damned, found each camp
      where hope had slowly died
        (some had never seen a plane).
       Instead of feathering himself, he exemplified
        the rule that, self-applied, omits the gold.
He said, "You may feel strange; nothing matters less.
Nobody notices; you'll find some happiness.
No new 'big fear'; no distress."
Yul can sing—twin of an enchantress—
elephant-borne dancer in silver-spangled dress,
     swirled aloft by trunk, with star-tipped wand, Tamara,
     as true to the beat as *Symphonia Hungarica.*

Head bent down over the guitar,
he barely seemed to hum; ended "all come home";
   did not smile; came by air;
did not have to come.
   The guitar's an event.
      Guests of honor can't dance; don't smile.
   "Have a home?" a boy asks. "Shall we live in a tent?"
      "In a house," Yul answers. His neat cloth hat
has nothing like the glitter reflected on the face
of milkweed-witch seed-brown dominating a palace
that was nothing like the place
where he is now. His deliberate pace
is a king's, however. "You'll have plenty of space."
   Yule—Yul log for the Christmas-fire tale-spinner—
   of fairy tales that can come true: Yul Brynner.

To Victor Hugo of My Crow Pluto

"Even when the bird is walking we know that it has wings."
                              —Victor Hugo

Of:
   my crow
   Pluto,

   the true
   Plato,

   azzurro-
   negro

   green-blue
   rainbow—

   Victor Hugo,
   it is true

   we know
   that the crow

   "has wings," how-
   ever pigeon-toe-

   inturned on grass. We do.
      (adagio)

   Vivo-
   rosso

   "corvo,"
   although

con dizio-
nario

io parlo
Italiano—

this pseudo
Esperanto

which, savio
ucello

you speak too—
my vow and motto

(botto e totto)
io giuro

è questo
credo:

lucro
è peso morto.

And so
dear crow—

gioièllo
mio—

I have to
let you go;

a bel bosco
generoso,

tuttuto
vagabondo,

serafino
uvaceo

Sunto,
oltremarino

verecondo
Plato, addio.

Impromptu equivalents for *esperanto madinusa* (made in U.S.A.) for those who might not resent them.

azzuro-negro: blue-black
vivorosso: lively
con dizionario: with dictionary
savio ucello: knowing bird
botto e totto: vow and motto
io giuro: I swear
è questo credo: is this credo
lucro è peso morto: profit is a dead
  weight

gioièllo mio: my jewel
a bel bosco: to lovely woods
tuttuto vagabondo: complete gypsy
serafino uvaceo: grape-black seraph
sunto: in short
verecondo: modest

Yvor Winters—

something of a badger-Diogenes—
we are indebted technically; and
attached personally, those of us who know him;
are proud of his hostility to falsity;
of his verse reduced to essence;
of a tenacity unintimidated by circumstance.
He does not hesitate to call others foolish,
and we do not shrink from imputations
of folly—of annoying a man to whom
compliments may be uncongenial;
—wise to be foolish when a sense of indebtedness
is too strong to suppress.

Baseball and Writing

Suggested by post-game broadcasts.

Fanaticism? No. Writing is exciting
and baseball is like writing.
　　You can never tell with either
　　　　how it will go
　　　　or what you will do;
generating excitement—
a fever in the victim—
pitcher, catcher, fielder, batter.
　　　　　　Victim in what category?
*Owl*man watching from the press box?
　　　　　To whom does it apply?
　　　　　Who is excited? Might it be I?

It's a pitcher's battle all the way—a duel—
a catcher's, as, with cruel
　　puma paw, Elston Howard lumbers lightly
　　　　back to plate. (His spring
　　　　de-winged a bat swing.)
They have that killer instinct;
yet Elston—whose catching
arm has hurt them all with the bat—
　　　　when questioned, says, unenviously,
"I'm very satisfied. We won."
　　　　　Shorn of the batting crown, says, "We":
　　　　　robbed by a technicality.

When three players on a side play three positions
and modify conditions,
　　the massive run need not be everything.
　　　　"Going, going . . ." Is
　　　　it? Roger Maris
has it, running fast. You will
never see a finer catch. Well . . .

"Mickey, leaping like the devil"—why
    gild it, although deer sounds better—
snares what was speeding towards its treetop nest,
    one-handing the souvenir-to-be
    meant to be caught by you or me.

Assign Yogi Berra to Cape Canaveral;
he could handle any missile,
   He is no feather. "Strike! . . . Strike *two!*"
    Fouled back. A blur.
    It's gone. You would infer
  that the bat had eyes.
  He put the wood to that one.
Praised, Skowron says, "Thanks, Mel.
  I think I helped a *little* bit."
    All business, each, and modesty.
  Blanchard, Richardson, Kubek, Boyer.
    In that galaxy of nine, say which
    won the pennant? *Each.* It was he.

Those two magnificent saves from the knee—throws
by Boyer, finesses in twos—
  like Whitey's three kinds of pitch and pre-
    diagnosis
  with pick-off psychosis.
  Pitching is a large subject.
  Your arm, too true at first, can learn to
  catch the corners—even trouble
    Mickey Mantle. ("Grazed a Yankee!
My baby pitcher, Montejo!"
    With some pedagogy,
    you'll be tough, premature prodigy.)

They crowd him and curve him and aim for the knees. Trying
indeed! The secret implying:
  "I can stand here, bat held steady."
    One may suit him;

none has hit him.
Imponderables smite him.
Muscle kinks, infections, spike wounds
require food, rest, respite from ruffians. (Drat it!
    Celebrity costs privacy!)
Cow's milk, "tiger's milk," soy milk, carrot juice,
      brewer's yeast (High-potency)—
      concentrates presage victory

sped by Luis Arroyo, Hector Lopez—
deadly in a pinch. And "Yes,
  it's work; I want you to bear down,
    but enjoy it
    while you're doing it."
  Mr. Houk and Mr. Sain,
  if you have a rummage sale,
  don't sell Roland Sheldon or Tom Tresh.
    Studded with stars in belt and crown,
the stadium is an adastrium.
    O flashing Orion,
    your stars are muscled like the lion.

Arthur Mitchell

Slim dragonfly
too rapid for the eye
  to cage—
contagious gem of virtuosity—
make visible, mentality.
Your jewels of mobility

  reveal
      and veil
          a peacock-tail.

Blue Bug

*Upon seeing Dr. Raworth Williams' Blue Bug with seven other ponies,
photographed by Thomas McAvoy,* Sports Illustrated.

    In this camera shot,
from that fine print in which you hide
(eight-pony portrait from the side),
    you seem to recognize
    a recognizing eye,
      limber Bug.
Only partly said, perhaps, it has been implied
that you seem to be the one to ride,

I don't know how you got your name
    and don't like to inquire.
      Nothing more punitive than the pest
    who says, "I'm trespassing," and
does it just the same.
    I've guessed, I think.
      I like a face that seems a nest,

a "mere container for the eye"—
    triangle-cornered—and
      pitchfork-pronged ears stiffly parallel:
    bug brother to an Arthur
Mitchell dragonfly,
    speeding to left,
      speeding to right; reversible,

like "turns in an ancient Chinese
    melody, a thirteen
      twisted silk-string three-finger solo."
    There they are, Yellow River–
scroll accuracies
    of your version
      of something similar—polo.

Restating it:
    pelo, I turn,
  on *polos*, a pivot.

If a little elaborate,
Redon (Odilon) brought it to mind,
    his thought of the eye,
of revolving—combined somehow with pastime—
    pastime that is work
muscular docility,
    also mentality,

as in the acrobat Li Siau Than,
      gibbon-like but limberer,
    defying gravity,
      nether side arched up,
      cup on head not upset—
    China's very most ingenious man.

Charity Overcoming Envy

Late-fifteenth-century tapestry, Flemish or French, in the Burrell Collection,
Glasgow Art Gallery and Museum.

   Have you time for a story
    (depicted in tapestry)?
   Charity, riding an elephant,
on a "mosaic of flowers," faces Envy,
the flowers "bunched together, not rooted."
Envy, on a dog, is worn down by obsession,
his greed (since of things owned by others
he can only take *some*). Crouching uneasily
in the flowered filigree, among wide weeds
    indented by scallops that swirl,
little flattened-out sunflowers,
thin arched coral steams, and—ribbed horizontally—
slivers of green, Envy, on his dog,
    looks up at the elephant,
cowering away from her, his cheek scarcely scratched.
    He is saying, "O Charity, pity me, Deity!
    O pitiless Destiny,
     what will become of me,
maimed by Charity—*Caritas*—sword unsheathed
over me yet? Blood stains my cheek. I am hurt."
In chest armor over chain mail, a steel shirt
to the knee, he repeats, "I am hurt."
The elephant, at no time borne down by self-pity,
    convinces the victim
that Destiny is not devising a plot.

The problem is mastered—insupportably
tiring when it was impending.
Deliverance accounts for what sounds like an axiom.

    The Gordian knot need not be cut.

To a Giraffe

If it is unpermissible, in fact fatal
to be personal and undesirable

to be literal—detrimental as well
if the eye is not innocent—does it mean that

one can live only on top leaves that are small
reachable only by a beast that is tall?—

of which the giraffe is the best example—
the unconversational animal.

When plagued by the psychological
a creature can be unbearable

that could have been irresistible;
or to be exact, exceptional

since less conversational
than some emotionally-tied-in-knots animal.

    After all
consolations of the metaphysical
can be profound. In Homer, existence

is flawed; transcendence, conditional;
"the journey from sin to redemption, perpetual."

"Avec Ardeur"

Dear Ezra, who knows what cadence is.

I've been thinking—mean, cogitating:

Make a fuss
and be tedious.

I'm annoyed?
Yes; am. I avoid

"adore"
and "bore";

am, I
say, by

the word
(bore) bored.

I refuse
to use

"divine"
to mean

something
pleasing:

"terrific color"
for some horror.

Though flat
myself, I'd say that

"Atlas"
(pressed glass)

looks best
embossed.

I refuse
to use

"enchant,"
"dement";

even "fright-
ful plight"
(however justified)

or "frivol-
ous fool"
(however suitable).

I've escaped?
am still trapped

by these
word diseases.

Without pauses,
the phrases

lack lyric
force, unlike

Attic
Alcaic,

or freak
calico-Greek.

This is not verse
of course.

I'm sure of this;

Nothing mundane is divine;
Nothing divine is mundane.

W. S. Landor

There
is someone I can bear—
   "a master of indignation . . .
meant for a soldier
   converted to letters," who could

throw
a man through the window,
   yet, "tender toward plants," say, "Good God,
the violets!" (below).
   "Accomplished in every

style
and tint"—considering meanwhile
   infinity and eternity,
he could only say, "I'll
   talk about them when I understand them."

The Master Tailor

For Ben Zuckerman
  "The Master Tailor"
by comparison with whose materials,
    zephyrs seem coarse;

  whose seaming is all of a piece,
      as Praxiteles would say,
  invisibly executed pockets,
    buttons: of ocean pearl—no two alike;
      each, a study, varying like the
          silvery face of the moon.
It is an event for anyone who admires
      perfection, to *own* it,

excited and thus disabled to use
      pen or write words.

An Expedient—Leonardo da Vinci's—and a Query

It was patience
    protecting the soul as clothing the body
from cold, so that "great wrongs
        were powerless to vex"—
        and problems that seemed to perplex
    him bore fruit, memory
making past present—
like "the grasp of the gourd,
            sure and firm."

"None too dull to
    be able to do one thing well. Unworthy
of praise, an orator
        who knows only one word,
        lacking variety." Height deterred
    from his verdure, any
polecat or snake that
might have burdened his vine:
            it kept them away.

With a passion,
    he drew flowers, acorns, rocks—intensively,
like Giotto, made Nature
        the test, imitation—
        Rome's taint—did not taint what he'd done.
    He saw as treachery
the all-in-one-mold.
Peerless, venerated
            by all, he succumbed

to dejection. Could not
   the Leda with face matchless minutely—
      have lightened the blow?
      "Sad" . . . Could not Leonardo
   have said, "I agree; proof refutes me.
If all is mobility,
   mathematics won't do":
instead of, "Tell me if anything
         at all has been done?"

Old Amusement Park

Before it became LaGuardia Airport.

Hurry, worry, unwary
visitor, never vary
 the pressure till nearly bat-blind.
  A predicament so dire could not
  occur in this rare spot—

where crowds flock to the tramcar
rattling greenish caterpillar,
 as bowling-ball thunder
  quivers the air. The park's elephant
  slowly lies down aslant;

a pygmy replica then rides
the mound the back provides.
 Jet black, a furry pony sits
  down like a dog, has an innocent air—
  no tricks—the best act there.

It's all like the never-ending
Ferris-wheel ascending
 picket-fenced pony rides (ten cents).
  A businessman, the pony-paddock boy
  locks his equestrian toy—

flags flying, fares collected,
shooting gallery neglected—
 half-official, half-sequestered,
  limber-slouched against a post,
  and tells a friend what matters least.

It's the old park in a nutshell,
like its tame-wild carrousel—
 the exhilarating peak
  when the triumph is reflective
  and confusion, retroactive.

LATE POEMS

1965–1972

Dream

*After coming on Jerome S. Shipman's comment concerning academic
appointments for artists.*

The committee—now a permanent body—
    formed to do but one thing,
discover positions for artists, was worried, then happy,
rejoiced to have magnetized Bach and his family
  "to Northwestern," besides five harpsichords
    without which he would not leave home.
For his methodic unmetronomic melodic diversity
contrapuntally appointedly persistently
  irresistibly Fate-like Bach—find me words.

Expected to create for university
    occasions, inventions with wing,
was no problem after stiff master-classes (stiffer in Germany) . . .

each week a cantata; chorales, fugues, concerti!
  Here, students craved a teacher and each student worked.
    Jubilation! Re-rejoicings! Felicity!
    Repeated fugue-like, all of it, to infinity.
  (Note too, that over-worked Bach was not irked.)

Haydn, when he had heard of Bach's billowing sail,
begged Prince Esterházy to lend him to Yale.
Master-mode expert fugue-al forms since, prevail.

    Dazzling nonsense? . . . I imagine it? Ah! nach
    enough. J. Sebastian—born at Eisenach:
    its coat-of-arms in my dream: BACH PLAYS BACH!

In Lieu of the Lyre

One debarred from enrollment at Harvard,
may have seen towers and been shown the Yard—
animated by Madame de Boufflers' choice rhymes:
Sentir avec ardeur: with fire; yes, with passion;
rime-prose revived also by word-wizard Achilles—
                Dr. Fang.

The *Harvard Advocate*'s select formal-informal
invitation to Harvard made grateful, Brooklyn's (or Mexico's)
                ineditos—
one whose "French aspect" was invented by
   Professor Levin,
a too outspoken outraged refugee from clichés particularly,
                who was proffered redress
                by the Lowell House Press—
Vermont Stinehour Press, rather. (No careless statements
to Kirkland House; least of all inexactness in quoting a fact.)

                To the *Advocate, gratia sum*
                unavoidably lame as I am, verbal pilgrim
like Thomas Bewick, drinking from his hat-brim,
drops spilled from a waterfall, denominated later by him
                a crystalline Fons Bandusian miracle.

It occurs to the guest—if someone had confessed it in time—
that you might have preferred to the waterfall, pilgrim and hat-brim,
                a valuable axiom such as
"a force at rest is at rest because balanced by some other force,"
or "catenary and triangle together hold the span in place"
                (of a bridge),

or a too often forgotten surely relevant thing, that Roebling cable
                was invented by John A. Roebling.

                These reflections, Mr. Davis,
                  in lieu of the lyre.

The Mind, Intractable Thing

even with its own ax to grind, sometimes
    helps others. Why can't it help me?

        O imagnifico,
wizard in words—poet, was it, as
Alfredo Panzini defined you?
Weren't you refracting just now
on my eye's half-closed triptych
    the image, enhanced, of a glen—
"the foxgrape festoon as sere leaves fell"
on the sand-pale dark byroad, one leaf adrift
    from the thin-twigged persimmon; again,

        a bird—Arizona
caught-up-with, uncatchable cuckoo
after two hours' pursuit, zigzagging
road-runner, stenciled in black
stripes all over, the tail
    windmilling up to defy me?
You understand terror, know how to deal
with pent-up emotion, a ballad, witchcraft.
    I don't. O Zeus and O Destiny!

Unafraid of what's done,
undeterred by apparent defeat,
you, imagnifico, unafraid
of disparagers, death, dejection,
have out-wiled the Mermaid of Zennor,
    made wordcraft irresistible:
reef, wreck, lost lad, and "sea-foundered bell"—
as near a thing as we have to a king—
    craft with which I don't know how to deal.

Granite and Steel

Enfranchising cable, silvered by the sea,
   of woven wire, grayed by the mist,
   and Liberty dominate the Bay—
   her feet as one on shattered chains,
   once whole links wrought by Tyranny.

   Caged Circe of steel and stone,
   her parent German ingenuity.
   "O catenary curve" from tower to pier,
   implacable enemy of the mind's deformity,
   of man's uncompunctious greed
   his crass love of crass priority
     just recently
   obstructing acquiescent feet
   about to step ashore when darkness fell
     without a cause,
   as if probity had not joined our cities
     in the sea.

"O path amid the stars
crossed by the seagull's wing!"
"O radiance that doth inherit me!"
—affirming inter-acting harmony!

Untried expedient, untried; then tried;
way out; way in; romantic passageway
first seen by the eye of the mind,
then by the eye. O steel! O stone!
Climactic ornament, a double rainbow,
as if inverted by French perspicacity,
   John Roebling's monument,
   German tenacity's also;
   composite span—an actuality.

Love in America—

Whatever it is, it's a passion—
a benign dementia that should be
engulfing America, fed in a way
   the opposite of the way
in which the Minotaur was fed.
It's a Midas of tenderness;
   from the heart;
nothing else. From one with ability
to bear being misunderstood—
   take the blame, with "nobility
   that is action," identifying itself with
   pioneer unperfunctoriness

   without brazenness or
   bigness of overgrown
   undergrown shallowness.

Whatever it is, let it be without
   affectation.

Yes, yes, yes, *yes.*

For Katharine Elizabeth McBride,
President of Bryn Mawr College

Dear Katharine McBride
words have no way
of conveying to you what achievement should say,
since we have not replicas of your insight enriching our school—
of your kindled vision discerning individual promise.

    What is a college?
a place where freedom is rooted in vitality,
where faith is the substance of things hoped for,
where things seen were not made with hands—
where the school's initiator being dead, yet speaketh,
where virtue trod a rough and thorny path,
finding itself and losing itself—
the student her own taskmaster,
tenacious of one hour's meaning sought
that could not be found elsewhere.

Students—foster-plants of scholarship—
at the beginning of the year,
bewildered by anxiety and opportunity
in the vibrant dried-leaf-tinctured autumn air,
pause and capitulate, compelled to ponder
intimations of divinity—
    recurrent words of an unaccompanied hymn:

    Ancient of Days, who sittest throned in glory.

O fosterer of promise, aware that danger is always imminent—
    The free believe in Destiny, not Fate.
O fortunate Bryn Mawr with her creatively unarrogant President
    unique in her exceptional unpresidential constant;

    a liking for people as they are.

Tippoo's Tiger

The tiger was his prototype.
The forefeet of his throne were tiger's feet.
He mounted by a four-square pyramid of silver stairs converging as they rose.

The jackets of his infantry and palace guard
bore little woven stripes incurved like buttonholes.

Beneath the throne an emerald carpet lay.
Approaching it, each subject kissed nine times
the carpet's velvet face of meadow-green.

Tipu owned sixteen hunting-cats to course the antelope
until his one great polecat ferret with exciting tail
escaped through its unlatched hut-door along a plank
above a ditch; paused, drank, and disappeared—
precursor of its master's fate.

His weapons were engraved with tiger claws and teeth
in spiral characters that said the conqueror is God.
The infidel claimed Tipu's helmet and cuirasse
and a vast toy, a curious automaton—
a man killed by a tiger; with organ pipes inside
from which blood-curdling cries merged with inhuman groans.
The tiger moved its tail as the man moved his arm.

This ballad still awaits a tiger-hearted bard.
Great losses for the enemy
can't make the owner's loss less hard.

The Camperdown Elm

Gift of Mr. A. G. Burgess to Prospect Park, Brooklyn, 1872.

I think, in connection with this weeping elm,
of "Kindred Spirits" at the edge of a rockledge
       overlooking a stream:
Thanatopsis-invoking tree-loving Bryant
conversing with Thomas Cole
in Asher Durand's painting of them
under the filigree of an elm overhead.

No doubt they had seen other trees—lindens,
maples and sycamores, oaks and the Paris
street-tree, the horse-chestnut; but imagine
their rapture, had they come on the Camperdown elm's
massiveness and "the intricate pattern of its branches,"
arching high, curving low, in its mist of fine twigs.
The Bartlett tree-cavity specialist saw it
and thrust his arm the whole length of the hollowness
of its torso and there were six small cavities also.

Props are needed and tree-food. It is still leafing;
still there. *Mortal* though. We must save it. It is
       our crowning curio.

Assistance

If unselfish ingenious
Mona Van Duyn Thurston—

could send me on a post-card
despite inconvenience and
a dearth of wild animals—
a wild moose making its way through
A Maine lake in deep water—

could I not ignore disability
and fly to Washington University?

Mercifully

I am hard to disgust,
but a pretentious poet can do it;
a person without a tap root; and
impercipience can do it; did it.

But why talk about it—
offset by Musica Antiqua's
"Legendary Performance"
of impassioned exactitude.

An elate tongue is music . . . . .
the plain truth—complex truth—
in which unnatural emphases,
"passi - on" and "divis - i - on,"
sound natural. Play it all; *do;*
except in uproars of conversation.

Celestial refrain . . . . . My mind
hears it again. Without music
life is flat—bare existence.
Dirgelike David and Absalom. That.
       Let it be that.

"Reminiscent of a Wave at the Curl"

On a kind of Christmas Day—
big flakes blurring everything—
cat-power matching momentum,
each kitten having capsized the other,
            one kitten fell;
the other's hind leg planted hard
on the eye that had guided the onslaught—
ears laid back, both tails lashing—
a cynic might have said,
"Sir Francis Bacon defined it:
'Foreign war is like the heat of exercise;
civil war is like the heat of a fever.'"

Not at all. The expert would say,
            "Rather hard on the fur."

A Christmas Poem

Santa Claus
How would it be
if you gave it to me
all at once for Christmas
Three dark sapphires
all the same size. Love,
                    Marianne Moore

Enough

1969

Am I a fanatic? The opposite.
     And where would I like to be?
     Sitting under Plato's olive tree
or propped against its thick old trunk,

        away from controversy
        or anyone choleric.

If you would see stones set right, unthreatened
     by mortar (masons say "mud"),
     squared and smooth, let them rise as they should,
Ben Jonson said, or he implied.

        In "Discoveries" he then said,
        "Stand for truth. It's enough."

The Magician's Retreat

of moderate height,
(I have seen it)
cloudy but bright inside
like a moonstone,
while a yellow glow
from a shutter-crack shone,
and a blue glow from the lamppost
close to the front door.
It left nothing of which to complain,
nothing more to obtain,
consummately plain.

A black tree mass rose at the back
almost touching the eaves
with the definiteness of Magritte,
was above all discreet.

Prevalent at One Time

I've always wanted a gig
semi-circular like a fig
for a very fast horse with long tail
for one person, of course;

and then a tiger-skin rug
for my Japanese pug,
the whole thing glossy black.
I'm no hypochondriac.

SELECTIONS FROM

THE FABLES OF LA FONTAINE

EDITOR'S NOTE: The following fables were translated by Marianne Moore and selected by her for her *Complete Poems* from *The Fables of La Fontaine* (New York: Viking, 1965). In a Foreword to that book, itself a selection, Moore acknowledges several major American poets, and two in particular for having inspired the edition. She writes of W. H. Auden as being "responsible for this undertaking—and is to be thanked in so far as the result is an asset, forgiven if a detriment." Of Pound, she asserts: "The influence here of Ezra Pound as translator may not be apparent, but for rhythm and syntax, unsatisfactory though the result may be to him, I reiterate with the immodesty of the amateur that the practice of Ezra Pound has been for me a governing principle—as deduced from his 'Guido Cavalcanti,' his 'Seafarer,' and certain French songs: the natural order of words, subject, predicate, object: the active voice where possible; a ban on dead words, rhymes synonymous with gusto."

The Fox and the Grapes

A fox of Gascon, through some say of Norman descent,
When starved till faint gazed up at a trellis to which grapes were tied—
      Matured till they glowed with a purplish tint
      As though there were gems inside.
Now grapes were what our adventurer on strained haunches chanced
                            to crave

      But because he could not reach the vine
He said, "These grapes are sour; I'll leave them for some knave."

Better, I think, than an embittered whine.

(Book Three, XI)

The Lion in Love

To Mademoiselle de Sévigné

Mademoiselle—goddess instead—
In whom the Graces find a school
Although you are more beautiful,
Even if with averted head,
Might you not be entertained
By a tale that is unadorned—
Hearing with no more than a quiver
Of a lion whom Love knew how to conquer.
Love is a curious master,
In name alone a felicity.
Better know of than know the thing.
If too personal and thus trespassing,
I'm saying what may seem to you an offense,
A fable could not offend your ear.
This one, assured of your lenience,
Attests its devotion embodied here,
And kneels in sworn obedience.

Before their speech was obstructed,
Lions or such as were attracted
To young girls, sought an alliance.
Why not? since as paragons of puissance,
They were at that time knightly fellows
Of mettle and intelligence
Adorned by manes like haloes.

The point of the preamble follows.
A lion—one in a multitude—
Met in a meadow as he fared,
A shepherdess for whom he cared.
He sought to win her if he could,
Though the father would have preferred
A less ferocious son-in-law.

To consent undoubtedly was hard;
Fear meant that the alternate was barred.
Moreover, refuse and he foresaw
That some fine day the two might explain
Clandestine marriage as the chain
That fettered the lass, bewitched beyond cure,
By fashions conducive to hauteur,
And a fancy that shaggy shoulder fur
Made her willful lover handsomer.
The father with despair choked down,
Said though at heart constrained to frown,
"The child is a dainty one; better wait;
You might let your claw points scratch her
When your heavy forepaws touch her.
You could if not too importunate
Have your claws clipped. And there in front,
See that your teeth are filed blunt,
Because a kiss might be enjoyed
By you the more, I should think,
If my daughter were not forced to shrink
Because improvidently annoyed."
The enthralled animal mellowed,
His mind's eye having been shuttered.
Without teeth or claws it followed
That the fortress was shattered.
Dogs were loosed; defenses were gone:
The consequence was slight resistance.

Love, ah Love, when your slipknot's drawn,
One can but say, "Farewell, good sense."

(Book Four, I)

The Animals Sick of the Plague

A malady smote the earth one year,
Felling beasts and infecting all with fear,
To prove to them what grave offenders they were;
Although plague was the name by which it was known,
For it literally congested Acheron,
Warring on creatures everywhere,
It did not bear off all but all were endangered.
Any that lingered barely stirred—
Could merely breathe and that diseasedly.
Nothing aroused their energy.
Neither wolf nor fox disappeared
To stalk young prey as it sunned.
The demoralized doves scattered
And love starved; life was moribund.

When the lion had called his constituency
He said, "Dear friends, this is heaven's remedy
For the sins we have thought a boon.
So he who is guiltiest
Should sacrifice his good to that of the rest
And possibly most of us will then be immune.
In accord with the past, history suggests to one,
Penance as atoning for evil done.
So without subterfuge, braving the consequence,
Let each search his conscience.
As for me, I have preyed on flocks of sheep so often
That I have become a glutton.
Because they had wronged me? not once.
Moreover I would devour him when I mastered
The shepherd.
Therefore let me be sacrificed in recompense,
But first make a clean breast, not just I say how I offend:
We must have justice and detect the trespass,
Then rend the culprit's carcass."
The fox said, "Sire, you are too good to rend;

Your sense of honor is excessively nice.
Eat sheep, Sire! Poor dolts, their loss is no sacrifice.
A sinful king? Oh, no. You prove when you devour
> The beasts that you thought them superior.
> As for the shepherd, one would swear
> That he went where he ought to go,
Having become to any of us, high or low,
> A monster none can endure."
When the fox said this, applause deafened the cur
> And no one dared to consider
A tiger, bear, or other beast of prominence
> Guilty of any offense.
In fact, quarrelers of evident spleen
Were canonized for their innocent mien.
When his turn came the ass said, "To take a backward glance,
> I recall passing clerical domain,
The herbs and grass and hunger close to sustenance.
> Fiend take me, how could I refrain?
I nipped off as much grass as would lie on my tongue;
So sinned, if what we say must be disinterested."
They made too much noise to hear what the donkey said.
A wolf pronounced the verdict, to which he clung,
Convinced they had found the animal they must kill—
The battered rapscallion who had made the world ill.
He deserved to be hung as an example.
Eat another's grass! What could be more horrible.
> Death, only death was suitable
For the criminal—inflicted at once by spite.
And so, as you are weak or are invincible,
The court says white is black or that black crimes are white.

(Book Seven, I)

The Bear and the Garden-Lover

A bear with fur that appeared to have been licked backward
Wandered a forest once where he alone had a lair.
This new Bellerophon, hid by thorns which pointed outward,
Had become deranged. Minds suffer disrepair
When every thought for years has been turned inward.
We prize witty byplay and reserve is still better,
But too much of either and health has soon suffered.
        No animal sought out the bear
        In coverts at all times sequestered,
        Until he had grown embittered
And, wearying of mere fatuity,
By now was submerged in gloom continually.
        He had a neighbor rather near,
        Whose own existence had seemed drear;
Who loved a parterre of which flowers were the core,
        And the care of fruit even more.
But horticulturalists need, besides work that is pleasant,
        Some shrewd choice spirit present.
When flowers speak, it is as poetry gives leave
        Here in this book; and bound to grieve,
Since hedged by silent greenery to tend,
The gardener thought one sunny day he'd seek a friend.
        Nursing some thought of the kind,
        The bear sought a similar end
        And the pair just missed collision
        Where their paths came in conjunction.
Numb with fear, how ever get away or stay there?
Better be a Gascon and disguise despair
In such a plight, so the man did not hang back or cower.
        Lures are beyond a mere bear's power
And this one said, "Visit my lair." The man said, "Yonder bower,
Most noble one, is mine; what could be friendlier
Than to sit on tender grass and share such plain refreshment
As native products laced with milk? Since it's an embarrassment
To lack what lordly bears would have as daily fare,

Accept what is here." The bear appeared flattered.
Each found, as he went, a friend was what most mattered;
Before they'd neared the door, they were inseparable.
        As confidant, a beast seems dull.
        Best live alone if wit can't flow,
And the gardener found the bear's reserve a blow,
But conducive to work, without sounds to distract.
Having game to be dressed, the bear, as it puttered,
        Diligently chased or slaughtered
Pests that filled the air, and swarmed, to be exact.
Round his all too weary friend who lay down sleepy—
        Pests—well, flues, speaking unscientifically.
One time as the gardener had forgot himself in dream
And a single fly had his nose at its mercy,
The poor indignant bear who had fought it vainly,
Growled, "I'll crush that trespasser; I have evolved a scheme."
Killing flies was his chore, so as good as his word,
The bear hurled a cobble and made sure it was hurled hard,
Crushing a friend's head to rid him of a pest.
With bad logic, fair aim disgraces us the more;
He'd murdered someone dear, to guarantee his friend rest.

Intimates should be feared who lack perspicacity;
Choose wisdom, even in an enemy.

(Book Eight, X)

The Mouse Metamorphosed into a Maid

A mouse fell from a screech-owl's beak—a thing that I can not pretend
      To be Hindoo enough to have cared
To pick up. But a Brahmin, as I can well believe, straightened
      The fur which the beak had marred.
      Each country has the code it's preferred;
      Though some scorn a mouse's pain—
We are hard; whereas a Brahmin would as soon disdain
      A relative's. He feels that he submits to a fate
      That transforms one at death, to a worm
Or beast, and lends even kings a transition state—
A tenet it pleased Pythagoras to affirm,
Deduced from that system, of which he was a ponderer.
Based on the same belief, the Brahmin sought a sorcerer,
Eager to right what had been unfair, and procured a key
To restore the mouse to her true identity.
      Well, there she was, a girl and real,
Of about fifteen, who was so irresistible
Priam's son would have toiled harder still to reward her
Than for Helen who threw the whole world in disorder.
The Brahmin said to her, marveling at the miracle,
      Charm so great that it scarcely seemed true—
"You have but to choose. Any suitor I know
      Contends for the honor of marrying you."
      —"In that case," she said, "the most powerful;
      I would choose the strongest I knew."
Kneeling, the Brahmin pled, "Sun, it shall be you.
      Be my heir; share my inheritance."
      —"No, a cloud intervening," it said,
"Would be stronger than I and I be discredited.
      Choose the cloud for her defense."
—"Very well," said the Brahmin to the cloud, sailing on,
"Were you meant for her?"—"Alas," it answered, "not the one.
The wind drives me from place to place; when whirled through the void:
I might affront Boreas and be destroyed."
      So the distracted Brahmin cried

To the wind he heard, "O Wind, abide.
Embrace my child in whom graces dwell."
Then Boreas blew hard, but met a mountainside.
Deterred lest interests coincide,
The ground demurred and sparred, "Scarcely suitable;
A rat might be incommoded
And weaken me by some tunnel he needed."
Rat! at the word, Love cast his spell
On an ear attuned. Wed? at last she knew.
A rat! A rat! Can names not do
Love service? Ah, you follow well:
Silence here between us two.

We retain the traits of the place from which we came. This tale
Bears me out; but a nearer view would seem good
Of what sophism never had quite understood:
We all love sun; yet more, what has a heart and will.
But affirm the premise? queer supposition
That when devoured by fleas, giants are outdone!
The rat would have had to transfer the maid in his care
And call him a cat; the cat, a wolf-hound;
The hound, a wolf. Carried around
By a force that was circular,
Pilpay would bear the maid to the sun's infinitude
Where the sun would blaze in endless beatitude.
Well, return if we can, to metamorphosis;
The Brahmin's sorcerer, as bearing upon this,
Had not proved anything but man's foolhardihood,
In fact had shown that the Brahmin had been wrong
In supposing, and far too long,
That man and worms and mice have in unison
Sister souls of identical origin—
By birth equally exempt
From change, whose diverse physiques, you'll own,
Have gradually won
Reverence or contempt.
Explain how a lass so fair, incomparably made,

        Could not earn for herself redress
And have married the sun. Fur tempted her caress.

        Now mouse and girl—both have been well weighed
And we've found them, as we have compared their souls,
        As far apart as opposite poles.
We are what we were at birth, and each trait has remained
In conformity with earth's and with heaven's logic:
        Be the devil's tool, resort to black magic,
None can diverge from the ends which Heaven foreordained.

                                    (Book Nine, VII)

MARIANNE MOORE'S NOTES

Editor's Note on Marianne Moore's Notes

Change was a constant in all of Marianne Moore's work. The notes were altered as radically as the poems, and changes occur even when a poem's text does not change. Rather than reprinting each note faithfully, which might confuse more than enlighten, I offer a partial view of the author's notes as they are found in all of her editions. Punctuation and spelling are presented in American style.

A Note on the Notes *by Marianne Moore*

A willingness to satisfy contradictory objections to one's manner of writing might turn one's work into the donkey that finally found itself being carried by its masters, since some readers suggest that quotation-marks are disruptive of pleasant progress; others, that notes to what should be complete are a pedantry or evidence of an insufficiently realized task. But since in anything I have written, there have been lines in which the chief interest is borrowed, and I have not yet been able to outgrow this hybrid method of composition, acknowledgements seem only honest. Perhaps those who are annoyed by provisos, detainments, and postscripts could be persuaded to take probity on faith and disregard the notes.

From *Observations*

TO A PRIZE BIRD
Bernard Shaw.

INJUDICIOUS GARDENING
Letters of Robert Browning and Elizabeth Barrett; Harper. Vol. I, p. 513; "the yellow rose? 'Infidelity,' says the dictionary of flowers." Vol. II, p. 38: "I planted a full dozen more rose-trees, all white—to take away the yellow-rose reproach!"

TO A STEAM ROLLER
"impersonal judgment": Lawrence Gilman.

TO A SNAIL
"compression is the first grace of style": Democritus.
"method of conclusions"; "knowledge of principles": Duns Scotus.

"THE BRICKS ARE FALLEN DOWN,"
Isaiah, 9:10.

GEORGE MOORE
Vale: Appleton, 1914; p. 82. "We certainly pigged it together. Pigs no doubt, but aspiring pigs."

TO THE PEACOCK OF FRANCE
"taking charge"; "anchorites": Molière: A Biography, H. C. Chatfield-Taylor (Chatto, 1907).

IN THIS AGE OF HARD TRYING
"it is not the business of gods": Dostoievsky.

POETRY
Diary of Tolstoy (Dutton, p. 84): "Where the boundary between prose and poetry lies, I shall never be able to understand. The question is raised in manuals of style, yet the answer to it lies beyond me. Poetry is verse: prose is not verse. Or else poetry is everything with the exception of business documents and school books."
"literalists of the imagination": Yeats, *Ideas of Good and Evil*, 1903; William Blake and his Illustrations to *The Divine Comedy*, p. 182. "The limitation of his view was from the very intensity of his vision; he was a too literal realist of imagination, as others are of nature; and because he believed that the figures seen by the mind's eye, when exalted by inspiration were 'eternal existences,' symbols of divine essences, he hated every grace of style that might obscure their lineaments."

PEDANTIC LITERALIST
All excerpts, from Richard Baxter, *The Saints' Everlasting Rest* (Lippincott, 1909).

"HE WROTE THE HISTORY BOOK"
At the age of five or six, John Andrews, son of Dr. C. M. Andrews, replied when asked his name: "My name is John Andrews. My father wrote the history book."

TO BE LIKED BY YOU
"Attack is more piquant than concord": Hardy.

SOJOURN IN THE WHALE
"water in motion is far from level": Literary Digest.

MY APISH COUSINS [*Editor's Note:* Also, "The Monkey's"]
An old gentleman during a game of chess: "It is difficult to recall the appearance of what one might call the minor acquaintances twenty years back."

IN THE DAYS OF PRISMATIC COLOR
"Part of it was crawling": Nestor, *Greek Anthology* (Loeb Classical Library), Vol. III, p. 129.

PETER
A black-and-white cat owned by Miss Magdalen Hueber and Miss Maria Weniger.

PICKING AND CHOOSING
feeling: T. S. Eliot, *The Little Review*, August, 1918. "James's critical genius comes out most tellingly in his mastery over, his baffling escape from, Ideas; a mastery and an

escape which are perhaps the last test of a superior intelligence. He had a mind so fine that no idea could violate it. . . . In England ideas run wild and pasture on the emotions; instead of thinking with our feelings (a very different thing) we corrupt our feelings with ideas; we produce the political, the emotional idea, evading sensation and thought."

"sad French greens": *The Compleat Angler.*

"top of a diligence": Prepatory school boy translating Cæsar; recollected by Mr. E. H. Kellogg.

"right good salvo of barks"; *"strong wrinkles"*: Xenophon, *Cynegeticus.*

"chrysalis of the nocturnal butterfly": Erté.

"I envy nobody": *The Compleat Angler.*

WHEN I BUY PICTURES

snipe-legged hieroglyphic: Egyptian low relief in The Metropolitan Museum.

"A silver fence was erected by Constantine to enclose the grave of Adam," *Literary Digest*, January 5, 1918. A descriptive paragraph with photograph.

"lit by piercing glances": A. R. Gordon, *The Poets of The Old Testament* (Hodder and Stoughton, 1912).

THE LABORS OF HERCULES

"charming tadpole notes": Review in the *London Spectator.*

"the negro is not brutal": The Reverend J. W. Darr.

NEW YORK

fur trade: in 1921, New York succeeded St. Louis as the center of the wholesale fur trade.

"as satin needlework": *The Literary Digest*, March 30, 1918, quotes *Forest and Stream*, March 1918—an article by George Shiras, 3rd: "Only once in the long period that I have hunted or photographed these animals (white-tailed deer) in this region, have I seen an albino, and that one lingered for a year and a half about my camp, which is situated midway between Marquette and Grand Island. Signs were put up in the neighborhood reading: 'Do not shoot the white deer—it will bring you bad luck.' But tho the first part of the appeal stayed the hand of the sportsman, and the latter that of most pot-hunters, it was finally killed by an unsuperstitious homesteader, and the heretofore unsuccessful efforts to photograph it naturally came to an end.

"Some eight years ago word came that a fine albino buck had been frequently seen on Grand Island and that it came to a little pond on the easterly part of the island. Taking a camping outfit, a canoe, and my guide, several days and nights were spent watching the pond; . . . the white buck did not appear.

"The next year the quest was no more successful, and when I heard that on the opening of the season the buck had been killed by a lumberjack, it was satisfactory to know that the body had been shipped to a taxidermist in Detroit, preparatory to being added to the little museum of the island hotel.

"About the middle of June, 1916, a white fawn only a few days old was discovered in a thicket and brought to the hotel. Here, in the company of another fawn, it grew rapidly. During the earlier months this fawn had the usual row of white spots on the back and sides, and altho there was no difference between these and the body color, they were conspicuous in the same way that satin needlework in a single color may carry a varied pattern. . . . In June, 1917, one of these does bore an albino fawn, which lacked, however, the brocaded spots which characterized the previous one.

"It may be of interest to note that the original buck weighed 150 pounds and possessed a rather extraordinary set of antlers, spreading twenty-six inches, with terminal points much further apart than any I have ever seen. The velvet on the antlers . . . was snow-white, giving them a most statuesque appearance amid the green foliage of the forest. The eyes of the three native albinos are a very light gray-blue, while the doe has the usual red eyeballs; . . . and in the absence of accident or disease, there should soon be a permanent herd of these interesting animals."

picardel: an Elizabethan ruff.

if the fur is not finer: Isabella, Duchess of Gonzaga. Frank Alvah Parrons, *The Psychology of Dress* (Doubleday), p. 63. "I wish black cloth even if it cost ten ducats a yard. If it is only as good as that which I see other people wear, I had rather be without it."

"accessibility to experience": Henry James.

PEOPLE'S SURROUNDINGS

"natural promptness": Ward's *English Poets*. Webbe—"a witty gentleman and the very chief of our late rhymers. Gifts of wit and natural promptness appear in him abundantly."

Persian velvet: Exhibition of Persian objects, Bush Terminal Building, December, 1919, under the auspices of the Persian Throne. Descriptive label—piece of 16th century brocaded velvet: "The design consists of single rose bushes in pearl white and pale black outline posed on a field of light brown ivory so that the whole piece bears the likeness of the leopard's spots."

Waterford: Irish glass.

municipal bat roost: Experiment in San Antonio, Texas, to combat mosquitoes.

Bluebeard's tower: Limestone tower at St. Thomas, Virgin Islands; purports to be the castle of the traditional Bluebeard.

"Chessmen carved out of moonstones": Anatole France.

"as an escalator cuts the nerve of progress": The Reverend J. W. Darr.

captains of armies: Raphael, *Horary Astrology*.

SNAKES, MONGOOSES

"the slight snake": George Adam Smith.

plastic animal: Hegel, *Philosophy of History*. The Greek state was plastic, i.e., all of a piece.

BOWLS

appear the first day: Advertisement in French magazine.

NOVICES

"Is it the buyer or the seller who gives the money?": Anatole France, *Petit Pierre*.

"dracontine cockatrices": Southey, *The Young Dragon*.

"lit by the half lights of more conscious art": A. R. Gordon, *The Poets of the Old Testament*.

"the smell of the cypress": Landor, *Imaginary Conversations* (Camelot Series, Walter Scott Publishing Company), p. 52. Petrarca: "The smell of box, although not sweet, is more agreeable to me than many that are. . . . The cypress too seems to strengthen the nerves of the brain."

"that tinge of sadness": Arthur Hadyn, *Illustrated London News*, February 26, 1921. "The Chinese objects of art and porcelain dispersed by Messrs. Puttick and Simpson on

the 18th, had that tinge of sadness which a reflective mind always feels; it is so little and so much."

"the authors are wonderful people": Leigh Hunt.

"much noble vagueness": James Harvey Robinson, *The Mind in the Making.*

"split like a glass against a wall": The Decameron, introduction by Morley (Cassell, 1908).

"precipitate of dazzling impressions": W. R. Gordon, *The Poets of the Old Testament.*

"fathomless suggestions of color": P. T. Forsyth, *Christ on Parnassus* (Hodder and Stoughton).

"ocean of hurrying consonants": George Adam Smith, *Expositor's Bible.*

"great livid stains": Faguet, *Gustave Flaubert* (Houghton Mifflin).

"flashing lances"; "molten fires": Leigh Hunt, *Autobiography.*

"with foam on its barriers": George Adam Smith, *Expositor's Bible*

"crashing itself out": George Adam Smith, *Expositor's Bible.*

MARRIAGE

"of circular traditions": Francis Bacon.

write simultaneously: Scientific American; January 1922; "Multiple Consciousness or Reflex Action of Unaccustomed Range." "Miss A———will write simultaneously in three languages, English, German, and French, talking in the meantime. (She) takes advantage of her abilities in everyday life, writing her letters simultaneously with both hands; namely, the first, third, and fifth words with her left and the second, fourth, and sixth with her right hand. While generally writing outward, she is able as well to write inward with both hands."

"See her, see her in this common world": George Shock.

"unlike flesh, stones": Richard Baxter, *The Saints' Everlasting Rest* (Lippincott, 1909).

"something feline, something colubrine": Philip Littell, *Books and Things;* Santayana's *Poems; New Republic,* March 21, 1923. "We were puzzled and we were fascinated, as if by something feline, by something colubrine."

"treading chasms": Hazlitt, *Essay on Burke's style.*

"past states": Baxter.

"he experiences a solemn joy": Anatole France, *Filles et Garçons.* A Travers Champs; "le petit Jean comprend qu'il est beau et cette idée le pénètre d'un respect profond de lui-même. . . . Il goûte une joie pieuse à se sentir devenu une idole."

"it clothes me with a shirt of fire": The Nightingale, a poem in Armenian by Dr. Hagoop Boghossian of the Department of Philosophy of Worcester College, Massachusetts.

"he dares not clap his hands": Edward Thomas, *Feminine Influence on the Poets* (Martin Secker, 1910). "The Kingis Quair—To us the central experience is everything—the strong unhappy king, looking out of the prison window and seeing the golden-haired maiden in rich attire trimmed with pearls, rubies, emeralds and sapphires, a chaplet of red, white and blue feathers on her head, a heart-shaped ruby on a chain of fine gold hanging over her white throat, her dress looped up carelessly to walk in that fresh morning of nightingales in the new-leaved thickets—her little dog with his bells at her side."

"illusion of a fire": Baxter.

"as high as deep": Baxter.

"very trivial object": Godwin: "marriage is a law and the worst of all laws . . . a very trivial object indeed."

"a kind of overgrown cupid": Brewer, *Dictionary of Phrase and Fable.*

"the crested screamer": Remark in conversation, Glenway Wescott.

"for love that will gaze an eagle blind": Anthony Trollope, *Barchester Towers,* Vol. II.

"no truth can be fully known": Robert of Sorbonne.

"darkeneth her countenance as a bear doth": Ecclesiasticus, "Women: Bad and Good—An Essay," *Modern Reader's Bible* (Macmillan).

"seldom and cold": Baxter.

"Married people often look that way": C. Bertram Hartmann.

"Ahasuerus tête à tête banquet": George Adam Smith, *Expositor's Bible.*

"Good monster, lead the way": The Tempest.

"Four o'clock does not exist": la Comtesse de Noailles, *Femina,* December, 1921. le Thè: "Dans leur impérieuse humilité elles jouent instinctivement leurs rôles sur le globe."

"What monarch": "The Rape of the Lock," a satire in verse by Mary Frances Nearing, with suggestions by M. Moore.

"the sound of the flute": A. Mitram Rhibany, *The Syrian Christ.* Silence on the part of women—"to an Oriental, this is as poetry set to music" although "in the Orient as here, husbands have difficulty in enforcing their authority"; "it is a common saying that not all the angels in heaven could subdue a woman."

"men are monopolists": Miss M. Carey Thomas, President Emeritus of Bryn Mawr College. Founders address, Mount Holyoke College, 1821: "Men practically reserve for themselves stately funerals, splendid monuments, memorial statues, membership in academies, medals, titles, honorary degrees, stars, garters, ribbons, buttons and other shining baubles, so valueless in themselves and yet so infinitely desirable because they are symbols of recognition by their fellow craftsmen of difficult work well done."

"the crumbs from a lion's meal": Amos: 3; 12. Translation by George Adam Smith, *Expositor's Bible.*

"a wife is a coffin": Quoted by John Cournos from Ezra Pound.

"settle on my hand": Charles Reade.

"some have rights": Burke. "Asiatics have rights; Europeans have obligations."

"leaves her peaceful husband": Simone A. Puget, Change of Fashion, advertisement, *English Review,* June, 1914. "Thus proceed pretty dolls when they leave their old home to renovate their frame, and dear others who may abandon their peaceful husband only because they have seen enough of him."

"Everything to do with love is mystery": F. C. Tilney, *The Original Fables of La Fontaine* (Dutton) *Love and Folly:* Book XII, No. 14.

"Liberty and Union": Daniel Webster.

SILENCE

My father used to say: a remark in conversation; Miss A. M. Homans, Professor Emeritus of Hygiene, Wellesley College. "My father used to say, 'superior people never make long visits, then people are not so glad when you've gone.' When I am visiting, I like to go about by myself. I never had to be shown Longfellow's grave nor the glass flowers at Harvard."

"make my house your inn": Edmund Burke to a stranger with whom he had fallen into conversation in a bookshop. *Life of Burke,* James Prior: "'Throw yourself into a coach,' said he. 'Come down and make my house your inn.'"

AN OCTOPUS

glass that will bend: Sir William Bell of the British Institute of Patentees has made a list of inventions which he says the world needs. The list includes glass that will bend; a smooth road surface that will not be slippery in wet weather; a furnace that will conserve 95 per cent. of its heat; a process to make flannel unshrinkable; a noiseless airplane; a motor engine of one pound weight per horse-power; methods to reduce friction; a process to extract phosphorus from vulcanized India rubber so that it can be boiled up and used again; practical ways of utilizing the tides.

"picking periwinkles": M. C. Carey, *London Graphic* (August 25, 1923).

"spider fashion": W. P. Pycraft, *Illustrated London News,* June 28, 1924.

"ghostly pallor": Francis Ward, *Illustrated London News,* August 11, 1923.

"magnitude of their root systems": John Muir.

"creepy to behold": W. P. Pycraft.

"each like the shadow of the one beside it": Ruskin.

"conformed to an edge": W. D. Wilcox, *The Rockies of Canada* (Putnam, 1903).

"thoughtful beavers": Clifton Johnson, *What to See in America* (Macmillan).

"blue stone forests": Clifton Johnson, *What to See in America.*

"grottoes": W. D. Wilcox, *The Rockies of Canada.*

"two pairs of trousers": W. D. Wilcox. "My old packer, Bill Peyto. He usually wears two pairs of trousers, one over the other, the outer pair about six months older. Every once in a while, Peyto would give one or two nervous yanks at the fringe and tear off the longer pieces, so that his outer trousers disappeared day by day from below upwards."

"deliberate wide eyed wistfulness": Olivia Howard Dunbar; review of Alice Meynell's prose; *Post Literary Review,* June 16, 1923. "There is no trace here of deliberate wild eyed wistfulness."

"glass eyes": W. D. Wilcox. "The Indian pony or cayuse probably owes its origin to a cross between the mustang and the horses introduced by the Spaniards in the conquest of Mexico. Some of them have 'glass eyes' or a colorless condition of the retina supposed to be the result of too much inbreeding."

"business men": W. D. Wilcox: "A crowd of the business men of Banff, who usually take about 365 holidays every year, stands around to offer advice."

"menagerie of styles": W. M., "The Mystery of an Adjective and of Evening Clothes," *London Graphic,* June 21, 1924: "Even in the Parisian menagerie of styles there remains this common feature that evening dress is always evening dress in men's wear. With women there is no saying whether a frock is meant for tea, dinner, or for breakfast in bed."

"bristling, puny, swearing men": Clifton Johnson.

"They make a nice appearance, don't they?": Comment overheard at the circus.

"Like happy souls in hell": Richard Baxter, *The Saints' Everlasting Rest.*

"so noble and so fair": Cardinal Newman, *Historical Sketches.*

"complexities . . . an accident": Richard Baxter.

"The Greeks were emotionally sensitive": W. D. Hyde, *The Five Great Philosophies* (Macmillan).

"creeping slowly": Francis Ward.

"tear the snow"; "flat on the ground"; "bent in a half circle": Clifton Johnson.

"with a sound like the crack of a rifle": W. D. Wilcox.

Quoted descriptions of scenery and of animals, of which the source is not given, have been taken from government pamphlets on our national parks.

SEA UNICORNS AND LAND UNICORNS

"mighty monoceroses": Spenser.

"disquiet shippers": Violet A. Wilson, *Queen Elizabeth's Maids of Honor* (Lane), quotes Olaus Magnus, *History of the Goths and Swedes*: "The sea serpent: he hath commonly hair hanging from his neck a cubit long, and sharp scales and is black, and he hath flameling shining eyes. This snake disquiets shippers and he puts up his head like a pillar, and catcheth away men."

a voyager: Violet A. Wilson, *Queen Elizabeth's Maids of Honor*. Thomas Cavendish: "He sailed up the Thames in splenour, the sails of his ship being cloth of gold and his seamen clad in rich silks. Many were the curiosities which the explorers brought home as presents for the ladies. The Queen naturally had first choice and to her fell the unicorn's horn valued at a hundred thousand pounds, which became one of the treasures of Windsor."

"abounding in land unicorns": Violet A. Wilson, "Hawkins affirmed the existence of land unicorns in the forests of Florida, and from their presence deduced abundance of lions because of the antipathy between the two animals, so that 'where the one is the other cannot be missing'."

"in politics, in trade": Henry James, *English Hours*.

"polished garlands"; "myrtle rods": J. A. Symonds.

"cobwebs, and knotts, and mulberries": Queen Elizabeth's dresses. Violet A. Wilson, *Queen Elizabeth's Maids of Honor*: "a forepart of white satten, embroidered all over with pansies, little roses, knotts, and a border of mulberries, pillars, and pomegranets, of Venice golde, sylver, and sylke of sondrye colours. One forepart of green satten embrodered all over with sylver, like beasts, fowles, and fishes." "A petticoat embroidered all over slightly with snakes of Venice gold and silver and some O's, with a faire border embroidered like seas, cloudes, and rainbowes."

the long tailed bear of Ecuador: In his *Adventures in Bolivia* (Lane, 1922), p. 193, C. H. Prodgers tells of a strange animal that he bought: "It was stuffed with long grass and cost me ten shillings, turning out eventually to be a bear with a tail. In his book on wild life, Rowland Ward says, 'Amongst the rarest animals is a bear with a tail; this animal is known to exist, is very rare, and only to be found in the forest of Ecuador,' and this was where the man who sold it to me said he got it."

"deriving agreeable terror": Leigh Hunt. "The lover of reading will derive agreeable terror from Sir Bertram and The Haunted Chamber."

"moonbeam throat": Medieval—anonymous poem in *Punch*, April 25, 1923.

an unmatched device: Bulfinch's *Mythology*. "Some described the horn as movable at the will of the animal, a kind of small sword in short, and which no hunter who has not exceedingly cunning in fence could have a chance. Others maintained that all the animal's strength lay in its horn, and that when hard pressed in pursuit it would show itself from the pinnacle of the highest rocks horn foremost, so as to pitch on it, and then quietly march off not a whit the worse for its fall."

"impossible to take alive": Pliny.

"as straight": Charles Cotton, "An Epitaph on M. H.

"As soft, and snowy, as that down

Adorns the Blow-ball's frizzled crown;
As straight and slender as the crest,
Or antlet of the one-beam'd beast;"
"with pavon high"; "upon her lap": Mediaeval—anonymous poem in *Punch*, April 25, 1923.

From *Selected Poems*

NO SWAN SO FINE

"There is no water so still as the dead fountains of Versailles." Percy Phillip, *New York Times Magazine*, May 10, 1931.

A pair of Louis XV candelabra with Dresden figures of swans belonging to Lord Balfour.

THE JERBOA

stone locusts: Toilet-box dating from about the twenty-second Egyptian Dynasty. *Illustrated London News*, July 26, 1930.

the king's cane: Description by J. D. S. Pendlebury. *Illustrated London News*, March 19, 1932.

folding bedroom: The portable bed-chamber of Queen Hetepheres presented to her by her son, Cheops. Described by Dr. G. A. Reisner. *Illustrated London News*, May 7, 1932.

"There are little rats called jerboas which run on long hindlegs as thin as a match. The forelimbs are mere tiny hands.": Dr. R. L. Ditmars: p. 274, *Strange Animals I Have Known*.

THE PLUMET BASILISK

Guatavita Lake: Associated with the legend of El Dorado, the Gilded One. The king, painted with gums and powdered with gold-dust as symbolic of the sun, the supreme deity, was each year escorted by his nobles on a raft, to the centre of the lake, in a ceremonial of tribute to the goddess of the lake. Here he washed off his golden coat by plunging into the water while those on the raft and on the shores chanted and threw offerings into the waters—emeralds or objects of gold, silver, or platinum. See A. Hyatt Verrill, *Lost Treasure* (Appleton-Century).

Frank Davis: "The Chinese Dragon." *Illustrated London News*, August 23, 1930. "He is the god of Rain, and the Ruler of Rivers, Lakes, and Seas. For six months of the year he hibernates in the depths of the sea, living in beautiful palaces. . . . We learn from a book of the T'ang Dynasty that 'it may cause itself to become visible or invisible at will, and it can become long or short, and coarse or fine, at its own good pleasure.' A dragon 'is either born a dragon (and true dragons have nine sons) or becomes one by transformation.' There is a 'legend of the carp that try to climb a certain cataract in the western hills. Those that succeed become dragons.'"

The Malay Dragon and the "basilisks": W. P. Pycraft, *Illustrated London News*, February 6, 1932. The basilisk "will when alarmed drop to the water and scuttle along the surface on its hindlegs. . . . An allied species (Deiropteryx) can not only run along the surface of the water, but can also dive to the bottom, and there find safety till danger is past."

The Tuatera or Ngarara: In appearance a lizard—with characteristics of the tortoise; on the ribs, uncinate processes like a bird's; and crocodilian features—it is the only living representative of the order Rhynchocephalia. Shown by Captain Stanley Osborne in motion pictures. Cf. *Animals of New Zealand,* by F. W. Hutton and James Drummond (Whitcombe and Tombs).

a fox's bridge: The South American vine suspension bridge.

A seven-hundred-foot chain of gold weighing more than ten tons was being brought from Cuzco, as part of the ransom for Atahualpa. When news of his murder reached those in command of the convoy, they ordered that the chain be hidden, and it has never been found. See A. Hyatt Verrill, *Lost Treasure* (Appleton-Century).

CAMELLIA SABINA

The Abbé Berlèse; Monographie du Genre Camellia: (H. Cousin).

The French are a cruel race, etc.: J. S. Watson, Jr.

a food-grape: In Vol. I, *The Epicure's Guide to France* (Thornton Butterworth), Curnonsky and Marcel Rouff quote Monselet: "Everywhere else you eat grapes which have ripened to make wine. In France you eat grapes which have ripened for the table. They are a product at once of nature and of art. . . . The bunch is covered and uncovered alternately, according to the intensity of the heat, to gild the grapes without scorching them. Those which refuse to ripen—and there are always some—are delicately removed with special scissors, as are also those which have been spoiled by the rain."

wild parsnip: Edward W. Nelson, "Smaller Mammals of North America," *National Geographic Magazine,* May 1918.

mouse with a grape: Photograph by Spencer R. Atkinson, *National Geographic Magazine,* February 1932. "Carrying a baby in her mouth and a grape in her right forepaw, a round-tailed wood rat took this picture."

The wire cage: Photograph by Alvin E. Worman of Attleboro, Massachusetts.

THE FRIGATE PELICAN

Fregata aquila: The Frigate Pelican of Audubon.

Giant tame armadillo: Photograph and description by W. Stephen Thomas of New York.

Red-spotted orchids: The blood, supposedly, of natives slain by Pizarro.

"If I do well, I am blessed," etc.: Hindoo saying.

NINE NECTARINES AND OTHER PORCELAIN

Alphonse de Candolle: *Origin of Cultivated Plants* (Appleton, 1886). "The Chinese believe the oval peaches which are very red on one side, to be a symbol of long life. . . . According to the work of Chin-noug-king, the peach *Yu* prevents death. If it is not eaten in time, it at least preserves the body from decay until the end of the world."

New York Sun, July 2, 1932. "The World To-day," by Edgar Snow, from Soochow, China; "An old gentleman of China, whom I met when I first came to this country, volunteered to name for me what he called the 'six certainties.' He said: 'You may be sure that the clearest jade comes from Yarkand, the prettiest flowers from Szechuen, the most fragile porcelain from Kingtehchen, the finest tea from Fukien, the sheerest silk from Hangchow, and the most beautiful women from Soochow.' . . ."

The kylin (or Chinese unicorn): Frank Davis: *Illustrated London News,* March 7, 1931. "It has the body of a stag, with a single horn, the tail of a cow, horse's hoofs, a yellow belly, and hair of five colors."

From *What Are Years*

RIGORISTS

Sheldon Jackson (1834–1909). Dr. Jackson felt that to feed the Esquimo at government expense was not advisable, that whales having been almost exterminated, the ocean could not be restocked as a river can be with fish, and having prevailed on the Government to authorize the importing of reindeer from Siberia, he made an expedition during the summer of 1891, procured 16 reindeer—by barter—and later brought others. *Report on Introduction of Domestic Reindeer into Alaska*, 1895; 1896; 1897; 1899, by Sheldon Jackson, General Agent of Education in Alaska. U.S. Educ. Bureau, Washington.

LIGHT IS SPEECH

A man already harmed: Jean Calas, unjustly accused of murdering his son, and put to death, March 9, 1762. In vindicating him and his household, Voltaire "fut le premier qui s'éleva en sa faveur. Frappé de l'impossibilité du crime dont on accusait Calas le père, ce fut lûy qui engagea la veuve à venir demander justice au Roy, . . ." *The History of the Misfortunes of John Calas, a Victim to Fanaticism, to which is added a Letter from M. Calas to His Wife and Children; Written by M. De Voltaire.* Printed by P. Williamson. Edinburgh, M, DCC, LXXVI.

Creach'h d'Ouessant aeromaritime lighthouse, the first observable—as planned—by ships and planes approaching the continent from North or South America.

Montaigne, captured by bandits and unexpectedly released, says "I was told that I owed my deliverance to my bearing and the uncowed resoluteness of my speech, which showed that I was too good a fellow to hold up"

Littré (1801–81) devoted the years 1839–62 to translating and editing Hippocrates.

Bartholdi's *Liberty.*

"Tell me the truth," etc. Marshal Pétain.

" 'animate whoever thinks of her' ": "Paradise Lost" by Janet Flanner in *Decision,* January 1941.

HE 'DIGESTETH HARDE YRON'

Lyly's *Euphues:* "the estrich digesteth harde yron to preserve his health."

The large sparrow Xenophon (Anabasis, I, 5, 2) reports many ostriches in the desert on the left . . . side of the middle Euphrates, on the way from North Syria to Babylonia. Animals for Show and Pleasure in Ancient Rome by George Jennison.

A symbol of justice, men in ostrich-skins, and other allusions: Ostrich Egg-shell Cups from Mesopotamia by Berthold Laufer, *The Open Court,* May 1926. "An ostrich plume symbolized truth and justice, and was the emblem of the goddess Ma-at, the patron saint of judges. Her head is adorned with an ostrich feather, her eyes are closed, . . . as Justice is blind-folded."

Six hundred ostrich brains: At a banquet given by Elagabalus. See above: *Animals for Show and Pleasure.*

egg-shell goblets, e.g. the painted ostrich-egg cup mounted in silver-gilt by Elias Geier of Leipzig about 1589. *Antiques in and About London* by Edward Wenham; *New York Sun,* May 22, 1937.

eight pairs of ostriches: See above: *Animals for Show and Pleasure.*

Sparrow-camel: στρουθιοκαμηλοζ

SMOOTH GNARLED CRAPE MYRTLE

J. I. Lawrence, *New York Sun*, June 23, 1934: "Bulbul is a broadly generic term like sparrow, warbler, bunting. . . . The legendary nightingale of Persia is the white-eared bulbul, *Pycnotus leucotis*, richly garbed in black velvet, trimmed with brown, white, and saffron yellow; and it is a true bulbul; . . . Edward FitzGerald told what Omar meant: that the speech of man changes and coarsens, but the bulbul sings eternally in the 'high-piping Pehlevi,' the pure heroic Sanskrit of the ancient poets."

"Those who sleep in New York, but dream of London": Beau Nash in *The Playbill*, January 1935.

"Joined in friendship, crowned by love": Battersea box motto.

"Without loneliness": Yoné Noguchi paraphrasing Saigyo. *The* (London) *Spectator*, February 15, 1935.

"By Peace Plenty by Wisdom Peace," framing horns of plenty and caduceus, above a clasped hands, on the first edition title-page of Lodge's *Rosalynde*.

BIRD-WITTED

Sir Francis Bacon: "If a boy be bird-witted."

VIRGINIA BRITANNIA

Cf. *Travaile into Virginia Britannia* by William Strachey.

a great sinner: Inscription in Jamestown churchyard: "Here lyeth the body of Robert Sherwood who was born in the Parish of Whitechapel near London, a great sinner who waits for a joyful resurrection."

ostrich and horse-shoe: As crest in Captain John Smith's coat of arms, the ostrich with a horse-shoe in its beak—i.e. invincible digestion—reiterates the motto, *vincere est vivere*.

Werewocomoco: Powhatan's capitol. Of the Indians of a confederacy of about thirty tribes of Algonquins occupying Tidewater Virginia, Powhatan was war-chief or head were-owance. He presented a deer-skin mantle—now in the Ashmolean—to Captain Newport when crowned by him and Captain John Smith.

"Strong sweet prison": Of Middle Plantation—now Williamsburg.

the one-brick-thick wall designed by Jefferson: in the grounds of the University of Virginia.

deer-fur crown: "He (Arahatec) gave our Captaine his Crowne which was of Deare's hayre, Dyed redd." *Travels and Works of Captain John Smith, President of Virginia and Admiral of New England, 1580–1631;* with Introduction by A. G. Bradley. Arber's Reprints.

the lark: The British Empire Naturalists' Association has found that the hedge-sparrow sings seven minutes earlier than the lark.

SPENSER'S IRELAND

Every name is a tune; it is torture; ancient jewellery; your trouble is their trouble: See *Ireland: The Rocks Whence I Was Hewn* by Don Byrne; *National Geographic Magazine*, March 1927.

the sleeves: In Maria Edgeworth—*Castle Rackrent* as edited by Professor Morley—Thady Quirk says, "I wear a long great-coat . . .; it holds on by a single button round my neck, cloak fashion."

Venus' mantle: Footnote, *Castle Rackrent*: "The cloak, or mantle, as described by Thady is of high antiquity. See Spenser, in his 'View of the State of Ireland.'"

"the sad-yellow-fly, made with the buzzard's wing"; and *"the shell-fly, for the middle of July,"* Maria Edgeworth: *The Absentee.*

the guillemot; the linnet: Happy Memories of Glengarry by Denis O'Sullivan.

Earl Gerald: From a lecture by Padraic Colum.

FOUR QUARTZ CRYSTAL CLOCKS

Bell T. leaflet, 1939, "The World's Most Accurate Clocks: In the Bell Telephone Laboratories in New York, in a 'time vault' whose temperature is maintained within 1/100 of a degree, at 41° centigrade, are the most accurate clocks in the world—the four quartz crystal clocks. . . . When properly cut and inserted in a suitable circuit, they will control the rate of electric vibration to an accuracy of one part in a million. . . . When you call MEridian 7-1212 for correct time you get it every 15 seconds."

Jean Giraudoux: "Appeler à l'aide d'un camouflage ces instruments faits pour la vérité qui sont la radio, le cinéma, la presse?" J'ai traversé voilà un an des pays arabes où l'on ignorait encore que Napoléon était mort." *Une allocation radiodiffusée de M. Giraudoux aux Françaises à propos de Sainte Catherine;* the *Figaro,* November 1939.

the cannibal Chronos: Rhea, mother of Zeus, hid him from Chronos who "devoured all his children except Jupiter (air), Neptune (water), and Pluto (the grave). These, Time cannot consume." Brewer's *Dictionary of Phrase and Fable.*

THE PANGOLIN

the "closing ear-ridge": and certain other detail, from "Pangolins" by Robert T. Hatt; *Natural History,* December 1935.

stepping peculiarly: See Lyddeker's *Royal Natural History.*

Thomas of Leighton Buzzard's vine: a fragment of ironwork in Westminster Abbey.

"A sailboat was the first machine": See F. L. Morse: *Power: Its Application from the 17th Dynasty to the 20th Century.*

From *Nevertheless*

ELEPHANTS

Data utilized in the above stanzas, from a lecture-film entitled *Ceylon, the Wondrous Isle* by Charles Brooke Elliott. And Cicero deploring the sacrifice of elephants in the Roman Games, said they "aroused both pity and a feeling that the elephant was somehow allied with man." *Animals for Show and Pleasure in Ancient Rome,* p. 52, by George Jennison.

Collected After *Nevertheless*

THE ICOSASPHERE

"In Buckinghamshire hedgerows," etc. Statement by E. McKnight Kauffer.

Someone's fortune: The $30,000,000 snuff fortune of a Mrs. Henrietta Edwardina Schaefer Garrett who died childless and without a will in 1930. Orphan's Court, Philadelphia, has reviewed more than 25,990 claims for the fortune. . . . Three persons were reportedly slain in quarrels; ten went to jail for perjury. . . . A dozen or more were fined, six died and two killed themselves. *New York Times,* December 15, 1949. The Mellon Institute is responsible for a steel globe of a design invented by J. O. Jackson, which "solves a problem which has long baffled draughtsmen and engineers. Anybody who has tried to wrap a rubber ball without wrinkling or waste . . . will understand the nature of the problem." Steel, like wrapping-paper, is delivered in rectangles . . . Mr. Jackson discovered that plexiglass . . . has the same plastic flow as steel and . . . will writhe back into its exact original shape if placed under proper heat. So he moulded a four-inch sphere out of flat plexiglass, studied the pattern and worked out a design whereby 'twenty equilateral triangles—the greatest number of regular sides geometrically possible—could be grouped into five parallelograms and cut from rectangular sheets with negligible scrap loss.'" Waldemar Kaemffert: "Economy in the Use of Steel," *New York Times,* February 5, 1950.

"KEEPING THEIR WORLD LARGE"
"All too literally, their flesh and their spirit are our shield": The Reverend James Gordon Gilkey, *New York Times,* June 7, 1944.

VORACITIES AND VERITIES
"grass-lamp glow": V. Locke-Ellis.
"The elephant's crooked trumpet doth write":
  "Elephants

  . . . Yea (if the Grecians doe not mis-recite)
  With's crooked trumpet he doth sometimes write."
Du Bartas: "The Sixth Day of the First Weeke."
Dance Index-Ballet Caravan Inc.: Clowns, Elephants, and Ballerinas, June 1946.

PROPRIETY
Bach's *Solfeggietto:* Karl Philipp Emanuel's (C minor).

ARMOR'S UNDERMINING MODESTY
hacked things out with hairy paws: "The very oldest relics of man's early ancestors are crudely chipped stones. He gripped them in his hairy paw and used them to hammer and chop with." Oscar Ogg: *The 26 Letters,* p. 6.
Arise for it is day: The motto of The John Day Company.
the bock beer buck: Poster unsigned, distributed by Eastern Beverage Corporation, Hammonton, New Jersey.
Ducs: "In England, in the Saxon times, the officers or commanders of armies, after the old Roman fashion, were called *dukes,* without any addition, but after the Norman conquest, the title was no longer used; till, in 1538, Edward III created his son, who was first called the Black Prince, Duke of Cornwall. . . . After Edward the Black Prince, more were made; . . . The Black Prince was created by a wreath on his head, a ring on his finger, and a silver rod." *The Book of the Ranks and Dignities of British Society,* lately attributed in the press and elsewhere to Charles Lamb. Charles Scribner's Sons, New York, 1924.

From *Like a Bulwark*

APPARITION OF SPLENDOR
"train . . . long": Oliver Goldsmith in one of his essays refers to "a blue fairy with a train eleven yards long, supported by porcupines."
"with . . . nurse": "All over spines, with the forest for nurse." "The Hedgehog, the Fox, and the Flies," Book Twelve, Fable XIII, *The Fables of La Fontaine* (New York: The Viking Press, 1954).

THEN THE ERMINE
"Rather . . . spotted": Clitophon; "his device was the Ermion, with a speach that signifie, Rather dead than spotted." Sidney's *Arcadia*, Book I, Chapter 17, paragraph 4. Cambridge Classics, Volume I, 1912; edited by Albert Feuillerat.
motto: Motto of Henry, Duke of Beaufort: *Mutare vel timere sperno.*
Lavater: John Kaspar Lavater (1741–1801), a student of physiography. His system includes morphological, anthropological, anatomical, histrionical, and graphical studies. Kurt Seligmann: *The Mirror of Magic* (New York: Pantheon Books, 1948, page 332).

TOM FOOL AT JAMAICA
Mule and jockey: A mule and jockey by "Giulio Gomez 6 años" from a collection of drawings by Spanish school children. solicited on behalf of a fund-raising committee for Republican Spain, sold by Lord and Taylor; given to me by Miss Louise Crane.

"There . . . said": The Reverend David C. Shipley, July 20, 1952.
Sentir avec ardeur: By Madame Boufflers—Marie-Françoise-Catherine de Beauveau, Marquise de Boufflers (1711–1786). See note by Dr. Achilles Fang, annotating Lu Chi's "Wên Fu" (A.D. 261–303)—his "Rhymeprose on Literature" ("rhyme-prose" from "Reimprosa" of German medievalists): "As far as notes go, I am at one with a

contemporary of Rousseau's: 'Il faut dire en deux mots / Ce qu'on veut dire'; . . . But I cannot claim 'J'ai réussi,' especially because I broke Mme. de Boufflers' injunction ('Il faut éviter l'emploi / Du moi, du moi.')" *Harvard Journal of Asiatic Studies*, Volume 14, Number 3, December 1951, page 529 (revised, *New Mexico Quarterly*, September 1952).

Air: Sentir avec ardeur

Il faut dire en deux mots
Ce qu'on veut dire;
Les long propos
Sont sots.

Il faut savoir lire
Avant que d'écrire,
Et puis dire en deux mots
Ce qu'on veut dire.
Les long propos
Sont sots.

Il ne faut pas toujours conter,
Citer,
Dater,
Mais écouter.
Il faut éviter l'emploi
Du moi, du moi,
Voici pourquoi:

Il est tyrannique,
Trop académique;
L'ennui, l'ennui
Marche avec lui.
Je me conduis toujours ainsi
Ici,
Aussi
J'ai réussi.

Il faut dire en deux mots
Ce qu'on veut dire;
Les long propos
Sont sots.

Master Atkinson: I opened *The New York Times* one morning (March 3, 1952) and a column by Arthur Daley on Ted Atkinson and Tom Fool took my fancy. Asked what he thought of Hill Gail, Ted Atkinson said, "He's a real good horse, . . . real good," and paused a moment. "But I think he ranks only second to Tom Fool. . . . I prefer Tom Fool. . . . He makes a more sustained effort and makes it more often." Reminded that Citation could make eight or ten spurts in a race, "That's it," said Ted enthusiastically. "It's the mark of a champion to spurt 100 yards, settle back and spurt another

100 yards, giving that extra burst whenever needed. From what I've seen of Tom Fool, I'd call him a 'handy horse.'" He mentioned two others. "They had only one way of running. But Tom Fool. . . ." Then I saw a picture of Tom Fool (*New York Times*, April 1, 1952) with Ted Atkinson in the saddle and felt I must pay him a slight tribute; got on with it a little way, then realized that I had just received an award from Youth United for a Better Tomorrow and was worried indeed. I deplore gambling and had never seen a race. Then in the *Times* for July 24, 1952, I saw a column by Joseph C. Nichols about Frederic Capossela, the announcer at Belmont Park, who said when interviewed, "Nervous? No, I'm never nervous. . . . I'll tell you where it's tough. The straightaway at Belmont Park, where as many as twenty-eight horses run at you from a point three quarters of a mile away. I get 'em though, and why shouldn't I? I'm relaxed, I'm confident and I don't bet."

In the way of a sequel, "Money Isn't Everything" by Arthur Daley (*New York Times*, March 1, 1955): "'There's a constant fascination to thoroughbreds,' said Ted, '. . . they're so much like people. . . . My first love was Red Hay . . . a stout-hearted little fellow . . . he always tried, always gave his best.' [Mr. Daley: 'The same description fits Atkinson.'] 'There was Devil Diver, . . . the mare Snow Goose. One of my big favorites . . . crazy to get going. . . . But once she swung into stride . . . you could ride her with shoelaces for reins. . . . And then there was Coaltown. . . . There were others of course, but I never met one who could compare with Tom Fool, my favorite of favorites. He had the most personality of all. . . . Just to look at him lit a spark. He had an intelligent head, an intelligent look and, best of all, was intelligent. He had soft eyes, a wide brow and—gee, I'm sounding like a lovesick boy. But I think he had the handsomest face of any horse I ever had anything to do with. He was a great horse but I was fond of him not so much for what he achieved as for what he was.' With that the sprightly Master Theodore fastened the number plate on his right shoulder and headed for the paddock."

"Chance . . . impurity": The *I Ching* or *Book of Changes,* translated by Richard Wilhelm and Cary Baynes, Bollingen Series XIX (New York: Pantheon Books, 1950).

Fats Waller: Thomas Waller, "a protean jazz figure," died in 1943. See *The New York Times,* article and Richard Tucker (Pix) photograph, March 16, 1952.

Ozzie Smith: Osborne Smith, a Negro chanter and drummer who improvised the music for Ian Hugo's *Ai-Yé.*

Eubie Blake: The Negro pianist in *Shuffle Along.*

THE WEB ONE WEAVES OF ITALY

"fount . . . spilt": "The Monkey and the Leopard," Book Nine, Fable III, *The Fables of La Fontaine* (Viking, 1954).

The greater part of stanzas 1 and 2 is quoted from an article by Mitchell Goodman, "Festivals and Fairs for the tourist in Italy," *New York Times,* April 18, 1954.

THE STAFF OF AESCULAPIUS

Suppose . . . one: Time, March 29, 1954, article on the Salk vaccine.

Selective . . . true: Sloan-Kettering Institute for Cancer Research, *Progress Report VII,* June 1954; pp. 20–21.

To . . . framework: Abbott Laboratories, "Plastic Sponge Implants in Surgery," *What's New,* Number 186, Christmas 1954.

THE SYCAMORE

nine . . . hairs: Imami, the Iranian miniaturist, draws "with a brush made of nine hairs from a newborn she camel and a pencil sharpened to a needle's point. . . . He was decorated twice by the late Riza Shah; once for his miniatures and once for his rugs." *New York Times,* March 5, 1954.

ROSEMARY

"hath . . . language": Sir Thomas More (see below).

According to a Spanish legend, rosemary flowers—originally white—turned blue when the Virgin threw her cloak over a rosemary bush, while resting on the flight into Egypt. There is in Trinity College Library, Cambridge, a manuscript sent to Queen Philippa of Hainault by her mother, written by "a clerk of the school of Salerno" and translated by "danyel bain." The manuscript is devoted entirely to the virtues of rosemary, which, we are told, never grows higher than the height of Christ; after thirty-three years the plant increases in breadth but not in height. See "Rosemary of Plesant Savour," by Eleanour Sinclair Rohde, *The Spectator,* July 7, 1930.

STYLE

Dick Button: See photograph, *New York Times,* January 2, 1956.

Etchebaster: Pierre Etchebaster, a machine-gunner in the First World War; champion of France in chistera (jai alai), pala, and mainnues. He took up court tennis in 1922, won the American championship in 1928, and retired in 1954. (*New York Times,* February 13, 1954, and February 24, 1955). *New York Times,* January 19, 1956: "Pierre Etchebaster, retired world champion, and Frederick S. Moseley won the pro-amateur handicap court tennis tournament at the Racquet and Tennis Club yesterday. . . . The score was 5-6, 6-5, 6-5. Moseley, president of the club, scored the last point of the match with a railroad ace. Johnson and McClintock had pulled up from 3-5 to 5-all in this final set."

Soledad: Danced in America, 1950–1951

Rosario's: Rosario Escudero, one of the company of Vincente Escudero, but not related to him.

LOGIC AND "THE MAGIC FLUTE"

Colorcast by NBC Opera Theater, January 15, 1956.

precious wentletrap: "wen′tle·trap′ (went′l·trap′), *n.* [D. *wenteltrap* a winding staircase; cf. G. *wendeltreppe.*] the genus *Epitonium,* or the family Epitoniidae.—*Webster's New International Dictionary.*

"What . . . it?'": Demon in Love by Horatio Colony (Cambridge, Massachusetts: Hampshire Press, 1955).

Banish sloth: "Banish sloth; you have defeated Cupid's bow," Ovid, *Remedia Amoris.*

BLESSED IS THE MAN

Blessed . . . scoffer: Psalm 1:1.

"characteristically intemperate": Campaign manager's evaluation of an attack on the Eisenhower Administration.

"excuse . . . heard": Charles Poore reviewing James B. Conant's *The Citadel of Learning* (New Haven: Yale University Press)—quoting Lincoln. *New York Times,* April 7, 1956.

Giorgione's self-portrait: Reproduced in *Life,* October 24, 1955.

"Diversity . . . learning": James B. Conant, *The Citadel of Learning.*

"takes . . . decision": Louis Dudek: "poetry . . . must . . . take the risk of a decision"; "to say what we know, loud and clear—and if necessary ugly—that would be better than to say nothing with great skill." "The New Laocöon," *Origin,* Winter–Spring 1956.

"Would . . . all?": "President Eisenhower Vetoes Farm Compromise [Agricultural Act of 1956]," *New York Times,* April 17, 1956: "We would produce more of certain crops at a time when we need less of them. . . . If natural resources are squandered on crops that we cannot eat or sell, all Americans lose."

Ulysses' companions: "The Companions of Ulysses," Book Twelve, Fable I, *The Fables of La Fontaine* (The Viking Press, 1954).

mitin (From *la mite,* moth): Odorless, non-toxic product of Geigy Chemical Corporation research scientists (Swiss). *New York Times,* April 7, 1956.

"private . . . shame": See note for line 13.

"things . . . appear": Hebrews 11:3.

From *O to Be a Dragon*

O TO BE A DRAGON

Dragon: see secondary symbols, Volume II of *The Tao of Painting,* translated and edited by Mai-mai Sze, Bollingen Series 49 (New York: Pantheon, 1956).

Solomon's wish: "an understanding heart." I Kings 3:9.

VALUES IN USE

Philip Rahv, July 30, 1956, at the Harvard Summer School Conference on the Little Magazine, Alston Burr Hall, Cambridge, Massachusetts, gave as the standard for stories accepted by the *Partisan Review:* "maturity, plausibility, and the relevance of the point of view expressed." "A work of art must be appraised on its own ground; we produce values in the process of living, do not await their historic progress in history." See *Partisan Review,* Fall 1956.

HOMETOWN PIECE FOR MESSRS. ALSTON AND REESE

Messrs. Alston and Reese: Walter Alston, manager of the Brooklyn Dodgers; Harold (Peewee) Reese, captain of the Dodgers.

Millennium: "The millennium and pandemonium arrived at approximately the same time in the Brooklyn Dodgers' clubhouse at the Yankee Stadium yesterday." Roscoe McGowen, *New York Times*, October 5, 1955.

Roy Campanella: Photograph: "Moment of Victory," *New York Times*, October 5, 1955.

Buzzie Bavasi: "The policemen understood they were to let the players in first, but Brooklyn officials—Walter O'Malley, Arthur (Red) Patterson, Buzzie Bavasi and Fresco Thompson—wanted the writers let in along with the players. This, they felt, was a different occasion and nobody should be barred." Roscoe McGowen, *New York Times*, October 5, 1955. E. J. Bavasi: Vice president of the Dodgers. William J. Briordy, "Campanella Gets Comeback Honors," *New York Times*, November 17, 1955.

When Sandy Amoros made the catch: [Joe Collins to Johnny Podres]: " 'The secret of your success was the way you learned to control your change-up. . . .' 'I didn't use the change-up much in the seventh game of the world series,' said Johnny. 'The background was bad for it. So I used a fast ball that really had a hop on it.' . . . 'Hey, Johnny,' said Joe, 'how did you feel when Amoros made that catch?' 'I walked back to the mound,' said Podres, 'and I kept saying to myself, "everything keeps getting better and better." ' " Arthur Daley, "Sports of the Times: Just Listening," *New York Times*, January 17, 1956.

"Hope springs eternal": Roscoe McGowen, "Brooklyn Against Milwaukee," *New York Times*, July 31, 1956.

8, Row 1: The Dodgers' Sym-Phoney Band sits in Section 8, Row 1, Seats 1 to 7, conducted by Lou Soriano (who rose by way of the snare-drum). "The Sym-Phoney is busy rehearsing a special tune for the Brooklyn income tax collector: It's "All of Me—Why Not Take All of Me?" William R. Conklin, "Maestro Soriano at Baton for 18th Brooklyn Season," *New York Times*, August 12, 1956.

"Four hundred feet": "Gilliam opened the game with a push bunt for a hit, and with one out Duke Snider belted the ball more than 400 feet to the base of the right-center-field wall. Gilliam came home but had to return to base when the ball bounced high into the stands for a ground-rule double." Roscoe McGowen, "Dodgers against Pittsburgh." Duke Snider "hit twenty-three homers in Ebbets Field for four successive years." John Drebinger, *New York Times*, October 1, 1956.

"stylish stout" [A catcher]: "He crouches in his wearying squat a couple of hundred times a day, twice that for double-headers." Arthur Daley, "At Long Last," *New York Times Magazine*, July 9, 1956.

Preacher Roe's number: 28. Venerated left-handed pitcher for Brooklyn who won 22 games in the season of 1951.

Jake: "He's a Jake of All Trades—Jake Pitler, the Dodgers' first-base coach and cheerleader." Joseph Sheehan, *New York Times*, September 16, 1956, "Dodgers Will Have a Night for Jake"—an honor accepted two years ago "with conditions": that contributions be for Beth-El Hospital Samuel Strausberg Wing. Keepsake for the "Night": a replica of the plaque in the Jake Pitler Pediatric Playroom (for underprivileged children).

Don Demeter: Center fielder, a newcomer from Fort Worth, Texas. "Sandy Amoros whacked an inside-the-park homer—the third of that sort for the Brooks this year—and Don Demeter, . . . hit his first major league homer, also his first hit, in the eighth inning." Roscoe McGowen, *New York Times*, September 20, 1956.

Shutting . . . do: Carl Erskine's no-hitter against the Giants at Ebbets Field, May 12, 1956. *New York Times,* May 27, 1956.

ENOUGH: JAMESTOWN, 1607–1957

On May 13, 1957—the 350th anniversary of the landing at Jamestown of the first permanent English settlers in North America—three United States Air Force super sabre jets flew non-stop from London to Virginia. They were the *Discovery,* the *Godspeed,* and the *Susan Constant*—christened respectively by Lady Churchill, by Mrs. Whitney (wife of Ambassador John Hay Whitney), and by Mrs. W. S. Morrison (wife of the speaker of the House of Commons). *New York Times,* May 12 and 13, 1957.

The colonists entered Chesapeake Bay, having left England on New Year's Day, almost four months before, "fell upon the earth, embraced it, clutched it to them, kissed it, and, with streaming eyes, gave thanks unto God . . ." Paul Green, "The Epic of Old Jamestown," *New York Times Magazine,* March 31, 1957.

If present faith mend partial proof: Dr. Charles Peabody, chaplain at Yale, 1896, author of *Mornings in College Chapel,* said past gains are not gains unless we in the present complete them.

MELCHIOR VULPIUS

"And not only is the great artist mysterious to us but is that to himself. The nature of the power he feels is unknown to him, and yet he has acquired it and succeeds in directing it." Arsène Alexander, *Malvina Hoffman—Critique and Catalogue* (Paris: J. E. Pouterman, 1930).

Mouse-skin-bellows'-breath: "Bird in a Bush . . . The bird flies from stem to stem while he warbles. His lungs, as in all automatons, consist of tiny bellows constructed from mouse-skin." Daniel Alain, *Réalités,* April 1957, page 58.

NO BETTER THAN "A WITHERED DAFFODIL"

"Slow, slow, fresh Fount" by Ben Jonson, from *Cynthia's Revels.*

A work of art: Sir Isaac Oliver's miniature on ivory of Sir Philip Sidney. (Collection at Windsor.)

IN THE PUBLIC GARDEN

Originally entitled "A Festival." Read at the Boston Arts Festival, June 15, 1958.

Faneuil Hall . . . glittered: "Atop Faneuil Hall, . . . marketplace hall off Dock Square, Boston, Laurie Young, Wakefield gold-leafer and steeple-jack, applies . . . finishing paint on the steeple rod after . . . gilding the dome and the renowned 204-year-old grasshopper." *Christian Science Monitor,* September 20, 1946.

Grasshopper: "Deacon Shem Drowne's metal grasshopper, placed atop old Faneuil Hall by its creator in 1749, . . . still looks as if it could jump with the best of its kind . . . thought to be an exact copy of the vane on top of the Royal Exchange in London." *Christian Science Monitor,* February 16, 1950, quoting *Crafts of New England,* by Allen H. Eaton (New York: Harper, 1949).

"My work be praise": Psalm 23—traditional Southern tune, arranged by Virgil Thomson. "President Eisenhower attributed to Clemenceau . . . the observation, 'Freedom is nothing . . . but the opportunity for self-discipline.' . . . 'And that means the work that you yourselves lay out for yourselves is worthwhile doing—doing without hope of reward.'" *New York Times,* May 6, 1958.

SAINT NICHOLAS

a chameleon: See photograph in *Life*, September 15, 1958, with a letter from Dr. Doris M. Cochran, curator of reptiles and amphibians, National Museum, Washington, D.C.

FOR FEBRUARY 14th

"Some interested law": From a poem to M. Moore by Marguerite Harris.

COMBAT CULTURAL

Nan-ai-ans: The Nanaians inhabit the frigid North of the Soviet Union.

One person: Lev Golanov: "Two Boys in a Fight." Staged by Igor Moiseyev, Moiseyev Dance Company, presented in New York, 1958, by Sol Hurok.

LEONARDO DA VINCI'S

See *Time*, May 18, 1959, page 73: "Saint Jerome," an unfinished picture by Leonardo da Vinci, in the Vatican; and *The Belles Heures of Jean, Duke of Berry, Prince of France*, with an Introduction by James J. Rorimer (New York: Metropolitan Museum of Art, 1958).

From *Tell Me, Tell Me*

GRANITE AND STEEL

See *Brooklyn Bridge: Fact and Symbol* by Alan Trachtenberg (New York: Oxford University Press, 1965).

Caged Circe: See Meyer Berger's story (retold in *Brooklyn Bridge: Fact and Symbol*) of a young reporter who in the 1870s was unaccountably drawn to climb one of the cables to the top of the bridge's Manhattan tower, became spellbound, couldn't come down, and cried for help; none came till morning.

O catenary curve: The curve formed by a rope or cable hanging freely between two fixed points of support. "Engineering problems of the greatest strength, greatest economy, greatest safety . . . are all solved by the same curve," John Roebling said. (Trachtenberg, p. 69.)

IN LIEU OF THE LYRE

Written in response to a request from Stuart Davis, president of the *Advocate*, for a poem.

Sentir avec ardeur: By Madame Boufflers—Marie-Françoise-Catherine de Beauveau, Marquise de Boufflers (1711–1786). See note by Dr. Achilles Fang, annotating Lu Chi's "Wên Fu" (A.D. 261–303)—his "Rhymeprose on Literature" ("rhyme-prose" from "Reimprosa" of German medievalists): "As far as notes go, I am at one with a contemporary of Rousseau's: *'Il faut dire en deux mots / Ce qu'on veut dire';* . . . But I cannot claim *'J'ai réussi,'* especially because I broke Mme. de Boufflers's injunction *('Il faut éviter l'emploi / Du moi, du moi').*" *Harvard Journal of Asiatic Studies*, Volume 14, Number 3, December, 1951, page 529 (revised, *New Mexico Quarterly*, September, 1952).

Professor Levin: Harry Levin, "A Note on Her French Aspect," p. 40, *Festschrift for Marianne Moore's Seventy-Seventh Birthday*, edited by T. Tambimuttu (1964).

Lowell House Press: Referring to a Lowell House *separatum: Occasionem Cognosce* (1963).

Gratia sum: Bewick tailpiece, "a trickle of water from a rock, underlined by a heart carved on the rock," p. 53, *Memoir of Thomas Bewick Written by Himself* (Centaur Classics).

A bridge: Brooklyn Bridge: Fact and Symbol, by Alan Trachtenberg (1965).

CARNEGIE HALL: RESCUED

"Saint Diogenes": "Talk of the Town," *The New Yorker,* April 9, 1960.

"Palladian majesty": Gilbert Millstein, *The New York Times Magazine,* May 22, 1960.

TELL ME, TELL ME

Lord Nelson's revolving diamond rosette: In the museum at Whitehall.

"The literal played in our education as small a part as it perhaps ever played in any and we wholesomely breathed inconsistency and ate and drank contradictions." Henry James, *Autobiography (A Small Boy and Others, Notes of a Son and Brother, The Middle Years),* edited by F. W. Dupee (New York: Criterion, 1958).

From *Complete Poems*

THE STUDENT

"In America": "Les Ideals de l'Éducation Française," lecture, December 3, 1931, by M. Auguste Desclos, Director-adjoint, Office National des Universités et Écoles Françaises de Paris.

The singing tree: "Each leaf was a mouth, and every leaf joined in concert." *Arabian Nights.*

"Science is never finished": Albert Einstein to an American student, *New York Times.*

Jack Bookworm: see Goldsmith's *The Double Transformation.*

A variety of hero: Emerson in *The American Scholar:* "There can be no scholar without the heroic mind"; "let him hold by himself; . . . patient of neglect, patient of reproach."

Wolf's wool: Edmund Burke, November 1781, in reply to Fox: "There is excellent wool on the back of a wolf and therefore he must be sheared. . . . But will he comply?"

"Gives his opinion": Henry McBride, *New York Sun,* December 12, 1931: "Dr. Valentiner . . . has the typical reserve of the student. He does not enjoy the active battle of opinion that invariably rages when a decision is announced that can be weighed in great sums of money. He gives his opinion firmly and rests upon that."

LOVE IN AMERICA

The Minotaur demanded a virgin to devour once a year.

Midas, who had the golden touch, was inconvenienced when eating or picking things up.

Unamuno said that what we need as a cure for unruly youth is "nobility that is action."

Without brazenness or bigness: Winston Churchill: "Modesty becomes a man."

TIPPOO'S TIGER

Derived from a Victoria and Albert Museum monograph, "Tippoo's Tiger," by Mildred Archer (London: Her Majesty's Stationery Office, 1959).

See Keats's *The Cap and Bells.*

"Tippoo" is the original form of the name used in the eighteenth century; "Tipu" is the accepted modern form.

A vast toy, a curious automaton: A mechanical tiger "captured by the British at Seringapatan in 1799, when Tipu Sultan, ruler of Mysore in Southern India, was defeated and killed." Mildred Archer.

Organ pipes: Cf. "Technical Aspects of Tipu's Organ" by Henry Willis, Jr., in Mildred Archer's monograph.

MERCIFULLY

An Evening of Elizabethan Verse and Its Music—W. H. Auden and the New York Pro Musica Antiqua; Noah Greenberg, Director. *Legendary Performances* (Odyssey 32160171).

"REMINISCENT OF A WAVE AT THE CURL"

Kittens owned by Mr. and Mrs. Richard Thoma.

THE MAGICIAN'S RETREAT

Drawing by Jean-Jacques Lequeu (1757–1825), *Arts Magazine,* December/January 1967–68.

René Magritte, Domain of Lights, 1953–54. *New York Times Magazine,* January 19, 1969, page 69.

EDITOR'S NOTES

With the Poetry's Attributions and Variants

Abbreviations

RML	The Rosenbach Museum and Library, Philadelphia, Pennsylvania
A	*The Arctic Ox* (London: Faber and Faber, 1964)
CP	*Collected Poems* (New York: Macmillan, 1951)
COMP	*The Complete Poems of Marianne Moore* (New York: Macmillan/Viking, 1967; rev. ed., 1981)
L	*Like a Bulwark* (New York: Viking, 1956)
MMR	*A Marianne Moore Reader* (New York: Viking, 1961)
N	*Nevertheless* (New York: Macmillan, 1944)
O	*Observations* (New York: Dial, 1924)
Others, 1917	*Others: An Anthology of the New Verse*, ed. Alfred Kreymborg (New York: Knopf, 1917)
OBD	*O to Be a Dragon* (New York: Viking, 1959)
P	*Poems* (London: Egoist Press, 1921)
PAN	*The Pangolin and Other Verse* (London: Brendin, 1936)
SP	*Selected Poems* (New York: Macmillan, 1935)
TM	*Tell Me, Tell Me: Granite, Steel, and Other Topics* (New York: Viking, 1966)
W	*What Are Years* (New York: Macmillan, 1941)
Uncollected	Designates poems that are not found in any of the author's poetry books.

Prelude, December 25, 1895

"Dear St. Nicklus;" (December 25, 1895). RML, Series 1, 1:01. The young poet illustrated this with drawings of the gifts she requested. Printed posthumously as a Christmas card. Note punctuation as part of the title, a practice that was to continue throughout her career. Uncollected.

Early Poems, 1907–1915

"Under a Patched Sail." *Tipyn o'Bob* 4 (February 1907): 12. Uncollected.
"To Come After a Sonnet." *Tipyn o'Bob* 4 (February 1907): 25. Uncollected.
"To My Cup-Bearer." *Tipyn o'Bob* 5 (April 1908): 21. Uncollected.

"The Sentimentalist." *Tipyn o'Bob* 5 (April 1908): 26. Uncollected.

"He Made This Screen." This, from *Poems,* 1921. First published in *Tipyn o'Bob* 6 (January 1909): 2–3, it appeared as "To a Screen-Maker" in *The Lantern* 17 (1909): 28; uncollected.

Compare with the version in *Tipyn o'Bob:*

To a Screen-Maker

I.

Not of silver nor of coral
But of weather-beaten laurel
Carve it out.

II.

Carve out here and there a face
And a dragon circling space
Coiled about.

III.

Represent a branching tree
Uniform like tapestry
And no sky.

IV.

And devise a rustic bower
And a pointed passion flower
Hanging high.

"Ennui." *Tipyn o'Bob* 6 (March 1909): 7. On May 26, 1907, Marianne Moore wrote home her response to *The Tempest,* produced by the Ben Greet Players at Bryn Mawr: "[Caliban] fauned on Prospero half rising from the ground and falling back heavily. His voice was from Hades direct, a rocky rain-crow utterance with a catch in it. The scene was funny beyond words where Trincolo finds him and says, 'A fish, or a man?' Arms where the fins should be, yet a fish, a fish.'" RML, Series I, 1:01. Uncollected.

"A Red Flower." *Tipyn o'Bob* 6 (May 1909): 14. Uncollected.

"A Jelly-Fish." *The Lantern* 17 (1909): 348. Uncollected.

"Progress" ("I May, I Might, I Must"). This, *Tipyn o'Bob* 6 (June 1909): 10. As "Progress," it appeared in the *Trinity Review* (Trinity College, Hartford) 11 (spring/summer 57): 23. As "I May, I Might, I Must," in *OBD, A, MMR, COMP.*

But for the title, and the removal of a comma in the last line, it is the same as in *COMP.* In manuscript c. 1907, the poem was called "Perseus to Polydectes." Its title has changed as follows: "Conservatism," ms. ca. February 1909 (RML, Series I, 1:01); "Progress," *Tipyn o'Bob* 6 (June 1909): 10; "Perseus to Polydectes," ms. ca. 1914; and "I May, I Might, I Must," *Trinity Review* 11 (spring/summer 1957), *OBD, A, MMR, COMP.*

"A Fish." RML Series I, 1:01. Ca. 1910. Unpublished.

"My Lantern." *The Lantern* 18 (1910): 28. "A Preciosity," "The Tentative Critic," and "The Fearful Critic" were found as alternate titles in her handwriting on the printed page. Possibly they allude to "Elfride, Making Epigrams" (see note, below). Uncollected.

"Tunica Pallio Proprior." *The Lantern* 18 (1910): 102. Uncollected.

"My Senses Do Not Deceive Me." *The Lantern* 18 (1910): 103. Uncollected.

"Qui S'Excuse, S'Accuse." *The Lantern* 18 (1910): 103. Uncollected.

"Elfride, Making Epigrams." This poem, composed about 1910, is found in a Rosenbach file accompanied by the following note, with an asterisk after the title: "The Court of Kellyon Castle, a Mediaeval Romance" by Ernest Field (Elfride Swancourt)—reviewed by Henry Knight in *The Present*. See "A Pair of Blue Eyes by Hardy." In the Hardy novel, Elfride, nineteen, has written the medieval romance under a pseudonym, "Ernest Field." Henry Knight reviews the book unfavorably, to Elfride's consternation, and the narrator concludes: "Attack is more piquant than concord." RML, Series I, 1:01, and *Marianne Moore Newsletter* 2, no. 2 (fall 1978). Uncollected.

"A Talisman." This version, *P*, 1921. Quoted by T. S. Eliot in *SP*. First publication, *The Lantern* 20 (1912): 61. Uncollected.

"Leaves of a Magazine." *The Lantern* 20 (1912): 10. Uncollected.

Draft found in file:

They open of their own will to the place
Where Piracy comes with a falcon's face
The tight strips of the sloping deck; a frame
Of knives lies interwoven with the name
Of Kyd and the close-printed poem made
In praise of him—a ragged block of shade,
Cut by the lead, with blurs and puckers where
Admiring hands have often brought to bear
Their pressure on the picture and the rhyme
Of buccaneering in the olden time.

"The Beast of Burden." *The Lantern* 22 (1913): 57. *Forfeit* was changed from *forget* in the manuscript. Uncollected.

"Things Are What They Seem." *The Lantern* 21 (1913): 109. Uncollected.

"This Is the Way Toads Talk:". RML, Series I, 1:01. Unpublished.

"To Pierrot Returning to His Orchid." RML, Series I, 1:01. Unpublished.

Unpublished variant in file:

To a Pierrette with Her Arm Around a Brass Vase as Tall as Herself

Orchid, with the pallor of a clown
    And sumptuous contortions of a gnome,
        How came you by that one bright object in my room
        That you could fitly call your own—upon whose flame you
            seemed unconsciously to drift
And like a moth to settle down.
    The forest is your home.

I shall not regret you, flower, no,
    You strayed exotic of the pantomime,
        You dog-flower carried by the stream, to drown yourself
        Like inland seaweed in a pond . . .
Content to thole the place? Say so
    For it is Christmastime.

"To Pharaoh's Baker Plucking Up Courage to Ask the Interpretation of His Dream, when a Favorable Interpretation Had Been Accorded the Dream of Pharaoh's Butler." RML, Series I, 1:01. Unpublished.

"Piningly." RML, Series I, 1:01. Unpublished.

"Artificers and the Alchemist." Manuscript dated November 20, 1915. RML, Series I, 1:01. Unpublished.

"To You—of the World, Not in the World." RML, Series I, 1:01. Unpublished.

"Wisdom at Last." RML, Series I, 1:01. Unpublished.

"To a Stiff-winged Grasshopper." RML, Series I, 1:01. Unpublished.

Variant in file:

To a stiff-winged grasshopper,
Dancing the price of admission
    To his own cage.

The momentum of this age
Can not be fastened in a cage.
    With wicker pins—

While the calling you forsook
Embodied motion and the look
    Of mental steel.

"Emeralds." RML, Series I, 1:01. Unpublished.

"Sun, Moon, and Stars:". RML, Series I, 1:01. Unpublished. Carlisle, Penn., 1909–16.

"Polyphonic Craftsman, Coated like a Zebra, Fleeing like the Wild Ass, Mourning like a Dove,". RML, Series I, 1:01. Unpublished.

"All of It, as Recorded." RML, Series I, 1:01. Unpublished.

"'Am I a Brother to Dragons and a Companion to Owls?'" RML, Series I, 1:01. Unpublished. Carlisle, Penn., 1909–16.

"'And Shall Life Pass an Old Maid By?'" RML, Series I, 1:01. Unpublished.

"As You Know." RML, Series I, 1:01. Unpublished. Carlisle, Penn., 1909–16.

"The Assassins." RML, Series I, 1:01. Unpublished.

"Axiomatic." RML, Series I, 1:01. Unpublished.

"Reprobate Silver." RML, Series I, 1:01. Unpublished.

"The Candle-Stick Maker." RML, Series I, 1:01. Unpublished. Carlisle, Penn., 1909–16.

"'Coral-and-Brown' Admiring Herself in the Mirror." RML, Series I, 1:01. Unpublished. Carlisle, Penn., 1909–16.

"'Crepe Hanger?' He." RML, Series I, 1:01. Unpublished. Carlisle, Penn., 1909–16.

"To a Cantankerous Poet Ignoring His Compeers—Thomas Hardy, Bernard Shaw, Joseph Conrad, Henry James." RML, Series I, 1:01. Unpublished. Carlisle, Penn., 1909–16.

"The Fashion, Poor Lady, Behaving Like a Dungeon, Looking Like a Church." RML, Series I, 1:01. Unpublished. Carlisle, Penn., 1909–16.

"Flints, Not Flowers." RML, Series I, 1:01. Unpublished. Carlisle, Penn., 1909–16. Author's note:

> See *The Letters of George Meredith*, collected and edited by his son, in two volumes; Charles Scribner's Sons New York, 1912—page 280, Vol. I. "Hack:" A "well-horse everlastingly pulling up the same buckets full of a similar fluid": See Volume I, page 280 (to Admiral Maxse).

"The Grass That Perisheth." RML, Series I, 1:01. Unpublished. Carlisle, Penn., 1909–16.

"Guillemots." RML, Series I, 1:01. Unpublished. Carlisle, Penn., 1909–16.

"He Did Mend It. His Body Filled a Substantial Interstice." RML, Series I, 1:01. Unpublished. Carlisle, Penn., 1909–16.

" 'I Like a Horse but I Have a Fellow Feeling for a Mule.' " RML, Series I, 1:01. Unpublished. Carlisle, Penn., 1909–16.

"I Tell You No Lie." RML, Series I, 1:01. Unpublished. Carlisle, Penn., 1909–16.

"Ichabod." RML, Series I, 1:01. Unpublished. Carlisle, Penn., 1909–16.

"Inheritance." RML, Series I, 1:01. Unpublished. Carlisle, Penn., 1909–16.

" 'It Makes No Difference to Balbus Whether He Drinks Wine or Water.' " RML, Series I, 1:01. Unpublished.

Variant in file:

He Said

To me,
" 'It makes no difference to Balbus whether he
    Drinks wine or water.' Wine is nothing

But sour
Water. As for the Egyptian darkness of our
    Mental life, it is no detriment

To my
Happiness. It is well that a country so dry
    And hostile as this should be peopled

With friends
And that one should know under just what unlikely ends
    of the sparse foliage to look for them.

As it
Is unfortunate that the desert, and unfit
    Determinants of everyday life

Should hold
Us all hostages, and presumably unfold
    To us our eternal limitations."

"Kay Nielson in *Cinderella*." RML, Series I, 1:01. Unpublished.

"Kay Nielson's Little Green Patch in the Midst of the Forest." RML, Series I, 1:01. Unpublished. Note on manuscript:

Illustrating the text of Sir George Dasent's tales from the Norse, "East of the Sun and West of the Moon"

"A Lady with Pearls, to a Blood Red Rook from Turkey, Who Has Depicted Her with Pathos in Surly Monotone." RML, Series I, 1:01. Unpublished. Carlisle, Penn., 1909–16. The poet's note found on the manuscript of "A Lady with Pearls . . .":

> The Chicago Tribune remarks that the foreign posters are hawks for audacity, while ours are barnyard chickens by comparison and dead ones at that. (Some of the hawks have been fashioned by the hand of commerce, to the detriment, but they are still recognizable as birds of prey.)

"Light through a Keyhole." RML, Series I, 1:01. Unpublished.
"Like Bertram Dobell, You Achieve Distinction by Disclaiming It." RML, Series I, 1:01. Unpublished.
"Majestic Haystack." RML, Series I, 1:01. Unpublished.
"Man's Feet Are a Sensational Device." RML, Series I, 1:01. Unpublished.
"Patriotic Sentiment and the Maker." RML, Series I, 1:01. Unpublished.
"As Has Been Said." RML, Series I, 1:01. Unpublished.
"Rencontre." RML, Series I, 1:01. Unpublished.
"Rodin's *Penseur*." RML, Series I, 1:01. Unpublished.
"Suaviter in Modo." RML, Series I, 1:01. Unpublished. Carlisle, Penn., 1909–16.
"To See It Is to Know that Mendelssohn Would Never Do:" Ca. 1909–16. RML, Series I, 1:01. Unpublished.
"To Worldly Wisemen Recommending the Town of Carnal Policy as a Substitute for the Celestial City." RML, Series I, 1:01. Unpublished. Carlisle, Penn., 1909–16.
"God Bless You, Sir." RML, Series I, 1:01. Unpublished.
"We All Know It." RML, Series I, 1:01. Unpublished.
"Why That Question:". RML, Series I, 1:01. Unpublished. Carlisle, Penn., 1909–16.
"You Are Very Pensive—Hammering Out in Darkness What Will Not Bear the Light of Day." RML, Series I, 1:01. Unpublished.

Little Magazines, 1915–1919

"Ezra Pound:" Published posthumously in the *Marianne Moore Newsletter* 3, no. 2 (fall 1979): 5; RML. A study of the poem's origin (pp. 5–8) dates its composition to March 4, 1915.
"To a Man Working His Way Through the Crowd." *Egoist* 2 (April 1, 1915): 62.
"To the Soul of 'Progress.'" Later, "To Military Progress." First published in the *Egoist*, 2 (April 1, 1915): 62. *O, SP, COMP*. An early manuscript had as its title "To Art Wishing for a Fortress into Which She may Flee from her Persecutors, Instead of Looking for a Jail in Which to Confine Them:"
"Pouters and Fantails," including "That Harp You Play So Well," "To an Intra-Mural Rat," "Conseil to a Bachelor," "Appellate Jurisdiction," and "The Wizard in Words" ("Reticence and Volubility"). First published as a sequence in *Poetry* 6 (May 1915): 71–72. Accepted by *Poetry* in July 1914, "Pouters and Fantails" is the first of Marianne Moore's poetic sequences. Here it is presented as a sequence, although two of the poems were published separately in *Observations*. As "Concell to a Bachelor," the third

poem appeared in the *Lantern* 21 (1913): 106. Of these poems, only "Reticence and Volubility" and "To an Intra-Mural Rat" have been collected, both in *O*. Versions used here are from *Poetry* but for "The Wizard in Words," which is from *O*.

Poetry's version of "Counseil to a Bachelor" follows:

Concell to a Bachelor

If thou bee younge
Then marie not yett.
If thou bee olde,
Then no wyfe gett,
For younge men's wyves
Will not bee taught,
And olde men's wyves
Bee good for naught.
      Elizabethan trencher.

"To William Butler Yeats on Tagore." This, from the *Egoist* 2 (May 1, 1915): 77. *P*.

"The North Wind to a Dutiful Beast Midway Between the Dial and the Foot of a Garden Clock." *Lantern* 23 (1915): 17. Uncollected.

"Isaiah, Jeremiah, Ezekial, Daniel." *Lantern* 23 (1915): 60. Uncollected.

"To a Strategist." This, from *O*. First appearance ("To Disraeli on Conservatism"), *Lantern* 32 (1915): 60. Uncollected.

"Injudicious Gardening." This, from *O*, p. 14. First published as "To Browning" in the *Egoist* 2 (August 2, 1915): 126. *O, SP, CP, COMP*.

"To a Prize Bird." This, from *O*, p. 13. First published as "To Bernard Shaw: A Prize Bird" in the *Egoist* 2 (August 2, 1915), 126. *O, COMP*.

"Diligence Is to Magic as Progress Is to Flight." This, from *O*, p. 22. First published in the *Egoist* 2 (October 1, 1915): 158. *P, O*.

"To a Steam Roller." This, from *O*, p. 21. First published in the *Egoist* 2 (October 1, 1915): 158. *P, O, SP, CP, COMP*.

"To Statecraft Embalmed." First published in *Others* 1, no. 6 (December 1915): 104. *O, SP, CP, COMP*.

"To a Friend in the Making." *Others* 1, no. 6 (December 1915): 105. Uncollected.

"Blake." *Others* 1, no. 6 (December 1915): 105. Uncollected.

"George Moore." This, from *O*, p. 25. First published in *Others* 1, no. 6 (December 1915): 105–6.

Variant in file:

George Moore

In speaking of "aspiration,"
    From the recesses of a pen more dolorous than blackness itself,
  Were you presenting us with one more form of imperturbable French drollery.
      Or was it self directed banter?
      What whim, familiarly
          Took from you, your invisible hot helmet of anaemia

And then replenished your " 'little glass' " from the decanter
　　　Of a transparent-murky, would-be-truthful "Hobohemia"?
　The strains of oddity
　Went down, drained by that swift supplanter
Of strong heads—the spirit of good narrative—and you've delineated briefly
The predicament: you have known beauty other than that of styes, on
Which to fix your admiration.

"The Past Is the Present." This. *COMP.* As *"So far as the future is concerned . . ."* in Others I, no. 6 (December 1915): 106. *O, SP, CP.* Note early syllabic pattern, 9-6-6-15-15 in first printed version:

　　So far as the future is concerned,
　"Shall we not say, with the Russian philosopher,
　　'How is one to know what one doesn't know?'"
　　So far as the present is concerned,

"Masks" ("A Fool, A Foul Thing, A Distressful Lunatic"). *Contemporary Verse* I (January 1916): 6. Uncollected.

"Diogenes." *Contemporary Verse* I (January 1916): 6. Uncollected. Ashtaroth (Astarte), ancient Syrian and Phoenician goddess of love and fertility. Uncollected.

"Sun." This, from *COMP*, p. 234. "Sun" ("Fear Is Hope," " 'Sun,' " " 'Sun!' " "Sun,") was first published as "Fear is Hope" in *Contemporary Verse* I, no. 7 (January 1916), and has evolved through eight published revisions. It has had a fifty-one-year life span of revision, settling in the poet's seventy-ninth year.

The following version of "Fear Is Hope" is from *O*, p. 15. Note that in the later versions, the typography has been changed to an hourglass.

Fear Is Hope

"No man may him hyde
From Deth holow eyed."
　　For us two spirits this shall not suffice,
　　　To whom you are symbolic of a plan
　　　Concealed within the heart of man.
　　　　Splendid with splendor hid you come, from your Arab abode,
　　　　An incandescence smothered in the hand of an astrologer
　　　　　who rode
　　Before you, Sun—whom you outran,
　　Piercing his caravan.

Sun, you shall stay
With us. Holiday
　　And day of wrath shall be as one, wound in a device
　　　Of Moorish gorgeousness, round glasses spun
　　　To flame as hemispheres of one
　　　　Great hourglass dwindling to a stem. Consume hostility;
　　　　Employ your weapons in this meeting place of surging enmity,
　　Insurgent feet shall not outrun
　　Multiplied flames, O Sun.

"'He Wrote the History Book.'" This, from *O*, p. 34. First appearance: *Egoist* 3 (May 1, 1916): 71. *P, O, SP, CP, COMP*.

"To a Chameleon." This, from *COMP*, p. 179. First published as "You Are Like the Realistic Product of an Idealistic Search for Gold at the Foot of the Rainbow," the *Egoist* 3 (May 1, 1916): 71. *P, O, OBD, MMR, A, COMP*.

"Is Your Town Nineveh?" This, from *O*, p. 17. First published in the *Lantern* 24 (1916): 59. The allusion is to Jonah, 5. *P* (stanzaic), *O* (free), *SP* (free); *COMP* (free).

"You are Fire Eaters." *Lantern* 24 (1916): 59. Uncollected. The allusion is to II Chronicles 20:15.

"Pedantic Literalist." This, from *COMP*, p. 37. First published in the *Egoist* 3 (June 1, 1916): 96. *P, O, SP, CP, COMP*.

"Critics and Connoisseurs." This, from *COMP*, p. 35–36. First published in *Others* 3 (July 1916): 4. *O, SP, CP, MM, COMP*.

"In This Age of Hard Trying, Nonchalance Is Good And." This, from *COMP*, p. 34. First published in *Chimaera* 1, no. 2 (July 1916): 52, 55. *P, O, SP, CP, COMP*.

"To Be Liked by You Would Be a Calamity." This, from *O*, p. 37. First published in *Chimaera* 1, no. 2 (July 1916): 56.

"Feed Me, Also, River God." *Egoist* 3 (August 1916): 118. *P*.

"Apropos of Mice." *Bruno's Weekly* 3 (October 7, 1916), 1137. Uncollected.

"'She Trimmed the Candles Like One Who Loves the Beautiful.'" RML, Series I, 1:01. Dated November 23, 1916. Unpublished.

"In 'Designing a Cloak to Cloak His Designs,' You Wrested from Oblivion, a Coat of Immortality for Your Own Use." *Bruno's Weekly* 3 (December 30, 1916): 1233. Uncollected.

"Holes Bored in a Workbag by the Scissors." *Bruno's Weekly* 3 (October 7, 1916): 1137. Uncollected.

"The Just Man And." *Bruno's Weekly* 3 (December 30, 1916): 1223. Uncollected.

"Those Various Scalpels." This, from *COMP*, pp. 51–52. First publication, *Lantern* 25 (1917): 50–51. *P, O, SP, CP*.

"Like a Bulrush." This, from *O*, p. 38. First publication, *Others*, 1917, p. 76. *O, P, SP*.

"To the Peacock of France" ("French Peacock"). This, from *COMP*, p. 87. First publication, *Others*, 1917, p. 77. *O, SP, CP, COMP*.

"Sojourn in the Whale." This, from *COMP*, p. 90. First published, *Others*, 1917, p. 78. *O, SP, P, COMP*.

"Roses Only." This, from *SP*, 42. First publication, *Others*, 1917, pp. 80–81. *P, O, SP*.

"The Monkeys" ("My Apish Cousins"). This, from *COMP*, p. 40. First publication, *Others*, 1917, p. 76. *P, O, SP, CP, COMP*.

"Melanchthon" ("Black Earth"). This, from *CP*, p. 45. First publication, *Egoist* 4 (April 1918): 55–56. *P, O, SP, CP*.

"An Ardent Platonist." *Lantern* 26 (1918): 22. Uncollected.

"Reinforcements." This, from the *Egoist* 5 (August 1918): 83. *P, O*.

"The Fish." This, from *COMP*, p. 32. First publication, *Egoist* 5 (August 1918): 95.

"Callot-Drecol-Cheruit-Jenny-Doucet-Aviotte-Lady." RML, Series I, 1:01. Dated November 26, 1918. Unpublished.

"You Say You Said." *Little Review* 5, no. 8 (December 1918): 21. Uncollected.

"Old Tiger." This, RML, Series I, 1:01. First publication: *Profile: An Anthology Collected in MCMXXXI*, ed. Ezra Pound (Milan: John Scheiwiller, 1932), pp. 61–64. Although the poem was not published in a journal until 1932, and was never collected, excerpts from it appeared in letters Moore exchanged with Ezra Pound in the winter of 1918–19. His suggested revisions embodied principles—the best word, lowered caps, naturalness, precision—that remained important to Moore throughout her writing career. The poem, like others of the period, including "Critics and Connoisseurs" and "Melanchthon," is built on the "intellectual, argumentative evolution" that Sir Herbert Grierson admired in the poems of Donne. Uncollected.

"Radical." *Others* 5 (July 1919): 5.

"Poetry." The version I have chosen for this edition is in the author's notes to the *Complete Poems*, given so that "the serious reader may look it up" (pp. 266–67). In *SP* (1935), there are no quotation marks around the famous phrase "imaginary gardens with real toads in them." This is significant especially because Patricia Willis, while at the Rosenbach Museum and Library, organized a contest to identify the quotation. The mystery was never solved.

First publication, *Others* 5 (July 1919): 5. Apart from collected editions, this poem has been reprinted twenty-seven times, and some are variants. *P, O, SP, MMR, CP, COMP*. The author's last revision, appearing in *COMP* to the devastation of many readers, goes as follows:

Poetry

I, too, dislike it.
    Reading it, however, with a perfect contempt for it, one discovers in
    it, after all, a place for the genuine.

Here are additional variants of "Poetry":

Poetry

I, too, dislike it:
there are things that are important beyond all this fiddle.
The bat, upside down; the elephant pushing,
a tireless wolf under a tree,
the base-ball fan, the statistician—
"business documents and schoolbooks"—
these phenomena are pleasing,
but when they have been fashioned
into that which is unknowable,
we are not entertained.
It may be said of all of us
that we do not admire what we cannot understand;
enigmas are not poetry.

                    —*Observations*, 2d ed. (New York: Dial, 1925)

Poetry

I, too, dislike it: there are things that are important beyond all this fiddle.
    Reading it, however, with a perfect contempt for it, one discovers in
    it after all, a place for the genuine.
        Hands that can grasp, eyes

      that can dilate, hair that can rise
         if it must, these things are important not because a

high-sounding interpretation can be put upon them but because they are
      useful. When they become so derivative as to become unintelligible,
        the same thing may be said for all of us, that we
           do not admire what
           we cannot understand: the bat
             holding on upside down or in quest of something to

eat, elephants pushing, a wild horse taking a roll, a tireless wolf under
      a tree, the immovable critic twitching his skin like a horse that feels a flea, the base-
      ball fan. the statistician—
        nor is it valid
          to discriminate against "business documents and

school-books"; all these phenomena are important. One must make a distinction
      however: when dragged into prominence by half poets, the result is not poetry,
      nor till the poets among us can be
        "literalists of
        the imagination"—above
          insolence and triviality and can present

for inspection, "imaginary gardens with real toads in them," shall we have
      it. In the meantime, if you demand on the one hand,
      the raw material of poetry in
        all its rawness and
        that which is on the other hand
          genuine, you are interested in poetry.

                                       —CP

"In the Days of Prismatic Color." This, from *COMP*, 41. First published in the *Lantern*, 27 (1919), 35. *P, O, SP, COMP*.

"Dock Rats." This, from *O*. First published in *Others for 1919*, ed. Alfred Kreymbourg (New York: Nicholas I. Brown, 1920), pp. 127–28.

"Picking and Choosing." This, *CP*. First publication, *Dial* 68 (April 1920): 421–22. *P, O, SP, CP, COMP*. In *P*, "Peter," "Picking and Choosing," "When I Buy Pictures," and "A Graveyard" have stanzaic versions. The freer version in *COMP* follows:

Picking and Choosing

Literature is a phase of life. If one is afraid of it,
the situation is irremediable; if one approaches it familiarly,
what one says of it is worthless.
The opaque allusion, the simulated flight upward,
accomplishes nothing. Why cloud the fact
that Shaw is self-conscious in the field of sentiment
but is otherwise rewarding; that James
is all that has been said of him. It is not Hardy the novelist
and Hardy the poet, but one man interpreting life as emotion.

The critic should know what he likes:
Gordon Craig with his "this is I" and "this is mine,"
with his three wise men, his "sad French greens" and his "Chinese cherry"
Gordon Craig, so inclinational and unashamed—a critic.
And Burke is a psychologist, of raccoon-like curiosity.
Summa Diligentia; to the humbug, whose name is so amusing—
very young and very rushed, Caesar crossed the Alps
on the top of a *"diligence"*!
We are not daft about the meaning,
but this familiarity with wrong meanings puzzles one.
Humming-bug, the candles are not wired for electricity.
Small dog, going over the lawn nipping the linen and saying
that you have a badger—remember Xenophon;
only rudimentary behavior is necessary to put us on the scent.
"A right good salvo of barks," a few strong wrinkles puckering the skin between the
ears, is all we ask.

The *Dial* Years, 1920–1925

"England." This, from *P*. First publication, *Dial* 68 (April 1920): 422–23. *P, O, SP, CP, COMP.*

"Lines on a Visit of Anne Carroll Moore to Hudson Park Branch." Quoted in a feature article about the library's fiftieth birthday celebration in the *Villager* 23, no. 42 (January 19, 1956): 16. Marianne Moore wrote this poem in March 1921, while working at the library. Here's what her mother had to say about the poem, in a letter to Moore's brother, John Warner Moore: "Rat [Marianne] doesn't admire Miss Moore, and grits his teeth over flattery—so was more than dour with the fear of being fulsome. I think he steered the narrows very well." Uncollected.

"When I Buy Pictures." This, from *CP*, p. 59. First publication, *Dial* 71 (July 1921): 33. *P, O, CP.* Stanzaic version in *P*:

When I Buy Pictures

or what is closer to the truth, when I look at
    that of which I may regard myself as the
        imaginary possessor, I fix upon that which would
    give me pleasure in my average moments: the satire upon curiosity
            in which no more is discernible than the intensity of the mood;

or quite the opposite—the old thing, the medieval decorated hat-box, in which there
        are hounds with waists diminishing like the waist of the hour-glass,
    and deer, both white and brown, and birds and seated people; it may be no more
                                                                        than a square
        of parquetry; the literal biography perhaps, in letters stand-

ing well apart upon a parchment-like expanse; or that which is better without words,
                                                                        which means
        just as much or just as little as it is understood to

mean by the observer—the grave of Adam, prefigured by himself; a bed of beans
　　or artichokes in six varieties of blue; the snipe-legged hiero-

glyphic in three parts; it may be anything. Too stern an
　　　intellectual emphasis, ironic or other—upon this quality or that, detracts
　　from one's enjoyment; it must not wish to disarm anything;
　　　　nor may the approved triumph easily be honoured—that
　　　　　which is great because something else is small.

It comes to this: of whatever sort it is, it must make known the fact that it has been
　　　　　　　　　　　　　　　　　　　　　　　　　　　　　displayed
　　　　to acknowledge the spiritual forces which have made it;
　　　and it must admit that it is the work of X, if X produced it; of Y, if made
　　　　by Y. It must be a voluntary gift with the name written on it.

"A Grave" ("A Graveyard"). This, from *COMP*. First publication, *Dial* 71 (July 1921): 34.
　　O, SP, CP, MMR, COMP.
"New York." This, from *COMP*. First publication, *Dial* 71 (December 1921): 637. *O, SP,*
　　CP, MMR, COMP.
"The Labors of Hercules." This, from *COMP*, p. 53–54. First publication, *Dial* 71 (De-
　　cember 1921): 637–38. *O, SP, CP, COMP*.

The first version from the *Dial* follows:

The Labors of Hercules

To popularize the mule, its neat exterior
expressing the principle of accommodation reduced to a minimum:
to persuade one of austere taste, proud in the possession of home, and a musician—
that the piano is a free field for etching; that his "charming tadpole notes"
belong to the past when one had time to play them:
to persuade those self-wrought Midases of brains
whose fourteen-karat ignorance aspires to rise in value
"till the sky is the limit,"
that excessive conduct augurs disappointment,
that one must not borrow a long white beard and tie it on
and threaten with the scythe of time, the casually curious:
to teach the bard with too elastic a selectiveness
that one detects creative power by its capacity to conquer one's detachment,
that while it may have more elasticity than logic,
it knows where it is going;
it flies along in a straight line like electricity
depopulating areas that boast of their remoteness,
to prove to the high priests of caste
that snobbishness is a stupidity,
the best side out, of age-old toadyism,
kissing the feet of the man above,
kicking the face of the man below;

to teach the patron-saints-to-atheists, the Coliseum
meet-me-alone-by-moonlight maudlin troubadour
that kickups for catstrings are not for life
nor yet appropriate to death—that we are sick of the earth,
sick of the pig-sty, wild geese and wild men;
to convince snake-charming controversialists
that it is one thing to change one's mind,
another to eradicate it—that one keeps on knowing
"that the negro is not brutal,
that the Jew is not greedy,
that the Oriental is not immoral,
that the German is not a Hun."

"Snakes, Mongooses, Snake-Charmers, and the Like." This, from *COMP*, p. 58. First
     publication, *Broom* 1 (January 1922): 193. *O, SP, CP, COMP.*
"People's Surroundings." This, from *COMP*, pp. 55–57. First publication, *Dial* 72 (June
     1922): 588–90. *O, SP, CP, COMP.*
"Novices." This, from *COMP*, pp. 60–61. First publication, *Dial* 74 (February 1923):
     183–84. *O, SP, CP, COMP.*
"Bowls." This, from *COMP*, p. 59. First publication, *Secession* 5 (July 1923): 12. *O, SP, CP,
     COMP.*
"Marriage." This, from *COMP*, pp. 62–70. First publication, *Maniken, Number Three*
     (New York: Monroe Wheeler, 1923). *O, SP, CP, MM, COMP.*

Undated version found in file:

Marriage

This institution out of respect for which one says one need not
     change one's mind about a thing one has believed in,
requiring public promises of one's intention to fulfill a private obligation—
I wonder what Adam and Eve think of it by this time:
this firegilt steel alive with goldenness; how bright it shows—
"of circular traditions and impostures, committing many spoils,"
requiring all one's criminal ingenuity to avoid:
Psychology which explains everything explains nothing and we are still in doubt.
Eve: beautiful woman—
I have seen her when she was so handsome she gave me a start,
able to write simultaneously in three languages—English, German
               and French and talk in the meantime.

"Silence." This, from *COMP*, p. 91. First publication, *Dial* 77 (October 1924): 290. *O,
     SP, CP, MM, COMP.*
"Sea Unicorns and Land Unicorns." This, from *COMP*, 77–79. First publication, *Dial* 77
     (November 1924): 411–13. *O, SP, CP, COMP.*
"An Octopus." This, from *COMP*, pp. 71–76. First publication, *Dial* 77 (December
     1924): 475–81. *O, SP, CP, COMP.*

"An Egyptian Pulled Glass Bottle in the Shape of a Fish." This, from *O*, p. 20. *O, SP, CP, MMR, COMP*. It has been pointed out that the poem depends for all but the title and the last two lines on one she wrote in Carlisle in 1915, "In Einar Jonsson's 'Cow,'" *Marianne Moore Newsletter* 2, no. 2 (spring 1978): 9–12. The full text reads:

Here we have thirst,
And patience from the first,
    And art—as in a wave held up for us to see—
    In its essential perpendicularity:

Not chilly but
Intense. The spectrum's cut
    Out of the body of the world, laid on its back
    And made subordinate. We recognize no lack.

"To a Snail." This, from *O*, p. 23. First publication, *COMP*, p. 85. "Compression is the first grace of style": Democritus. "A knowledge of principles": Duns Scotus. *O, SP, CP, COMP*.

"'The Bricks Are Fallen Down, We Will Build with Hewn Stones. The Sycamores Are Cut Down, We Will Change to Cedars.'" *O*, p. 24. Title: Isaiah 9:10.

"'Nothing Will Cure the Sick Lion but to Eat an Ape.'" This, from *O*, p. 26. *O, SP, CP, COMP*.

"Peter." This, *O*, p. 51. Like "Picking and Choosing," "Peter" was revised extensively for *COMP* from the syllabic stanzaic pattern used frequently in poems of the period. In 1967, the author said she revised "Peter" after "I realized that the spoken word is different from the one on the page." *O, SP, CP, COMP*. The version in *COMP* follows:

Peter

      Strong and slippery,
built for the midnight grass-party
confronted by four cats, he sleeps his time away—
the detached first claw on the foreleg corresponding
to the thumb, retracted to its tip; the small tuft of fronds
or katydid-legs above each eye still numbering all units
in each group; the shadbones regularly set about his mouth
to droop or rise in unison like the porcupine's quills.
He lets himself be flattened out by gravity,
as seaweed is tamed and weakened by the sun,
compelled when extended, to lie stationary.
Sleep is the result of his delusion that one must
do as well as one can for oneself,
sleep—epitome of what is to him the end of life.
Demonstrate on him how the lady placed a forked stick
on the innocuous neck-sides of the dangerous southern snake.
One need not try to stir him up; his prune shaped head
and alligator-eyes are not party to the joke.
Lifted and handled, he may be dangled like an eel

or set up on the forearm like a mouse;
his eyes bisected by pupils of a pin's width,
are flickeringly exhibited, then covered up.
May be? I should have said might have been;
when he has been got the better of in a dream—
as in a fight with nature or with cats, we all know it.
Profound sleep is not with him a fixed illusion.
Springing about with froglike accuracy, with jerky cries
when taken in the hand, he is himself again;
to sit caged by the rungs of a domestic chair
would be unprofitable—human. What is the good of hypocrisy?
It is permissible to choose one's employment,
to abandon the wire nail, or roly-poly,
when it shows signs of being no longer a pleasure,
to score the adjacent magazine with a double line of strokes.
He can talk, but insolently says nothing. What of it?
When one is frank, one's very presence is a compliment.
It is clear that he can see the virtue of naturalness,
that he is one of those who do not regard the published fact as a surrender.
As for the disposition invariably to affront,
an animal with claws should have to use them;
The eel-like extension of trunk into tail is not an accident.
To leap, to lengthen out, divide the air, to purloin, to pursue,
To tell the hen: fly over the fence, go in the wrong way
in your perturbation—this is life;
to do less would be nothing but dishonesty.

"The Monkey Puzzle" ("The Monkey Puzzler.") This, from *COMP*. First publication,
    Dial 78 (January 1925): 8. *SP*, *O* (1925 edition), *CP*, *COMP*.
Compare with these versions, c. 1909–16:

Garter Snake—

Thin like a rail and harmless, with
    That "music on your tongue which is speech—"
        I am at a loss to know how you should
            Have come to this part of the earth;
To account for your origin
    At all: You were born in Ireland? How
        Can that be? There are no snakes there; but
            "We prove, we do not explain our birth."

Eloquence

A species of basilisk, with
"That music on your tongue which is speech."
One is at a loss to know how you should
        Have come to this part of the earth—

To account for your origin
At all. Born upon a great estate
In Ireland! There are no snakes there; but
> We prove, we do not explain our birth.

—RML, series I, 1:01

"A Fool, a Foul Thing, A Distressful Lunatic." *O*, p. 18.

Lyrics and Sequences: 1926–1940

"The Steeple-Jack," "The Student," "The Hero." "Part of a Novel, Part of a Poem, Part of a Play." Versions here follow the order in *Poetry* 40, 3 (June 1932): 119–28, but are from *CP* ("The Steeple-Jack" and "The Hero") and *COMP* ("The Student"). Marianne Moore had a predilection for sequences, though sometimes she reprinted individual poems separately. In *SP* (1935) and in *CP* (1951), "The Steeple-Jack" is followed by "The Hero," and not on a separate page, but "The Student" is omitted. In *MMR* (1961), the collective title, "The Hero," and "The Student" are omitted. In *COMP* (1967–81), the collective title is omitted and "The Hero" follows "The Steeple-Jack," but on a separate page. "The Student" is included, but follows much later in the edition. "The Steeple-Jack" is published as the first poem of every edition in which it appears. Although the line, "Revised, 1961," appears in *MMR* and *COMP*, many of the "new" lines are actually taken from *SP* (1935). *CP* (1951) represents the most dramatic revision of "The Steeple-Jack," and the 1961 version is more of a restoration of the *SP* version. "The Steeple-Jack," *SP, CP, MMR, COMP.* "The Student," *W, COMP.* "The Hero," *CP, COMP.*

The sequence originally appeared this way, as "Part of a Novel, Part of a Poem, Part of a Play," in *Poetry* 40, 3 (June 1932): 119–28.

Part of a Novel, Part of a Poem, Part of a Play

The Steeple-Jack

Dürer would have seen a reason for living
> in a town like this, with eight stranded whales
to look at; with the sweet sea air coming into your house
on a fine day, from water etched
> with waves as formal as the scales
on a fish.

One by one, in two's, in three's, the seagulls keep
> flying back and forth over the town clock,
or sailing around the lighthouse without moving the wings—
rising steadily with a slight
> quiver of the body—or flock
mewing where

a sea the purple of the peacock's neck is
> paled to greenish azure as Dürer changed
the pine green of the Tyrol to peacock blue and guinea

grey. You can see a twenty-five-
    pound lobster and fish-nets arranged
to dry. The

whirlwind fife-and-drum of the storm bends the salt
    marsh grass, disturbs stars in the sky and the
star on the steeple; it is a privilege to see so
much confusion. Disguised by what
    might seem austerity, the sea-
side flowers and

trees are favored by the fog so that you have
    the tropics at first hand; the trumpet-vine,
fox-glove, giant snap-dragon, a salpaglossis that has
spots and stripes; morning-glories, gourds,
    or moon-vines trained on fishing-twine
at the back

door; cat-tails, flags, blueberries and spiderwort,
    striped grass, lichens, sunflowers, asters, daisies—
the yellow and the crab-claw blue ones with green bracts—toad-plant,
petunias, ferns; pink lilies, blue
    ones, tigers; poppies; black sweet-peas.
The climate

is not right for the banyan, frangipan, the
    jack-fruit tree; nor for exotic serpent
life. Ring lizard and snake-skin for the foot if you see fit,
but here they've cats not cobras to
    keep down the rats. The diffident
little newt

with white pin-dots on black horizontal spaced
    out bands lives here; yet there is nothing that
ambition can buy or take away. The college student
named Ambrose sits on the hill-side
    with his not-native books and hat
and sees boats

at sea progress white and rigid as if in
    a groove. Liking an elegance of which
the source is not bravado, he knows by heart the antique
sugar-bowl shaped summer-house of
    interlacing slats, and the pitch
of the church

spire, not true, from which a man in scarlet lets
    down a rope as a spider spins a thread;
he might be part of a novel, but on the sidewalk a
sign says C. J. Poole, Steeple-jack,

in black and white; and one in red
and white says

Danger. The church portico has four fluted
    columns, each a single piece of stone, made
modester by white-wash. This would be a fit haven for
waifs, children, animals, prisoners,
    and presidents who have repaid
sin-driven

senators by not thinking about them. There
    are a school-house, a post-office in a
store, fish-houses, hen-houses, a three-masted schooner on
the stocks. The hero, the student,
    the steeple-jack, each in his way,
is at home.

It could not be dangerous to be living
    in a town like this, of simple people,
who have a steeple-jack placing danger signs by the church
while he is gilding the solid-
    pointed star, which on a steeple
stands for hope.

The Student

"In America everybody must have a degree," the French man
says, "but the French do not think that all can have it; they don't
    say everyone must go to college." We
    may feel as he says we do; five kinds of superiority

might be unattainable by all, but one degree is not too much.
In each school there is a pair of fruit-trees like that twin tree
    in every other school: tree-of-knowledge—
    tree-of-life—each with a label like that of the other college:

lux, or *lux et veritas, Christo et ecclesiae, sapiet
felici,* and if science confers immortality,
    these apple-trees should be for everyone.
    Oriental arbor vitae we say lightly. Yet you pardon

it as when one thinking of the navy does not know not to infer
dishonorable discharge from a D. D. It is a
    thoughtful pupil has two thoughts for the word
    valet; or for bachelor, child, damsel; though no one having heard

them used as terms of chivalry would make the mediaeval use of
them. Secluded from domestic strife, Jack Bookworm led a
    college life says Goldsmith. He might not say
    it of the student who shows interest in the stranger's resumé

by asking "when will your experiment be finished, Doctor Einstein?"
and is pleased when Doctor Einstein smiles and says politely
   "science is never finished." But we're not
   hypocrites, we're rustics. The football huddle in the vacant lot

is impersonating calculus and physics and military
books; and is gathering the data for genetics. If
   scholarship would profit by it, sixteen
   foot men should be grown; it's for the football men to say. We must lean

on their experience. There is vitality in the world of sport.
If it is not the tree of knowledge, it's the tree of life.
   When Audubon adopted us he taught
   us how to dance. It was the great crab-flounder of Montana caught

and changed from that which creeps to that which is angelic. He taught us how
to turn as the airport wind-sock turns without an error;
   like Alligator, Downpour, Dynamite,
   and Wotan, gliding round the course in a fast neat school, with the white

of the eye showing; or as sea-lions keep going round and round the
pool. But there is more to learn—the difference between cow
   and zebu; lion, tiger; barred and brown
   owls; horned owls have one ear that opens up and one that opens down.

The golden eagle is the one with feathered legs. The penguin wing is
ancient, not degenerate. Swordfish are different from
   gars, if one may speak of gars when the big
   gamehunters are using the fastidious singular—say pig,

and that they have seen camelsparrow, tigerhorse, rat, mouse, butterfly,
snake, elephant, fruit-bat, et cet'ra. No fact of science—
   theology or biology—might
   not as well be known; one does not care to hold opinions that fright

could dislocate. Education augments our natural forces and
prompts us to extend the machinery of advantage
   to those who are without it. One fitted
   to be a scholar must have the heroic mind, Emerson said.

The student concentrates and does not like to fight; "gives his opinion
firmly and rests on it"—in the manner of the poet;
   is reclusive, and reserved; and has such
   ways, not because he has no feeling but because he has so much.

Boasting provokes jibes, and in this country we've no cause to boast; we are
as a nation perhaps, undergraduates not students.
   But anyone who studies will advance.
     Are we to grow up or not? They are not all college boys in France.

The Hero

Where there is personal liking we go.
    Where the ground is sour; where there are
    weeds of beanstalk height,
    snakes' hypodermic teeth, or
    the wind brings the "scarebabe voice"
    from the neglected yew set with
    the semi-precious cats' eyes of the owl—
awake, asleep, "raised ears extended to fine points," and so
on—love won't grow.

We do not like some things and the hero
    doesn't; deviating head-stones
    and uncertainty;
    going where one does not wish
    to go; suffering and not
    saying so; standing and listening where something
    is hiding. The hero shrinks
as what it is flies out on muffled wings, with twin yellow
eyes—to and fro—

with quavering water-whistle note, low,
    high, in bass-falsetto chirps
    until the skin creeps.
    Jacob when a-dying, asked
    Joseph: Who are these? and blessed
    both sons, the younger most, vexing Joseph. And
    Joseph was vexing to some.
Cincinnatus was; Regulus; and some of our fellow
men have been, although devout,

like Pilgrim having to go slow
    to find his roll; tired but hopeful—
    hope not being hope
    until all ground for hope has
    vanished; and lenient, looking
    upon a fellow creature's error with the
    feelings of a mother—a
    woman or a cat. The decorous frock-coated Negro
by the grotto

answers the fearless sightseeing hobo
    who asks the man she's with, what's this,
    what's that, where's Martha
    buried, "Gen-ral Washington
    there; his lady, here"; speaking
    as if in a play—not seeing her; with a
    sense of human dignity

and reverence for mystery, standing like the shadow
of the willow.

Moses would not be grandson to Pharaoh.
    It is not what I eat that is
    my natural meat,
    the hero says. He's not out
    seeing a sight but the rock
    crystal thing to see—the startling El Greco
    brimming with inner light—that
covets nothing that it has let go. This then you may know
as the hero.

"No Swan So Fine." This, *COMP*, 19. First published in *Poetry* 41 (October 1932): 7. *SP, CP, COMP*.

"The Jerboa." This, *COMP*, pp. 10–15. First publication, *Hound and Horn* 6 (October–December 1932): 108–13. *SP, CP, COMP*.

"To Peace." June 30, 1933. ("To Peace" was found typed on the reverse side of Beethoven's "Ode to Joy." Also typed there was "To peace/Schiller, tr by Henry G. Chapman," acknowledging Friedrich Schiller's poem. The poet also referred to a hymn contest to *"emphasize International Co-operation,"* and not to exceed three verses, sponsored by the League of Nations Association.) Unpublished, uncollected. RML, Series 1.

"The Plumet Basilisk." This, *COMP*, pp. 20–24. First publication, *Hound and Horn* 7 (October–December 1933): 29–34. *SP, CP, COMP*.

"Camellia Sabina." This, *COMP*, pp. 16–18. First publication, *Active Anthology*, ed. Ezra Pound (London: Faber & Faber, 1933): 189–91. *SP, CP, COMP*.

"The Frigate Pelican." This, *COMP Criterion* 12 (July 1934): 557–60. This, *Complete Poems*, pp. 25–26. *SP, CP, COMP*.

"Imperial Ox, Imperial Dish."
    "The Buffalo" and "Nine Nectarines and Other Porcelain" comprise the sequence called "Imperious Ox, Imperial Dish," first seen in *Poetry* 45 (November 1934): 61–67. Both poems presented here are from *COMP*, pp. 29–30 and pp. 61–64, respectively. "The Buffalo," *SP, CP, MMR, COMP*. "Nine Nectarines," *SP, CP, MM, COMP*.

"Pigeons." *Poetry* 47 (November 1935): 61–63. Uncollected.

The following five poems—"Virginia Britannia," "Bird-Witted," "Half Deity," "Smooth Gnarled Crape Myrtle," and "The Pangolin"—were presented as a sequence, "The Old Dominion," in *PAN*. "Virginia Britannia," which appears in the main text from *COMP*, pp. 107–11, was first published in *Life and Letters Today* 13 (December 1935): 66–70. *PAN, W, CP, COMP*. "Bird-Witted," which appears in the main text from *COMP*, pp. 105–6, was first in the *New Republic* 85 (January 22, 1936): 311. *PAN, W, CP, MMR, COMP*. "Half Deity," which appears in the main text from *W*, pp. 17–19, was first in *Direction* 1 (January–March 1935): 74–75. *Pan, W*. "Smooth Gnarled Crape Myrtle," which appears in the main text from *COMP*, pp. 103–4, was first published in *New English Weekly* 8 (October 17, 1935): 13. *PAN, W, CP, MMR, COMP*. "The Pangolin," which appears in the main text from *COMP*, pp. 116–20, appears with the sequence for the first time. *PAN, W, MMR, COMP*.

Here is the sequence, "Old Dominion," from *PAN:*

Virginia Britannia

Pale sand edges England's old
dominion. The air is soft, warm, hot,
    above the cedar-dotted emerald shore
known to the redbird,
    the redcoated muskateer,
    the trumpet-flower, the cavalier,
the parson, and the
    wild parishioner. A deer-
track in a church-floor
brick and Sir George Yeardlery's
coffin-tacks and tombs remain.
The now tremendous vine-en-
compassed hackberry,
       starred with the ivy-flower,
       shades the church tower.
And "a great sinner lyeth here" under
    the sycamore.
A fritillary zigzags
toward the seemly resting-place of this
    unusual man and pleasing sinner who
"waits for a joyful
       resurrection." We-re-wo-
       comoco's fur crown could be no
odder than we were
    with ostrich, Latin motto,
    and small gold horse-shoe,
as arms for an able
sting-ray-hampered pioneer,
painted as a Turk it seems,
the incessantly
       exciting Captain Smith
       who patient with
his inferiors, was a pugnacious
    equal; and to

Powhattan obliged, but not
a flatterer. Rare Indian, crowned by
    Christopher Newport! The Old Dominion has
all-green grass-hoppers
       in all-green, box-sculptured grounds;
       an almost English green surrounds
them. Care has formed a-
       mong un-English insect sounds,
    the white wall-rose. As

thick as Daniel Boone's grape-
vine, the stem has wide-spaced great
blunt alternating ostrich-
skin warts that were thorns.
        Care has formed walls of yew
        since Indians knew
the Fort Old Field and narrow neck of land
    that Jamestown was.

Observe the terse Virginian,
the mettlesome gray one that drives the
    owl from tree to tree and imitates the call
of whippoorwill or
        lark or katydid—the lead-
        gray lead-legged mocking-bird with head
held half way, and
            meditative eye as dead
    as sculptured marble
eye, alighting noiseless,
musing in the semi-sun,
standing on tall thin legs as
if he did not see,
        conspicuous, alone,
        on the stone-
topped table with lead cupids grouped to form
    the pedestal.

Narrow herring-bone-laid bricks,
a dusty pink beside the dwarf box-
    bordered pansies, share the ivy-arbor shade
with cemetery
        lace settees, one at each side,
        and with the bird: box-bordered tide-
water gigantic
        jet black pansies (splendor; pride;)
    not for a decade
dressed, but for a day, in
over-powering velvet; and
gray-blue-Andalusian
cock-feather pale ones
            ink-lined on the edge, fur-
            eyed, with ochre
on the cheek. The slowmoving glossy, tall
    quick cavalcade

of buckeye-brown surprising
jumpers, the contrasting work-mule and
    show-mule & witch-cross door & "strong sweet prison"

are a part of what
         has come about—in the Black
         idiom—from advancing back-
ward in a circle;
         from taking the Potomac
    cowbirdlike; and on
the Chickahominy
establishing the Negro, opportunely bought, to strength-
en protest against
         tyranny. Rare unscent-
         ed, provident-
ly hot, too sweet, inconsistent flower-bed!
    Old Dominion

earth makes sunflower-heads grow large;
hibiscus and so-called mimosa
    close at night; scarlet peculiarly-quilled
pomegranate petals,
         the African violet,
         and camellia, perfumeless. Yet
house-high glistening green
         magnolia trees with velvet-
    textured flower, are filled
with anaesthetic scent
enough to make one die; as
the gardenia is, though its
two-toned green-furled buds
         and dark leaf-vein on green-
         er leaf when seen
against the light attract no pigmy beeds
    such as the frilled

silk substanceless faint flower of
the crape-myrtle does. Old Pamunkey
princess, birdclaw-earringed; with a pet raccoon
from the Mattapo-
         ni (what a bear!). Feminine
         odd Indian young lady! Odd thin-
gauze-and-taffeta-
         dressed English one! Terrapin
    meat and crested spoon
feed the mistress of French
plum-and-turquoise-piped chaise-longue;
of brass-knobbed slat front-door and
everywhere open
         shaded house on Indian-
         named Virginian

streams, in counties named for English lords. The
  rattlesnake soon

said from our once dashingly
undiffident first flag, "don't tread on
  me"—tactless symbol of a new republic.
Priorities were
      cradled in this region not
      noted for humility; spot
that has high-singing
      frogs, cotton-mouth snakes and cot-
      ton fields; clay for brick,
Lawrence jugs with Persian
loping wolf design; and hounds.
Here the poor unpoisonous
terrapin likes to
      idle near the sea-top;
      tobacco-crop
gains have church tablets; Devil's Woodyard swamps
  and one-brick-thick-

wall serpentine shadows star-
tle strangers. The strangler fig, the dwarf-
  fancying Egyptian, the American,
the Dutch, the noble
      Roman, in taking what they
      pleased—colonizing as we say—
were not all intel-
      lect and delicacy. A
  black savage or such
as was subject to the
deer-fur Crown is not all brawn
and animality. The
limestone tea-table,
      the mandolin-shaped big
      and little fig,
and the now disused silkworm-trees, imply
  amity; much

kind tyranny made ha-has
that kept back cows; clock-strengthened stocking
  and drooping cotton dress with handmade edge, mark
tyrant taste; the song-
      bird wakes too soon, to enjoy
      excellent idleness, destroy-
ing legitimate
      laziness, this unbought toy

even in the dark
risking loud whee whee whee
of joy, the caraway-seed-
spotted sparrow perched in the
dew-drenched juniper
      beside the window-ledge;
      this little hedge-
sparrow that wakes up seven minutes soon-
   er than the lark

they say. The live oak's rounded
mass of undulating boughs, the white
   pine, the agèd hackberry—handsomest vis-
itor of all—the
      cedar's etched solidity,
      the cypress, lose identity
and are one tree, as
      sunset flames increasingly
  against their leaf-chis-
elled blackening ridge of green;
and the redundantly wind-
widened clouds expanding to
earth size above the
      town's bothered with wages
      childish sages,
are to the child an intimation of
  what glory is.

Bird-Witted

With innocent wide penguin eyes, three
  grown fledgling mocking-birds below
the pussy-willow tree,
  stand in a row,
wings touching, feebly solemn,
  till they see
    their no longer larger
    mother bringing
something which will partially
feed one of them.
    Towards the high-keyed intermittent squeak
    of broken carriage-springs, made by
the three similar, meek-
    coated bird's-eye
freckled forms she comes; and when
    from the beak
    of one, the still living

beetle has dropped
out, she picks it up and puts
it in again.
    Standing in the shade till they have dressed
        their thickly filamented, pale
    pussy-willow-surfaced
        coats, they spread tail
and wings, showing one by one,
    the modest
                white stripe lengthwise on the
                tail and crosswise
on the under wing, and the
accordion
    is closed again. What delightful note
        with rapid unexpected flute-
    sounds leaping from the throat
        of the astute
    grown bird comes back to one from
    the remote
                unenergetic sun-
                lit air before
the brood was here? Why has the
bird's voice become
    harsh? A piebald cat observing them,
        is slowly creeping toward the trim
    trio on the tree-stem.
    Unused to him
the three make room—uneasy
    new problem.
                A dangling foot that missed
                its grasp is raised
and finds the twig on which it
planned to perch. The
    parent darting down, nerved by what chills
        the blood, and by hope rewarded—
    of toil—since nothing fills
        squeaking unfed
mouths, wages deadly combat,
    and half kills
with bayonet beak and
        cruel wings, the
intellectual, cautious-
ly c r e e ping cat.

Half Deity

half worm. We all, infant and adult, have
    stopped to watch the butterfly, last of the
    elves, and learned to spare the wingless worm
        that hopefully ascends the tree. The well-known
    silk tiger-swallowtail
        of South America, with body light-
ly furred, was that bearing pigments which engrave
the lower wings with dragon's blood, weightless.
    They that have wings must not have weights. This more
    peninsula-tailed one with a black
        pitchfork-scalloped edge on sunburnt zebra-skin,
    tired by the trip it made
        with drover-like tenacity, has been
sleeping upright on the elm. Its yellowness
that of the autumn poplar leaf by day
    has been observed. Disguised in butterfly-
    bush Wedgewood blue, Psyche follows it
        to that small tree, *Micromalus,* the midget
    crab, to the mimosa;
        and from that, to the flowering pomegranate.
Baffled not by the quick-clouding serene gray
moon but forced by the hot hot sun to pant,
    she stands on rug-soft grass; though "it is not
    permitted to gaze informally
        on majesty in such a manner as might
    well happen here." The blind
        all-seeing butterfly, fearing the slight
finger, wanders, as though it were ignorant,
across the path and lights on Zephyr's palm,
    planting forefeet soberly; then pawing
    like a horse, turns round,—apostrophe-
        tipped brown antennae porcupining out as
    it arranges nervous
        wings. Vexed because curiosity has
been pursuing it, it cannot now be calm.
The butterfly's round unglazed china eyes,
    pale tobacco brown, with the large eyes of
    the Nymph on them—gray eyes that now are
        black, for she with controlled agitated glance
    observes the insect's face
        and all's a-quiver with significance—
enact the scene of cats' eyes on the magpie's
eyes, by Goya. Butterflies do not need
    home advice. As though Zephyr and Psyche
    were patent-leather cricket singing
        loud, and gnat-catching garden-toad, the swallow-

tail, bewitched and danger-
ous, springs away, zebra half-deified,
trampling the air as it trampled the flowers, feed-
ing where it pivots. Twig-veined irascible
fastidious stubborn undisciplined
zebra! Sometimes one is grateful to
a stranger for looking very nice. But free
to leave the outspread hand
it flies, drunken with triviality
or guided by visions of strength, off until,
diminishing like wreckage on the sea,
rising and falling easily, it mounts
the swell and keeping its true course with
what swift majesty, indifferent to
us, is gone. Deaf to ap-
proval, magnet-nice, as it flutters through
airs now slack now fresh. It has strict ears when the
West Wind speaks. It was he, with mirror eyes
of strong anxiety, who had no net
of flowering shrewd-scented tropical
device, or lignum vitae perch in half-shut
hand; for ours is not a
canely land; nor was it Oberon, but
this quiet young man with piano replies,
named Zephyr, whose hand spread out was enough
to tempt the fiery tiger-horse to stand,
eyes staring skyward and chest arching
bravely out—historic metamorphoser
and saintly animal
in India, in Egypt, anywhere.
His talk was as strange as my grandmother's muff.

Smooth Gnarled Crape Myrtle

A brass-green bird with grass-
green throat smooth as a nut, springs from
twig to twig askew, copying the
Chinese flower piece—businesslike atom
in the stiff-leafed tree's blue-
pink, dregs-of-wine, pyramids
of mathematic
circularity—one of a
pair. A redbird with a hatchet
crest lights straight, on a twig
between the two, bending the
peculiar
bouquet down; and there are

several black antique
bootjack fireflies touched with weak bright
    hunting-pink. "The legendary white-
eared black bulbul that sings
        only in pure Sanskrit" should
        be here—"tame clever
        true nightingale." The cardinal-
    bird that is usually a
    pair looks somewhat odd, like
    "the ambassadorial
            Inverness
            worn by one who dresses

    in New York but dreams of
London." It was artifice saw,
        on a patch-box pigeon-egg, room for
fervent script, and wrote as with a bird's claw
        under the pair on the
        hyacinth-blue lid—"joined in
        friendship, crowned by love."
        As aspect may deceive; as the
        elephant's columbine-tubed trunk
        held waveringly out—
        an at will heavy thing—is
            delicate.
            Art is unfortunate.

    One may be a blameless
bachelor and it is but a
        step to Congreve. A Rosalindless
redbird comes where people are, knowing they
        have not made a point of
        being where he is—this bird
        which says not sings, "with-
        out loneliness I should be more
        lonely, so I keep it"—half in
        Japanese. And what of
        our clasped
hands that swear "By Peace
            Plenty; as
            by Wisdom Peace." Alas!

The Pangolin

· Another armoured animal—scale
        lapping scale with spruce-cone regu-
        larity until they
    form the uninterrupted central

tail-row! This near artichoke
    with head and legs and grit-equipped giz-
zard, the night miniature artist-
        engineer is   Leonardo's
            indubitable son? Im-
        pressive animal
and toiler, of whom we seldom hear.
            Armor seems extra. But for him,
    the closing ear-
        ridge—or bare
        ear, lacking even this small
        eminence—and similarly safe

contracting nose and eye apertures,
    impenetrably closable,
    are not;—a true ant-eat-
er, not cockroach-eater, who endures
    exhausting solitary
        trips through unfamiliar ground at night,
    returning before sunrise; stepping
        in the moonlight,   on the moonlight
            peculiarly, that the out-
    side edges of his
hands may bear the weight and save the claws
        for digging. Serpentined about
the tree, he draws
    away from
    danger unpugnaciously,
    with no sound but a harmless hiss; keep-

ing the fragile grace of the Thomas-
    of-Leighton Buzzard Westminster
    Abbey wrought-iron vine, or
rolls himself into a ball that has
    power to defy all effort
        to unroll it; strongly intailed, neat
    head for core, on neck not breaking off,
        with curled-in feet.   Nevertheless
            he has sting-proof scales; and nest
        of rocks closed with earth
from inside, which he can thus darken.
    Sun and moon & day and night &
        man and beast
    each with a splen-
        dor which man
        in all his vileness cannot
        set aside; each with an excellence!

"Fearful yet to be feared," the armored
   ant-eater met by the driver
   ant does not turn back, but
engulfs what he can, the flattened sword-
   edged leafpoints on the tail and
       artichoke-set leg and body plates
   quivering violently when it
     retaliates   and swarms on him.
         Compact like the furled fringed frill
     on the hat-brim of
Gargallo's hollow iron head of a
        matador, he will drop and will
then walk away
   unhurt, al-
   though if unintruded on
he will come slowly down the tree, helped

by his tail. The giant-pangolin
   tail, graceful tool, as prop or hand
   or broom or axe, tipped like
the elephant's trunk with special skin,
   is not lost on this ant and
       stone swallowing uninjurable
   artichoke, which simpletons thought a
     living fable   whom the stones had
       nourished whereas ants had done
   so. Pangolins are
   not aggressive animals; between
       dusk and day, they have the not-un-
chainlike, machine-
   like form and
   frictionless creep of a thing
   made graceful by adversities, con-

versities. To explain grace requires
   a curious hand. If that which
   is at all were not for
ever, why would those who graced the spires
   with animals and gathered
       there to rest, on cold luxurious
   low stone seats—a monk and monk and monk—
     between the thus   ingenious roof-
       supports, have slaved to confuse
   grace with a kindly
manner, time in which to pay a debt,
   the cure for sins, a graceful use
   of what are yet

approved stone
mullions branching out across
the perpendiculars? A sailboat

was the first machine. The manis, made
for moving quietly also,
is neither a prisoner
nor a god; on hind feet plantigrade,
with certain postures of a
man. Beneath sun and moon, man slaving
to make his life more sweet, leaves half the
flowers worth having,   needing to choose
wisely how to use the strength;—
a paper-maker
like the wasp; a tractor of foodstuffs,
like the ant; spidering a length
of web from bluffs
above a
stream; in fighting, mechanicked
like the pangolin; capsizing in

disheartenment. Bedizened or stark
naked, man, the self, the being
so-called human, writing-
master to this world, griffons a dark
"Like does not like like that is
obnoxious"; and writes error with four
r's. Among animals, *one* has a
sense of humour   then, which saves a
few steps, which saves years—unig-
norant, modest and
unemotional, and all emo-
tion, one with everlasting vig-
our, power to grow,
though there are few of him—who can make one
breathe faster and make one erecter.

Not afraid of anything is he,
and then goes cowering forth, tread paced
to meet an obstacle
at every step. Consistent with the
formula—warm blood, no gills,
two pairs of hands and a few hairs—that
is a mammal; there he sits in his
own habitat,   serge-clad, strong-shod.
The prey of fear, he, always
curtailed, extinguished,
thwarted by the dusk, work partly done,
says to the alternating blaze,

"Again the sun!
    anew each
    day; and new and new and new,
    that comes into and steadies my soul."

"The Being So-Called Human," built on the third stanza of "The Pangolin," appeared in
    print in the *Living Age* 360, no. 4498 (July 1941): 500.

Not afraid of anything is he
    and then goes cowering forth, tread paced
    to meet an obstacle
at every step. Consistent with the
    formula—warm blood, no gills,
    two pairs of hands and a few hairs—that
    is a mammal; there he sits in his
        own habitat,   serge-clad, strong-shod.
    The prey of fear; he, always
    curtailed, extinguished
thwarted by the dusk, work partly done,
    says to the alternating blaze,
"Again the sun!
    anew each
    day; and new and new and new,
    that comes into and steadies my soul."

"Walking-Sticks and Paper-Weights and Water Marks." This, from *W*. First published in
    Poetry 49 (November 1936): 59–64. Moore's handwritten revision of stanza three ap-
    pears in a Bryn Mawr Library edition. The altered stanza reads:

shapes matter as a die is hid
while used; and that such power, unavid
    since secure, can
mold an at first fluid solid
glass weight. Amid
    the wax the seal is safe. Also
    as the water mark's translucence had obscured
itself, through claws, the vivid
        though hid white flower attracts one lightly

"See in the Midst of Fair Leaves." *New Directions in Prose and Poetry*, vol. 1, ed. James
    Laughlin IV (Norfolk, Conn.: New Directions, 1936), pages unnumbered.

World War II and After, 1940–1956

"Four Quartz Crystal Clocks." This, *COMP*, pp. 115–16. First publication, *Kenyon Review*
    2 (summer 1940); 284–85. *W, CP, MMR, COMP*.
"What Are Years." This, *COMP*. First, *Kenyon Review* 2 (summer 1940): 286. *W, CP,
    MMR, COMP*. In 1967, Miss Moore told me that she did not want the question mark
    after the title. "In my 'What Are Years' the printers universally have insisted on put-
    ting a question mark after the title: "What Are Years?" It's not that at all! It's a medi-

tation: 'What Are Years. What Are Years.' You're not thinking about it, not asking anyone to come and answer you. But they won't have it that way." Since the poem appears in many publications with a question mark, I show it that way, but with a cautionary note.

"The Paper Nautilus" ("A Glass-Ribbed Nest"). This, *COMP*, pp. 121–22. First publication, *Kenyon Review* 2 (summer 1940): 287–88. *W, CP, MMR, COMP*.

"Rigorists." This, *COMP*, 96. First seen in *Life and Letters Today* 26 (September 1940): 243–44. *W, CP, MMR, COMP*.

"Light Is Speech." This, *COMP*, pp. 97–98. First seen in *Decision* 1 (March 1941): 26. *W, CP, MMR, COMP*.

"He 'Digesteth Harde Yron,'" This, *COMP*, pp. 99–100. First published in *Partisan Review* 8 (July–August 1941): 312. *W, CP, MMR, COMP*.

"Spenser's Ireland." This, *COMP*, pp. 112–14. First published in *Furioso* 1 (summer 1941): 24–25. *WN, CP, MMR, COMP*.

"The Wood-Weasel." This, *COMP*, p. 127. First published in the *Harvard Advocate* 128 (April 1942): 11. *N, CP, COMP*.

"Pale Morning Moon, Dark Blue Black Sea," RML, Series I, 1:01. Unpublished.

"You, Your Horse." RML, Series I, 1:01. Unpublished.

"In Distrust of Merits." This, *COMP*, pp. 136–38. First published in the *Nation* 156 (May 1, 1943): 636. *N, CP, MMR, COMP*.

"Nevertheless" ("It Is Late, I Can Wait"). This, *COMP*, p. 125–26. First published in *Contemporary Poetry* 3, no. 2 (summer 1943): 5. *N, CP, MMR, COMP*.

"Elephants." This, *COMP*, 128–30. First published in the *New Republic* 109 (August 23, 1943): 250–51. *N, CP, COMP*.

"The Mind Is an Enchanting Thing." This, *COMP*, pp. 134–35. First published in the *Nation* 157 (December 18, 1943): 735. *N, CP, MM, COMP*.

"A Carriage from Sweden." This, *COMP*, pp. 131–33. First published in the *Nation* 158 (March 11, 1944): 311. *N, CP, COMP*.

"'Keeping Their World Large.'" This, *COMP*, pp. 145–46. First published in *Contemporary Poetry* 4 (autumn 1944): 5–6. *CP, COMP*.

"His Shield." *Title* (Bryn Mawr College), November 1944, p. 4. *CP, COMP*.

"Propriety." This, *COMP*, pp. 149–50. First published in the *Nation* 159 (November 25, 1944): 656. *CP, MMR, COMP*. The *Nation*'s version:

Propriety

It's a chord
like one word
   Brahms had heard
   from a bird
warbling at the root of its throat
It's the little downy woodpecker
     spiraling a tree
       . . . up up up like mercury

  A bird song
  is not long,

a wayside
of hayseed
tune; a reticence with rigor
from strength at the source. Propriety's
Bach's *Sofegietto*,
harmonica, and basso.

The fish-spines
of fir pines—
somber trees
by the sea's
walls of waveworn rock—have it; and
a moonbow and Bach's cheerful firmness
in a minor key
It's an owl-and-pussy

both content
agreement.
Come, come. It's
mixed with wits;
it's not a graceful sadness. It's
resistance with bent head, like foxtail-
millet's, Brahms and Bach,
no; Bach and Brahms. To thank Bach

for his song
first, is wrong.
Pardon me;
both are the
unintentional pansy-face
uncursed by self-inspection; blackened
because born that way;
blackened because born that way.

"Advent." *Lafayette Record*, January 1946, p. 11. Uncollected.

"A Face." This, *COMP*, p. 141. First publication, *Horizon* 16 (October 1947): 58.

"Efforts of Affection." This, *COMP*, p. 147. First published in the *Nation* 167 (October 16, 1948): 430.

"At Rest in the Blast." *Botteghe Oscure* 2 (1948): 287. Uncollected.

"Like a Bulwark" ("Bulwarked Against Fate"). This, *COMP*, p. 157. First published in the *New York Times* 2 (1948): 121.

"Voracities and Verities Sometimes Are Interacting." This, *COMP*, p. 148. First published in *Spearhead: Ten Years' Experimental Writing in America* (New York, 1947), p. 190.

"By Disposition of Angels." This, *COMP*, p. 142. First publication, *Quarterly Review of Literature* 4, no. 2 (1948): 1921. *CP*, *COMP*.

"Armor's Undermining Modesty." This, *COMP*, 151–52. First published in the *Nation* 170 (February 25, 1950): 181. *CP*, *COMP*.

"The Stuttering Quagmires Speak." C. April 5, 1950. RML, Series I, 1:01.Unpublished.

"The Icosasphere." This, *COMP*, p. 143. First published in *Imagi*, 5, no. 5 (1950): 2. *CP*, *COMP*.

"Pretiolae." *Wake*, no. 9 (1950): 4. Uncollected. Author's note on manuscript:

> The Hartford Fire Insurance Company and Hartford Accident and Indemnity Company building—690 Asylum Avenue, Hartford, Connecticut—as part of its classic facade, has six granite columns supporting the pediment; all of solid granite.
>
> Pretiolae are thought by the *New York Times* to have been originally Roman—little pieces of baked dough, symbolizing the folded arms of a suppliant, presented to children for dutifully said prayers. "Little pretzels" were introduced to America in the 18th Century from Germany, by bakeries in Lititz and Reading, Pennsylvania, in accordance with a secret recipe—hand-twisted for factory ovens.

"Quoting an Also Private Thought." This, from *Nine* 2, no. 2 (May 1950): 109. First published in the *University of Kansas City Review* 16 (spring 1950): 163. Uncollected.

"We Call Them the Brave." *Nation* 172 (May 5, 1951): 423. Uncollected.

"Then the Ermine:" This, *COMP*, pp. 160–61. First published in *Poetry* 81 (October 1952): 55–56. *COMP*.

"Apparition of Splendor." This, *COMP*, pp. 158–59. First published in the *Nation* 175 (October 1952): 383. *L, MMR, COMP*.

"Tom Fool at Jamaica." This, *COMP*, pp. 162–63. First published in the *New Yorker* 29 (June 13, 1953): 32. *L, MMR, COMP*.

"The Web One Weaves of Italy." This, *COMP*, p. 164. First published in the *Times Literary Supplement*, September 17, 1954, p. xlvii ("American Writing Today" issue). *L, MMR, COMP*.

"Rosemary." This, *COMP*, p. 168. First published in *Vogue* 124 (December 1954): 101. *L, MMR, COMP*.

"The Staff of Aesculapius." This, *COMP*, pp. 165–66. First published in *What's New* (Abbott Laboratories) 186 (December 1954): 9. *COMP*.

"The Sycamore." This, *COMP*, p. 167. First published in *Art News Annual* 24 (1955): 94–95. *COMP*.

The Magic Flute, 1956–1965

"Style." This, *COMP*, pp. 169–70. First published in the *Listener* 55 (April 12, 1956): 423. *MMR, COMP*.

"Logic and 'The Magic Flute.'" This, *COMP*, pp. 171–72. First published in *Shenandoah* 7 (summer 1956): 18–19. *L, MMR, COMP*.

"Blessed Is the Man." This, *COMP*, pp. 173–74. First published in *Ladies' Home Journal* 73 (August 1956): 101. *L, MMR, COMP*.

"Values in Use." This, *COMP*, p. 181. First published in *Partisan Review* 23 (fall 1956): 506. *OBD, MMR, COMP*.

"Hometown Piece for Messrs. Alston and Reese." This, *COMP*, pp. 182–84. First published in the *New York Herald Tribune*, October 3, 1956, p. 1. *OBD, MMR, A, COMP*.

"O to Be a Dragon." This, *COMP*, p. 177. First published in *Sequoia* 3, no. 1 (autumn 1957): 20. *OBD, MMR, A, COMP*.

"Enough: Jamestown, 1607–1957." This, *COMP*, pp. 185–87. First published in *Virginia Quarterly Review* 33 (fall 1957): 500–502. *OBD, MMR, A, COMP*.

"Melchior Vulpius." This, *COMP*, p. 188. First published in *Atlantic* 201 (January 1958): 59. *OBD, MMR, A, COMP*. Note found in file, RML, Series I, 1:01: "Is it possible that Melchior Vulpius and Saint Jerome are in reality T. S. Eliot?"

"In the Public Garden." This, *COMP*, pp. 190–92. First published in the *Boston Globe*, June 15, 1958, as "A Festival." Also seen as "Boston." *OBD, MMR, A, COMP*.

"The Arctic Ox (or Goat)." This, *COMP*, pp. 193–95. First published in *New Yorker* 34 (September 13, 1958): 40. *OBD, MMR, A, COMP*.

"Saint Nicholas," This, *Complete Poems*, pp. 196–97. First published in *New Yorker* 34 (December 27, 1958): 28. *OBD, MMR, A, COMP*.

"For February 14th." This, *COMP*. First publication, *New York Herald Tribune* (February 13, 1959), p. 1. *OBD, A, COMP*.

"No Better Than 'A Withered Daffodil.'" This, *COMP*, p. 188. First published in *Art News* 58 (March 1959): 44. *OBD, MMR, A, COMP*. "Sir Isaac Oliver's miniature on ivory of Sir Philip Sidney, now in the collection at Windsor." Moore's note on ms. dated May 13, 55. RML, Series I, 1:01.

"Combat Cultural." This, *COMP*, pp. 199–200. First published in *New Yorker* 35 (June 6, 1959): 40. The author has used this spelling consistently, although the correct phrase, in French, is *"Combat Culturel." OBD, MMR, A, COMP*.

"Leonardo da Vinci's." This, *COMP*, pp. 201–2. First published in *New Yorker* 35 (July 18, 1959): 22. *OBD, MMR, A, COMP*.

"Saint Valentine," This, *COMP*, p. 233. First published in *New Yorker* 35 (February 13, 1960): 30. *TM, COMP*.

"Lines for Narrator." Program for Schola Cantorum, Carnegie Hall, April 27, 1960. Uncollected.

"Tell Me, Tell Me." This, *COMP*, p. 231–32. First published in *New Yorker* 36 (April 30, 1960): 44. *MMR, TM, A, COMP*.

"Carnegie Hall: Rescued." This, *COMP*, pp. 229–30. First published as "Glory" in *New Yorker* 36 (August 13, 1960): 37. *MMR, TM, A, COMP*.

"Rescue with Yul Brynner." This, *COMP*, pp. 227–28. First published in *New Yorker* 37 (May 20, 1961): 40. *MMR, TM, A, COMP*.

"To Victor Hugo of My Crow Pluto." This, *COMP*, pp. 224–26. First published in *Harper's Bazaar* 94 (October 1961): 185. *MMR, TM, A, COMP*.

"Yvor Winters—" This, RML, Series I, 1:01. Published as "To Yvor Winters" in *Sequoia* 6 (1961): facing page 1.

"Baseball and Writing." This, *COMP*, pp. 221–23. First published in *New Yorker* 37 (December 9, 1961): 48. *TM*.

"Arthur Mitchell." This, *COMP*, p. 220. City Center Music and Drama Souvenir Program, January 1962. *TM*.

"Poetry as Expression." *Writer* 75 (April 1962), 35. Uncollected.

"Blue Bug." This, *COMP*, pp. 218–19. First published in *New Yorker* 38 (May 26, 1962): 40. *A, TM, COMP*.

"Charity Overcoming Envy." This, *COMP*, pp. 216–17. First published in *New Yorker* 39 (March 30, 1963): 44. *TM, COMP*.

"To a Giraffe." This, *COMP*, p. 215. First published in `Poetry in Crystal: Steuben Glass, Inc* (New York: Spiral Press, 1963), p. 44. *A, TM, COMP*. Author's note on ms.: "Ennis Rees summarizes the Odyssey, I feel, when he finds expessed in it, 'the conditional nature of existence, the consolation of the metaphysical: the journey from sin to redemption.'"

"'Avec Ardeur.'" This, *COMP*, 237–39. Published as "I've Been Thinking" in the *New York Review of Books*, October 31, 1963, 19. First published as "Occasionem Cognosce" in a broadside (Lunenberg, Vt.: Stinehour Press, 1963). *COMP*.

"W. S. Landor." This, *COMP*, p. 214. First published in *New Yorker* 40 (February 22, 1964): 26. *COMP*.

"The Master Tailor." *New York Herald Tribune*, November 27, 1963, p. 19.

"An Expedient—Leonardo da Vinci's—and a Query." This, *COMP*, pp. 201–2. First published in *New Yorker* 40 (April 18, 1964): 52. *A, TM, COMP*.

"Old Amusement Park." This, *COMP*, pp. 210–11. First published in *New Yorker* 40 (August 29, 1964): 34. *TM, COMP*.

Late Poems, 1965–1972

"Dream." This, *COMP*, p. 209. First published in *New Yorker* 41 (October 16, 1965): 52. *TM, COMP*.

"In Lieu of the Lyre." This, *COMP*, pp. 206–7. First published in *Harvard Advocate* 100 (November 1965). *TM, COMP*.

"The Mind, Intractable Thing." This, *COMP*, p. 208. First published in *New Yorker* 41 (November 27, 1965): 60. *TM, COMP*.

"Granite and Steel." This, *COMP*, p. 205. First published in *New Yorker* 42 (9 July 1966): 32. *TM, COMP*.

Draft of Granite and Steel:

"O radiance that doth inherit me,"
confirming inter-acting amity!

Untried expedient, untried; then tried:
sublime elliptic two-fold egg;
way out; way in; romantic passageway—
first seen by the eye of the mind;
then by the eye . . . O steel, O stone!
Climactic ornament, double half-rainbow,
as if inverted by French perspicacity,
    John Roebling's monument,
    German tenacity's also; composite span
        an actuality.

                                        —RML, Series I, 1:01.

"Love in America—" This, *COMP*, p. 240. First published in *Saturday Evening Post* 239 (December 31, 1966): 78. *COMP*.

"For Katharine Elizabeth McBride." Printed on a sheet inserted in a program for a dinner honoring Katharine Elizabeth McBride, president of Bryn Mawr College, March

1, 1967. Unpublished. In manuscript, the poem is signed "Marianne Moore, 09," and is followed by the author's note:

> Inconsiderable as derived from its sources, the foregoing lines attempt to thank Miss McBride for an article in the *Christian Science Monitor,* naming a number of constants which make for continuity; Mr. John W. Gardner for concepts set forth in his monographs, EXCELLENCE and SELF-RENEWAL (Harper Colophon Books); and Cornelia Meigs, '07 for WHAT MAKES A COLLEGE? (Macmillan).

"Tippoo's Tiger." This, *COMP,* p. 241. Thanks to Patricia Willis, we know that the manuscript of this poem is dated June 16, 1967, and given to Robert Wilson, who issued it in his "Oblong Octavo Series" in 1967. *COMP.*

"The Camperdown Elm." This, *COMP,* p. 242. First published in the *New Yorker* 43 (September 23, 1967): 48. *COMP.*

"Assistance." *Tambourine* (Washington University), 1967–68, p. 1. Uncollected.

"Mercifully." This, *COMP,* p. 243. First published in *New Yorker* 44 (July 20, 1968): 34. *COMP.*

"'Reminiscent of a Wave at the Curl.'" This, *COMP,* p. 244. First published as "Like a Wave at the Curl," *New Yorker* 45 (November 29, 1969): 50. *COMP.*

"A Christmas Poem." *New York Times Magazine,* December 21, 1969, p. 5. Uncollected.

"Enough." This, *COMP,* p. 245. First published in *New Yorker* 45 (January 17, 1970): 28. *COMP.*

"The Magician's Retreat." This, *COMP,* p. 246. First published in *New Yorker* 46 (February 21, 1970): 40. *COMP.*

"Prevalent at One Time." This, *COMP,* p. 247. *COMP.*

"The Fox and the Grapes," "The Lion in Love," "The Animals Sick of the Plague," "The Bear and the Garden-Lover," "The Mouse Metamorphosed into a Maid." Selected by Moore for *COMP,* pp. 251–58, from *The Fables of La Fontaine,* tr. Marianne Moore (New York: Viking, 1965). *COMP.*

INDEX OF TITLES AND FIRST LINES

Titles are in *italics*.